All Those Wonderful Names

All Those Wonderful Names

A Potpourri of People, Places, and Things

J. N. Hook

JOHN WILEY & SONS, INC.
New York   Chichester   Brisbane   Toronto   Singapore

Parts of this book were published in J. N. Hook, *The Book of Names* (New York: Franklin Watts, 1983). Copyright © 1983 by J. N. Hook.

Library of Congress Cataloging-in-Publication Data

Hook, J. N. (Julius Nicholas). 1913–
    All those wonderful names : a potpourri of people, places, and things / by J.N. Hook.
        p.   cm.
    Includes index.
    ISBN 0-471-53011-5
    1. Onomastics.   2. Language and languages—Etymology.
    3. Names—History.   I. Title.
    P321.H64   1991   90-44827
    929.9'7—dc20

Printed in the United States of America

91 92 10 9 8 7 6 5 4 3 2 1

❦ Acknowledgments

The author is grateful to the following persons who contributed items to *All Those Wonderful Names*: Pierre DuPont of Dover, DE; Edward N. Hook of Mesa, AZ; Julian L. Hook of Chicago, IL; Rachel G. Hook of Waveland, IN; Elmer Johnson of St. Cloud, FL; and Frederic Luther of Waveland, IN.

❦ Contents

All Those Wonderful Names

❦ PART I

The Names People Give Their Defenseless Children

🍎 1
Choosing Names for Girls

Ballad of Beautiful Names

Emily, Rachel, Bernadette,
Ellen, Astrid, Fawn,
Cecilia, Tamar, Christabel,
Lolita, Inez, Dawn.

Marguerite, Rita, Angeline,
Keiko, Moira, Mae,
Corinne, Denise, May-Ree-Lynn,
Mahalia, Pauline, Faye.

Heidi, Haidee, Isabel,
Kathryn, Lucette, or Joy
(In Heaven yclept Euphrosyne).
Thank God you're not a boy.

Women Who Get into the *Who's Whos*

You hold your newborn daughter in your arms for the first time. Perhaps her father stands beside your hospital bed. You brush your lips across the baby's forehead and gaze adoringly, wonderingly, at her.

You say, "I wonder what she'll be like, what she'll become. Will she be a great actress, dancer, teacher, politician, business person, industrial tycoon? Maybe she'll get into *Who's Who*."

"Maybe," your husband agrees. "A person doesn't have to be in *Who's Who* to be great, though. I'm not in it, and you're not, but you're great anyhow."

"I wonder if a girl's name helps to get her in or keep her out?"

"Probably not. It might be fun to browse in *Who's Who* in the library and see whether any first names keep popping up over and over. Does an unusual name help, or are *Who's Who* names like everybody else's?"

If you ever did look in *Who's Who in the United States*, *Who's Who in Canada*, or the British *Who's Who*, representative samplings of the names would look something like the following three lists. For each list, pages in a *Who's Who* were selected randomly, and women's names were recorded to a total of 250. (Men's names exceed women's by about 11 or 12 to 1, but that one-sided ratio is declining.)

Who's Who in the United States

Name and Close Variants	Number	Percentage of Sample
Ann (8), Anne (5), Anna (1), Annette (1), Anni (1)	16	6.4
Barbara	13	5.2
Suzanne (7), Susan (5)	12	4.8
Ruth	9	3.6
Maria (5), Mary (4)	9	3.6
Margaret	8	3.2
Elizabeth	7	2.8
Linda (4), Lynda (1)	5	2.0
Kathryn (2), Catherine (1), Katherine (1)	4	1.6
Helen	4	1.6
Joan	4	1.6
Louise	4	1.6
Patricia	4	1.6
Carolyn	3	1.2
Elaine	3	1.2
Jane	3	1.2
Janet	3	1.2
Jean	3	1.2

Women listed in a 1989 or 1990 *Who's Who* were born, on average, in the 1930s. At that time, almost all the names on the previous list were also among the 50 most popular in the United

States, with Mary, Barbara, Linda, Ruth, and Patricia ranking especially high.

But women with less popular birth names of that period certainly have not been shut out. Jane ("plain Jane," some people called her) has three entries, as the list shows, but relatively few girls were given that name in the 1930s (Dunkling, *First Names First*). Similar comments apply to many other names with only one or two appearances in the *Who's Who* sampling, for example, Cynthia, Daisy, Gilda, Leona, Manuela, Rebecca, Regina, Rosemarie, Sherry, Sandy, Violet. And women with still more uncommon names also got into *Who's Who*: Exina, Jhane (she's no plain Jane), Luginia, Mara, Maya, Otti, Selena, Vali. So unique Vali finds herself in the Peerage of Great Accomplishment alongside the much more numerous Barbaras and Elizabeths. It's not the name that bring the fame; it's what the girl becomes and the woman does.

Similar conclusions may be drawn from the names of Canadian and British women included in the pantheons of the famous.

Who's Who in Canada

Name and Close Variants	Number	Percentage of Sample
Mary (12), Marie (4)	16	6.4
Ann (7), Anne (4), Annette (11)	12	4.8
Margaret	10	4.0
Jane	7	2.8
Elizabeth	6	2.4
Janet (3), Jan (1), Janette (1)	5	2.0
Alice	4	1.6
Jean (3), Jeannine (1)	4	1.6
Marjorie	4	1.6
Phyllis	4	1.6
Ruth	4	1.6
Audrey	3	1.2
Joy	3	1.2
Louise	3	1.2
Miriam	3	1.2
Patricia	3	1.2
Sylvia	3	1.2

In Canada, too, the most common names in the *Who's Who* list are not far different from those most popular in the country at large. But once more, much less popular names can be found in the bright red book: Adina, Alexia, Christilot, Inger, Iby, Milada. . . .

Who's Who (British)

Name and Close Variants	Number	Percentage of Sample
Margaret	20	8.0
Mary (15), Marie (2)	17	6.8
Ann (8), Anne (6), Annie (1)	15	6.0
Elizabeth	12	4.8
Barbara	8	3.2
Joan	6	2.4
Patricia	5	2.0
Constance	4	1.6
Helen	4	1.6
Kathleen	3	1.2
Rose	3	1.2
Shirley	3	1.2

Some grand old names there: The first four belonged to various queens and princesses. In the 1930s, those names also ranked high among non-*Who's Who* Britishers. So did Barbara, Joan, and some of the others.

But a British girl need not be named for a queen to be allowed through the gates with the other mighty. She might be—and has been—named Atarah, Chicele, Daphne, Elspeth, Felicity, Olwen, Olwyn, Psyche, Romola, or even Trixie. (What parents, peering at their newborn, could have supposed that their little Trixie would someday share pages with little girls named for queens?)

How to Avoid a Baby's Name You Dislike

Use tact. That's what one husband, Raymond Roberts, did.

His wife, Alice, said, "If the baby is a girl, let's call her Lana."

Raymond detested that name, but didn't want to argue.

"Great!" he said. "The first girl I ever dated seriously was named Lana. She was beautiful, intelligent, and sexy. I've always liked that name."

Alice was silent for a few moments and then said, "Of course, we should talk over some other possibilities. What do you think of Marie, or Claudette, or Melanie?"

A Book about Some Modern Trends

In 1988 *Beyond Jennifer and Jason*, by Linda Rosenkrantz and Pamela R. Satran, was published by St. Martin's Press. Unlike most books on selecting a baby's name, it does not discuss the ancestral meaning of a name, but rather describes current (1980s) attitudes toward hundreds of names.

Fifteen pages are devoted to names that celebrities chose for their children. Ted Danson has a daughter named Alexis, Kim Alexis has a son Jamie, but Jamie is also the name of a Joan Lunden daughter. Mia Farrow seems to be the most versatile in choice of names: the old-fashioned Daisy, Dylan (a girl), Fletcher (a boy), the ethnically mixed name Gigi Soon Yi, Matthew Phineas, Satchel, and the beautifully poetic Lark Song. The son of Susan St. James is Harmony. The daughter of Mick and Bianca Jagger is Jade. Charlene Tilton's daughter is Cherish, and Sonny and Cher raised eyebrows by naming their daughter Chastity. Sylvester Stallone's son is Sage Moon Blood.

But more traditional names far outnumber the unusual, even among celebrities. A few examples: Katharine (Jane Seymour), Mary and Stella (Paul and Linda McCartney), Matthew (Christopher Reeve), Rachel (Kathleen Turner), William and Hannah (Mel Gibson), and Benjamin Simon (Carly Simon and James Taylor).

Rosenkrantz and Satran are interested not only in name-styles of the rich and famous. For example, they combine into one list the birth names most popular in five states: California, New York, Oregon, Tennessee, and Wisconsin. They report that in these states the ten most popular girls' names were, in order, Jessica, Amanda, Ashley, Jennifer, Sara(h), Nicole, Megan, Stephanie, Elizabeth, and Heather.

New York City's Favorite Given Names

In 1988 Jessica was the name most often given to New York City's newborn girls. Jessica supplanted Jennifer, which had been the leader since 1972. Other girls' names high on the list during the seventies and eighties, but changing order frequently, were Melissa, Nicole, Michelle, Elizabeth, Stephanie, Lisa, Tiffany, Amanda, Ashley, Samantha, Christina, and Danielle—sometimes in variant forms such as Christine, Kristin, or Daniella.

Among boys born in the late eighties, Michael led in popularity as usual (ever since 1963). Other favorites of the seventies and eighties, in shifting order, were Christopher, David, John, Joseph, Anthony, Jason, Daniel, Robert, Jonathan, Matthew, Andrew, and James.

In those lists, Michelle, Stephanie, Christina, and Danielle are feminine forms of the biblical names Michael, Stephen, Christ(ian), and Daniel. Samantha, Elizabeth, and its derivative, Lisa, also are rooted in the Bible. The boys' names based on the Bible are Christopher, David, Joseph, John, Daniel, Jonathan, Andrew, Matthew, and James.

Almost a hundred years ago, the biblical influence in New York City name-giving was about equally evident in the most-chosen names. In the following lists of the 1898 leaders, Bible-based names are italicized:

Girls—*Mary*, Catherine, Margaret, *Annie*, Rose, *Marie* (variant of *Mary*), *Esther*, *Sarah*, Frances, Ida
Boys—*John*, William, Charles, George, *Joseph*, Edward, *James*, Louis, Francis, *Samuel*

Adams without Eves

In *Oregon Health Trends* for April 1987, Joseph D. Carney, state registrar, reported on a sad state of affairs in the naming of Oregon children: "Romance in 1986 seemed to be one-sided. There were 16 Tristans, but alas, no Isolde; 183 Adams but no Eve; one Romeo and not a Juliet; one Samson but no Delilah!"

Feminissima

Rosenkrantz and Satran, the authors of *Beyond Jennifer and Jason*, prepared a list, based on their own impressions, of about a hundred girls' names they describe as "feminissima," saying that "If these names were dresses, they would be pale pink, with ruffles and lace and big bows and springs of flowers. . . . They are the sweetest of the sweet."

Examples: Adora, Allegra, Camilla, Cherie, Desiree, Giselle, Heather, Lacey, Melody, Priscilla, Serena, Tiffany, Yvette.

The authors rate such names as Annette, Elena, and Margo as feminine but not feminissima.

If You Were a Girl in Old London

Back in the London of the eleventh to fourteenth centuries, the chances that a girl's or woman's name would be Edith was greater than for any other name, although it often was spelled with *y* instead of *i*, or with a final *e*.

If you weren't named Edith, the chances of having one of the following names was also fairly good, each with variant spellings: Alice, Amice, Emma, Isabel(la), Jocelyn, Johanna, Katherine, Laura, Margery, Maud, and Yvonne.

Most other female names of the period have vanished or now are disguised somewhat. Estrilda is only infrequently found today, as are Godeva or Godiva, although the suggestion of nudity makes the latter rare. Etheldreda has lost its second half (the first means 'noble.') Aedeleva may survive as Adelaide. The now unusual Aldith or Aldeth was spelled with a final *a* in the Middle Ages.

There seem to be few or no survivors of many other names of the early period, such as Alueua, Godid, Godgifu 'God's gift.' Goldcorna, Gun(n)ilda 'battle helmet,' Gonona, Leofdaeg 'love day,' Reganilda (an older form of Regan, King Lear's daughter in Shakespeare's play), Saefaru 'seafarer,' Swanhild 'swan war,' Swetleofu 'sweet love,' T(h)urgund, and Wulfgifu 'wolf gift.'

Late in the fourteenth century, Londoner Geoffrey Chaucer wrote his *Canterbury Tales*. Because of the subject matter, most of the names he used came from either Greek and Roman sources or the Bible. He did, however, use some women's names that reflected his own time. The lascivious Wife of Bath and the carpenter's unfaithful wife were both named Alys (equivalent to Alice or Alison), a nun was Madame Eglantine, and Jill was a housemaid. Maudy was another adulterous wife, but Griselda was unbelivably patient and completely virtuous. Maia (May) was married to January (with the usual unhappy results). Other Chaucerian names representative of his time include Mag, Custance (Constance), Susanna, Lady Donegild, Prudence, Sophia, Mabely, Elpheta, Canace, and Dorigen. (Incidentally, a ewe in one story was Moll, and a hen was Pertelote—whose companion was called by the traditional rooster's name, Chanticlere.)

The Most Popular Names for English and Welsh Girls (since 1925)

In England and Wales, girls' names fluctuate much more in popularity than do boys' names, and also more than girls' or boys' names in the United States. No single girls' name has ranked in the top ten in each of the years 1925, 1950, 1965, 1975, and 1981. In fact, very few have remained among the top 50 for each of those years (surprisingly, not even Mary, although Elizabeth has bounced about between 23d and 43d).

Here are the top ten for 1925, 1975, and 1981, according to Leslie Dunkling's *First Names First*:

1925	1975	1981
1. Joan	Claire	Sarah
2. Mary	Sarah	Emma
3. Joyce	Nicola	Claire
4. Margaret	Emma	Kelly
5. Dorothy	Joanna	Rebecca
6. Doris	Helen	Gemma
7. Kathleen	Rachel	Rachel
8. Irene	Lisa	Lisa
9. Betty	Rebecca	Victoria
10. Eileen	Karen	Laura
	Michelle (tie)	

In the 1975 and 1981 lists, note the interesting mixture of biblical names (Rachel, Rebecca, Sarah), "elderly" or "middle-aged" names (Emma, Helen, Joanne, Victoria), and "relatively modern" (Claire, Nicola, Lisa, Kelly, and Gemma), the last perhaps deriving from "Solo," a then-popular British TV series in which Gemma was the lead character.

How About *Etta Candy Barr*?

Thomas Pyles, a noted linguist and student of Americana, must have had fun when he wrote for the magazine *Names* an article about his beloved Southland: "Bible Belt Onomastics or Some Curiosities of Anti-Pedobaptist Nomenclature" (1959). He listed a number of pairings of given and last names that, in combination, proved amusing. The following are taken from his longer list:

Candy Barr (also the stage name of
   a famous stripper)
Okla Bobo
Pinkie Bottom
Girlie Burns
Sandy Candy
Royal Child
Melody Clinkenbeard
Honey Combs
French Crown
Pamela Gay Day
Merry English
Charming Fox
Golden Gamble
Fawn Gray
Fairy Guy

Bunker Hill
Early Hawaiian McKinnon
Rocky Mountain
Virgin Muse
Percy Nursery
France Paris
Dill L. Pickle (who sold pickles)
English Piper
Diamond Queen
Summer Robbins
Paris Singer
Lovie Slappy
Shellie Swilley
Drew Swords
Etta Turnipseed
Early Wages
Pleasant Weathers

H. L. Mencken's Unusual Names for Girls

In *The American Language* and its *Supplement Two*, H. L. Mencken, that great collector of oddities of the American language, listed several hundred girls' names that were found in newspapers of the 1930s and 1940s, mainly in the South and Southwest. Here are some of the especially remarkable ones:

Armadilla
Attaresta
Ava Maria
Buena Vista
Cementa
Cherubim
Chlorine
Coita
Credilla
Dardanella
Delector
Dewdrop
Dicey Mae
Dinette
Dreamy
Dullere
Echo

Elicious
El Louise
Endamile
Exum
Fairy
Faucette
Febe
Flouzelle
Flowanna
Fra
Fragoletta
Gazelle
Glanda
Gloriola
G'Ola
Gommeray
Halloween

Hygiene
Iceyphobia
Jaann
Jennyberry
Johnny-v
Kewpie
Kiwanis
La Duska
Ladye
La Lahoma
Larceny (*lar-CEE-nee*)
Livera
Locust
Lush
Madame
Malta Jean
Mecca

Navelle	Ravola	Vasoline
Nordamyrth	Roseola	Venajulia
Okla	Rumba Jo	Windi
Ova	Satyra	Wroberta
Pencilla	Sing	Zdenka
Phalla	Swan	Zoya
Pleasantina	Twitty	Zula Bell
Polo	Ulyssia	Zylphia
Qay	Ureatha	Zzelle

Charlton Laird, in *Language in America*, adds the following:

Acid	Dimple	Orchid Favia
Charm	Dovey	Pixianne
Dawn Robin	Kitty Bit	Satire
Delyte (also a name for men, one of whom became a university president)	Lance Amorus Mary Sunshine	Tyty

Leslie Dunking's *First Names First* credits George Hubbard, a New York name collector, with finding these and many other strange-sounding full names. Note how much difference a middle name can make. Some of them show that almost any name that suggests a verb may cause problems.

Barbara Womble Groat	Lil Lovey Dove
Diana Brown Beard	Margery Ready First
Dorothy May Grow	Mary Hatt Box
Ima June Bugg	Mary Rhoda Duck
Icie Snow Furr	Ruth Pinches Finch
Janet Isadore Bell	Wava White Flagg
Juliet Seashell Moonbeam Gamba	Welcome Baby Darling

Do Teachers Favor Conformists?

Herbert Harari, a psychologist at the University of California in San Diego, made a study in 1973 of whether children's first names affect the grades that teachers give.

Eight essays said to be of identical quality were duplicated and given to 80 fifth- and sixth-grade teachers to evaluate. Four of the papers bore names considered ordinary: Michael, David, Karen, and Lisa. The other four had less common names: Elmer, Hubert, Bertha, and Adelle.

Michael and David outscored Elmer and Hubert by a full letter grade. Karen and Lisa outscored Bertha by a small margin—a point and a half. Adelle's grades were reported as "not significantly lower."

Like other such research, this study should not be considered conclusive unless confirmed by further investigations.

Misnomer

Who could be more trustworthy than a young woman named Virtue Innocent?

Sad to say, this nineteenth-century woman was found guilty of short-weighting the customers in her shop.

Why *Freelove* Didn't Last

Although most Puritans had such ordinary given names as Mary and William, some parents liked to emphasize their religious convictions through the names they gave their children. A male might go through life as Persistence even if he gave up easily, and Preserved 'saved' was sometimes teamed with an unsuitable surname, as was true of one Preserved Puddifoot.

Compound or hyphenated names were somewhat less common: Everlasting-Mercy or Avoid-Illness. Gary Jennings, for his *Personalities of Language*, found these names in a 1658 jury panel list: Faint-Not Hewett, Stand-Fast-on-High Stringer, Search-the-Scriptures Moreton, Fly-Debate Roberts, and Be-of-Good-Comfort Small.

Jennings adds: "One poor girl was baptized Through-Much-Tribulation-We-Enter-into-the-Kingdom-of-Heaven Crabb. Her friends called her Tribby."

Among the jury panelists not mentioned by Jennings were Repentant Hazel, The-Work-of-God Farmer, Be-Thankful Playnard, God-Reward Smart, More-Fruit Flower, Fight-the-Good-Fight-of-Faith White, and Hope-for Bending.

Other Puritan names, likely to be masculine but sometimes feminine, include Thankful, Submit, Godly, Faynt-Not, Experience, Sorry-for-Sin, Tamesin (Tame Sin), and Prosper (short for Prosper-Thy-Works). Increase Mather, the son of one prominent Puritan pastor and the father of another, made Increase a familiar given name in his day.

Two men whose last names originally may have been Barbon perhaps inevitably found it corrupted to Barebone. One of them was Jesus-Christ-Came-into-the-World-to-Save Barebone; the other, If-Christ-Had-Not-Died-for-Thee-Thou-Hadst-Been-Damned Barebone. The latter, it is said, was called Damned Barebone for short.

Some girls were named Faith or Faithful, Faith-My-Joy, Hope, Gracious, Charity, Prudence (a favorite), Blessing, Comfort, Constant or Constancy, Felicity, Virtue, Diligence, and Obediencia. Flora Loughead's *Dictionary of Given Names* has this to say about another name:

> *Freelove* ... This name was bestowed upon girls of highly respected New England families in late Puritan days, evidently through a misconception of the practices advocated by the apostles of its creed; but enlightenment evidently came, for within a few years it was discarded abruptly.

100 Traditional-Modern Names for Girls

The names in this list are centuries old and remain in use today in the United States, Canada, and the British Isles.

Common variants are included for some names. The generally accepted meanings are in single quotes. (Some meanings, and also some derivations, are in doubt. Some of each may indeed be double or multiple.)

Adele: (Adela, Adelaide, Adelia, Adelina, Della) Teutonic 'noble or kind lady'

Agnes: (Agnella, Annis, Ines, Inez, Neysa) Greek, Late Latin 'pure, gentle'

Alice: (Alicia, Alisa, Allison, Allie, Althea, Alyce, Alys, Elissa, Elsa [sometimes]) Teutonic (possibly derived from Adelaide) 'noble princess'

Amanda: (Aimee, Amie, Amorita, Amy) Latin 'loving, lovable'

Andrea: (Andreanna) Greek (feminine of Andrew) 'womanly, a man's woman'

Ann: (Anabel, Anabella, Anita, Anna, Annette, Annie, Annis, Hannah, Nana, Nancy, Nanette, Nina, Nita) Hebrew 'graceful'

Arlene: (Arlana, Arleen, Arlena, Arline) Celtic 'a pledge'

Barbara: (Babette, Barbarita, Barbette) Greek 'a stranger'

Bernice: (Berenice, Berni, Berniz, Bronislava, Bronna) Greek 'she brings victory'

Blanche: (Bela, Bianca, Blanch) French 'white, fair-skinned'

Brenda: Scandinavian 'fiery, flaming sword'

Carmen: (Carman, Carmencita, Carmina, Carmita) Latin through Spanish 'rosy,' 'a song'

Caroline: (Carla, Carlotta, Carol, Carola, Carolina, Carolyn, Carrie, Caryl, Charlotte, Karla, Karlina, Karline, Karolyn, Lola[?]) Teutonic (feminine of Charles) 'noble-spirited, strong'

Catherine: (Catalina, Caterina, Catharina, Catharine, Katerina, Katharine, Katherine, Kathryn, Kathy, Katy, Kay, Rina, Trina) Greek 'pure'

Cheryl: English (probably from *cherry*)

Christine: (Chris, Christa, Christiana, Christina, Chrystabel, Crystal [sometimes], Kristin, Kristina, Teena, Tina) Greek through English (feminine of Christian) 'fair Christian'

Claudia: (Claudette, Claudina, Claudine, Klaudia) Latin (feminine of Claude) 'lame, frail'

Colleen: (Coleen, Colena) Irish 'a girl'

Cora: (Corena, Coretta, Corinna, Corinne) Greek 'a maiden'

Cynthia: (Cynthe) Greek 'moon goddess'

Darlene: (Darleen, Darline, Daryl) English 'dearly beloved'

Deborah: (Debora, Debra) Hebrew 'the bee, industrious'

Diana: (Deanna, Diane, Dina, Dinah) Latin 'goddess of the moon'

Dolores: (Delores, Deloris, Dolora) Latin 'our lady of sorrows'

Donna: (Donia, Donica, Donnabel) Latin through Italian or Spanish 'lady, mistress'

Dorothy: (Dora, Doratea, Dorathea, Feodora, Teodora) Greek (feminine of Theodore) 'gift of God'

Edith: (Eadith, Edetta, Edita, Editha, Edyth) Teutonic 'rich gift,' 'happiness'

Elizabeth: (Bess, Bessie, Beth, Betsy, Bette, Bettina, Betty, Elisa, Elisabeth, Eliza, Elka, Elsa, Else, Ilse, Isabel[?], Liesel, Liza) Hebrew 'consecrated to God'

Emma: (Emmy, Manuela) Teutonic 'industrious,' 'the healer'

Esmeralda: Latin through Spanish 'emerald'

Esther: (Essie, Estella, Estelle, Ester, Hester, Hestera, Stella) Hebrew, Persian, Latin, French 'star'

Eunice: Greek 'happily triumphant'

Eva: (Eve, Eveline, Evelyn, Evita, Ewa, Yeva) Hebrew 'life'

Faye: (Fae, Faith, Fay) Old French 'faithful'

Florence: (Firenza, Flora, Florenca, Florencia, Florentia, Florentina, Lora) Latin 'flower, flourishing'

Frances: (Chica, Francesca, Francisca, Francine, Francoise) Teutonic (feminine of Francis) 'free'

Genevieve: (Beba, Genoveva, Genevieffa, Genowewa) Celtic 'white wave'

Geraldine: (Geralda, Geraldine, Giralda) Teutonic (feminine of Gerald) 'maid of battle'

Gertrude: (Gertrud, Gerty, Trudy) Teutonic 'space maid'

Gladys: (Glad, Gladine, Gladis) Latin 'delicate, frail'

Glenna: English (feminine of Glen) 'from a mountain valley'

Gloria: (Glora, Gloriana, Glory) Latin 'glory, glorious'

Grace: (Engracia, Gracia, Graciana, Gratia, Grazia, Grazielle) Latin 'graceful'

Hazel: English 'hazel'

Helen: (Eileen, Elaine, Eleanor, Elena, Ella, Ellen, Elnore, Helena, Ilka, Ilonka, Olenko, and many more) Greek 'light'

Hilda: (Heidi, Hilde, Hildegarde, Matilda, Tilda) English 'battle maiden'

Hope: (Nada, Nadzia, Esperanza) English 'desire for good'

Imogene: Greek 'beloved daughter'

Inez: (Ines, Necha) Portuguese or Spanish 'gentle, pure'

Irene: (Irena, Ireneo, Iryna, Renata, Renee) Greek 'peace'

Irma: (Erma, Erme, Irwinia) Teutonic 'highborn,' 'strong'

Isabel: (Bella, Belle, Isabella, Isobel, Mabel [?]) Hebrew (possibly through Elizabeth) 'consecrated to God'

Jane: (Gianina, Giovanna, Ioanna, Ivanna, Jana, Janina, Jeanne, Jeannette, Joan, Joanna, Johanna, Juana, Juanita, Nita) Hebrew (feminine of John) 'God's precious gift'

Jessica: (Gessica, Jessie, Jesslyn) Hebrew 'God's grace'

Jocelyn: (Jocelin, Lyn, or Lynne [sometimes]) Latin 'fair,' 'playful'

Josephine: (Finette, Giuseppina, Iosifa, Josepha, Josephina, Jozia, Pepe, Pepina, Pepita) Hebrew (feminine of Joseph) 'God will increase her'

Judith: (Juditha, Judy) Hebrew 'praise God, admired, praiseworthy'

Julia: (Jill, Jule, Juliana, Julie, Julienne, Juliet, Julieta, Juliette, Julita) Latin (feminine of Julius) 'youthful,' 'soft-haired'

June: (Junette, Junia, Juniata, Junilla) Latin 'ever-young'

Karen: (Kara, Karena, Karene, Karin, Karyn) Greek (perhaps derived from Catherine) 'pure'

Kathleen: (Kathlyn) Celtic or Greek (perhaps sometimes derived from Catherine) 'beautiful eyes,' 'pure'

Lana: (Alana, Alina, Lanette) Celtic 'attractive'

Laura: (Lara, Laureana, Laurel, Laurette, Lavra) Latin 'the laurel'

Leah: (Lea, Leigh [sometimes]) Hebrew 'weary'

Lillian: (Lela, Lelia, Lila, Lileana, Lilie, Olena) Latin 'the lily'

Linda: (Lynda; often part of another name, as Rosalind) Latin (often through Spanish) 'beautiful, daintily pretty'

Louise: (Aloisa, Eloise, Heloise, Lois, Louisa, Luisa, Luiza) Teutonic (feminine of Louis) 'war heroine'

Lucille: (Lucia, Lucie, Lucile, Lucilla, Lucinda, Lucine, Lucy) Latin (feminine of Luke) 'light, dawn'

Marcia: (Marcella, Marsha) Latin (feminine of Martius) 'of Mars,' 'little hammer'

Margaret: (Gretchen, Gretel, Marga, Margarita, Margery, Margie, Margo, Margret, Marguerite, Marjorie) Greek 'pearl'
Martha: (Marfa, Marthe, Marta, Martella, Marty, Mattie) Aramaic 'lady'; patron saint of housewives
Mary: (Mara, Maria, Marian, Marie, Marianka, Marika, Marilyn, Marya, Miriam [?], Molly, Polly, and many more) Hebrew 'bitter tears'
Maude: (Magdalene) Teutonic 'brave in battle'
Maxine: Latin 'the greatest'
Melba: (Melbia) English 'woman of Melbourne'
Michelle: Hebrew (feminine of Michael) 'godly'
Mildred: (Millie) English 'gentle adviser'
Muriel: Greek? Hebrew? Celtic? 'sweet, bittersweet'
Myra: (Mira, Myrrha) Latin 'admirable, wonderful'
Naomi: (Naemi, Noemi) Hebrew 'pleasant, sweet'
Norma: Latin (sometimes a feminine of Norman) 'pattern, model'
Paula: (Paulette, Paulina, Pauline, Paulita, Pavla, Pavlina, Pawlina) Latin (feminine of Paul) 'little'
Rachel: (Rachael, Rachelle, Rae, Raquel, Rochelle) Hebrew 'ewe, lamblike, innocent'
Rhoda: (Rodas, Ryza) Greek 'rose'
Roberta: (Bobbie, Robin, Robina, Ruberta, Ruperta) Teutonic (feminine of Robert) 'bright,' 'famous'
Rosalind: (Rosalee, Rosaleen, Rosalyn, Roslyn) Latin 'pretty as a rose'
Ruby: (Rubetta) Latin through English 'ruby'
Ruth: Hebrew 'beautiful friend'
Sara: (Sadie, Sally, Sarah, Sarena, Saretta, Sarita) Hebrew 'princess'
Sharon: Hebrew (for a coastal plain; popularized by the biblical "roses of Sharon")
Shirley: English (a place name, then a man's name) 'from the shire meadow'
Sophia: (Fifi, Sofia, Sonya, Sophie, Sophronia, Zofia) Greek 'wise'
Stephanie: (Estefana, Stefanie, Stephenia) Greek (feminine of Stephen) 'wearing a garland or crown'
Susan: (Sue, Susanna, Suzanna, Suzette, Zuzana) Hebrew 'a lily'
Sylvia: (Silva, Silvia, Silvie, Silvya) Latin 'forest maiden'
Teresa: (Teresita, Theresa, Therese, Tracey, Tess, Tessa, Tessie) Greek 'harvester'
Valerie: (Valentina, Valeria, Valeriana) Latin 'valiant, strong'
Victoria: (Victoire, Victoriana, Viktoria, Vittoria) Latin (feminine of Victor) 'victorious'
Virginia: (Ginia, Virgilia, Virginie, Ginger, Ginny, Virgy) Latin 'maidenly'
Vivian: (Vivien, Vivienne, Vivia) Latin 'lively'

250 Slightly Offbeat Names for Girls

Excluded from this list are the most conventional names such as Mary and Elizabeth, currently very popular names such as

Jennifer and Karen, and seemingly far-out names such as Satinka and Semiramis.

Included are some old-fashioned names such as Abigail and Edwina that perhaps should be given another chance, a variety of rather infrequently used but attractive names such as Astrid and Mona, and other names such as Benita and Almira now popular among certain segments of the population.

Where appropriate, some of the alternative forms or approximate synonyms are listed. A few pronunciations are given, although some individuals or groups may prefer another pronunciation. The usual national or linguistic origin is shown, but some names are derived from other sources and may have different meanings. Many girls' names that came from ancient Greek or Latin have undergone changes in modern languages.

Abigail: (Abbey, Abbie, Abby, Gail, Gale) Hebrew 'father's joy'
Adelaide: (Adeline, Addie, Adele, Della) Teutonic 'noble and kind'
Adora: Latin 'adored'; Greek 'a gift'
Adorna: Latin 'she makes beautiful'
Adrienne: (Adria, Adriana, Adriane, Adrianna, Adrianne) Greek 'girl
    from Adria,' 'girl from the sea'
Agatha: (Aga, Agata, Atka) Greek, or southern or central European
    'good'
Agnella: (Agna, Agnola; same as Agnes) Greek, Italian 'pure'
Aida: (*ah-EE-duh*): Italian 'happy'
Alameda: (*ah-la-MAY-duh*): North American Indian 'cottonwood
    grove'; Spanish 'parade, promenade'
Alana: (Alanna, Lana) Celtic 'fair, harmonious'; Hawaiian 'light and
    airy'
Alberta: (Albertina, Berta) Teutonic (feminine of Albert) 'noble and
    bright'
Alda: Teutonic 'rich'
Alesia: Greek 'helper'
Aleta: Greek 'wanderer'
Alicia (*uh-LEE-see-uh*): (Alice, Alisa, Alison, Alyce, Elissa, Alys, Alika)
    Greek, Italian, Spanish, Swedish, Hawaiian 'truth'
Aline (*uh-LEEN*): (Alina) Teutonic 'noble'; Russian, Polish 'bright'
Alita (*uh-LEE-tuh*): (Leta, Adelita) Spanish 'noble, truthful'
Alma (*AL-muh* or *AHL-muh*): Latin 'nourishing, supportive, spiritually
    helpful'
Almira: (Elmira, Mira) Arabic 'complete truth'; Hindustani 'clothing
    container'
Althea: (Althaia, Thea) Greek 'wholesome, healing'
Amabel: (Amabelle, Amabella, Amybelle) Latin 'beautiful loved one'
Amata: (Ama, Amanda, Amy) Latin, Spanish 'loved one'

Amber: Arabic 'jewel'; Gaelic 'fierce'
Amelia: (Amalie, Amelie, Emilia, Emilie, Emily) Latin 'industrious,' but
    with overtones of 'affectionate'
Amity: Latin 'friendship'
Anastasia: (Anastassia, Nessa, Stacy, Stasey, Tasya) Greek 'resurrection,
    Easter, who shall rise again'
Andreanna: Greek 'a man's woman, fearless'
Angela: (Angel, Angelica, Angeline, Angelique, Angelita, Angie) Greek
    'angelic, heavenly messenger'
Annis: (Annys) Greek 'whole, complete'
Ardeen: Latin 'ardent'
Ardis: (Arda, Ardella, Ardelle, Ardelia, Ardene) Latin 'fervent, zealous'
Arina: (Arona) Hebrew (feminine of Aaron) of uncertain meaning
    'mountain' (?) 'singer' (?) 'inspired' (?)
Astrid: Teutonic, especially Scandinavian 'strong in love'
Aurelia: (Aurel, Aurelie) Latin 'golden'
Aurore: (Aurora) Latin 'dawn'
Avis: (Ava) Latin 'birdlike'
Aviva: (Avivah) Hebrew 'springtime, youthfully fresh'
Babette: (Hawaiian Babara *buh-BAH-ruh*) Greek 'little Barbara,'
    'stranger, foreigner'; sometimes considered a diminutive of Elizabeth
    'God has promised'
Benita: Spanish 'little Benedicta,' 'blessed'
Bernadette: Teutonic, French (feminine of Bernard) 'little strong one,
    little masterful one'
Bertha: Teutonic, French 'bright, beautiful'
Bonita: Spanish 'pretty and good'
Brenna: Celtic 'with raven tresses'
Brigid: (Birgit, Bride, Bridget, Brietta, Brigette, Brighid, Brigida,
    Brigitta) Celtic, with forms in other languages 'protective, strong'
Camille: (Camila, Camilla, Camellia) Greek, Latin 'assistant in
    religious ceremonies'
Cara: Gaelic 'friend'; Vietnamese 'precious jewel'
Carli: (Carla, Carlita, Carlina, Karla) Teutonic (pet name for Caroline,
    feminine of Charles) 'little womanly one'
Carmel: Hebrew 'vineyard, fruitful field'
Carlotta: Italian form of Caroline, Carla
Cecilia: (Cecelia, Cecile, Cecily, Celia) Latin (feminine of Cecil)
    original means 'blind,' but St. Cecilia is the patron saint of music,
    hence 'musical'
Celesta: (Celeste, Celestina, Celestine) Latin 'heavenly'
Chandra (*CHAHN-druh*): Hindi 'moon'
Charmaine (shar-MANE): (Charmain, Charma, Charmian) Greek 'joy,
    delight'
Claudia: (Claudette, Claudina, Claudine, Cladys) Latin (feminine of
    Claude or Claudius) 'little lame one'; sometimes interpreted as
    'magnanimous' because Emperor Claudius treated captives so well

Cora: (Corena, Coretta, Corette, Corinna, Corinne) Greek 'maiden'
Coral: Greek, Latin 'coral'
Cordelia: Celtic 'daughter of the sea'; Latin 'warm-hearted'
Cornelia: (Cornella, Nella, Nellie) Latin (feminine of Cornelius) 'queenly, womanly, enduring'
Dagmar: Teutonic, especially Danish 'glory of the Danes, joy of the land'
Damita (*duh-MEE-tuh*): Spanish 'little noble lady'
Daphne: (Daphna) Greek 'laurel tree, laurel maiden, victorious'
Dawn: English 'dawn = Aurora'
Deirdre: Celtic 'sorrow, compassion'
Delia: Greek 'from the island of Delos'; also short for Cordelia, Adele
Delphine: (Delphina, Delphinia) Greek 'calm, serene,' 'loving sister'
Desiree (*DEZ-uh-REE*): Latin 'desired, desirable'
Dora: Greek, unclear
Dorene: (Doreen, Dorena, Dorenn, Dorine, Dorina) Greek 'bountiful'
Dorinda: Greek 'she has been given to us'
Dorisa: (variant of Greek Doris) Hawaiian 'from the sea'
Edwina: Teutonic (feminine of Edwin) 'rich friend'
Eldora: Teutonic 'gift of wisdom'
Elfrida: (Elfreda) Teutonic 'wise and peaceful'
Elise: (variant of Elizabeth) Hebrew 'God's promise'
Elma: Greek 'pleasant, lovable'; English 'like an elm'; Turkish (*el-MUH*) 'apple'
Elvira (*el-VI-ruh*): Spanish 'elfin'
Emilia: (Emilie, Emily) Latin 'industrious'
Enid: Celtic 'pure in soul'; English 'fair'
Enola (*ay-NO-luh*): Native American, meaning unknown
Erica: (Erika; feminine of Eric) Greek 'the heather flower'; Teutonic 'ever regal'
Erlinda: Hebrew 'lively'
Ertha: (Eartha, Erda) Teutonic 'child of the earth, earthly, earthy, worldly, realistic'
Esmeralda: Latin 'adorned'; Spanish 'emerald'
Eudice (*ee-oo-DEES*): Modern Israeli form of Hebrew Judith 'praise'
Eudora: (Eudore) Greek based on Dora 'gift', 'splendid gift'
Eugenia: (Eugenie, Gena, Gina) Greek (feminine of Eugene) 'well-born, of fortunate parents'
Eula: (Eulalia, Eulalie) Greek 'sweet in speaking'
Eustacia: (Eustacie) Greek 'rich in flowering,' 'steady'
Evadne (*ee-VAD-ne* or *ay-VAD-ne*): Greek 'sweet singer'
Evangeline: Greek 'bearer of good news'
Faith: Teutonic 'ever true, always faithful'
Felcia (*FEL-shuh*): Polish, from Latin Felicia 'happy'
Felicidad: (Feliciana) Spanish, from Latin Felicia 'happy'
Fenella: (Finella) Celtic 'white-shouldered'
Fiona: Greek 'violet'; Celtic 'fair-complexioned'

Flavia: Latin (feminine of Flavius) 'light-haired'
Fleur: (Fleurette) French 'flower'
Flora: (Florence, Floria, Florinda, Floris) Latin 'flowers, blossoming'
Gabrielle: (Gabriella) Hebrew (feminine of Gabriel 'heroine of God, God gives me strength'
Gari: Teutonic (feminine of Gary) 'spear maiden'
Gerda: Scandinavian 'protected'
Gianina (*juh-NEE-nuh*): Italian (feminine of Giovanni =John) 'God is gracious'
Gillian: (one of the most popular names in the Middle Ages; variant of Julia) English, from Latin 'youthful'
Gina: (sometimes a variant of Eugenia) also Japanese 'silvery'
Gleda (*GLED-uh*): Icelandic 'make happy, gladden'
Golda: Teutonic, Israeli 'golden-haired'
Greta: German, from Latin Margarita (Margaret, etc.) 'pearl'
Gunda: Norwegian 'battle maiden'
Gwendolyn: (Gwen, Gwendaline, Gwendolen, Gwendoline, Gwyn, Gwyneth, Wendy) Celtic 'white-haired, lady of the new moon'
Haidee: (Haida) Greek 'modest'
Haley: modern U.S. 'clever, ingenious'
Helga: Scandinavian 'religious, pious'
Hilary: (Hilaria) Latin 'cheerful, merry'
Iantha: (Ianthe, Ianthine) Greek 'violet'
Ilona: (Ilone) Greek 'a light'; Hungarian 'beautiful'
Ilse: (Elsa, Else, Ilsa) Teutonic 'noble maiden' (also sometimes defined as a variant of Elizabeth)
Inessa: Russian equivalent of Ines
Ingrid: Scandinavian, probably referring to Ingi, an early king
Iona: (Ione, Ionia) Greek 'violet=Ianthe'), also Celtic, the name of a revered island where many Celtic kings are buried
Irena: (Irene, Russian Irina) Greek 'peace'
Iris: (Russian Irisa: *i-REES-uh*): Greek 'rainbow,' 'goddess of the rainbow'
Isolde: (Isolda) Celtic 'fair'
Ivy: Teutonic 'a clinging vine, affectionate and dependent'
Jacinta (*jah-SIN-tuh*): (Spanish: hah-SEEN-tah) Greek 'hyacinth, purple'
Jamila (*jah-MEE-lah*): Arabic 'beautiful'
Jasmine: (in India, Yasmine, Yasiman) Greek for the flower of a climbing shrub
Jocasta: Italian 'lighthearted'
Jocelyn: (Jocelin) Latin 'playful, merry'
Joella: (Joela, Joelle) Hebrew (feminine of Joel) 'the Lord is willing'
Johanna: Hebrew (feminine of Johann=John) 'God is gracious'
Joline: (modern form of Josephine) Hebrew (feminine of Joseph) 'she will increase'
Juanita: (feminine of Juan=John) Hebrew through Spanish 'God is gracious'

Juliet: (Spanish Julieta *hoo-lee-ET-ah*=Julia) Latin 'youthful'
Justina: (Justine, Tina) Latin 'the just one'
Kalila (*kah-LEE-lah*): Arabic 'sweetheart, loved one'
Kari: modern U.S. for Carol, Caroline, or Carrie 'strong'; Hungarian form of Karoly
Karla: (Carla) also modern U.S. for Carol, Caroline 'strong, womanly'
Kelilah (*kuh-LEE-lah*): Kelula, Kyla, Kyle) Hebrew 'laurel, crown, victory'
Kenda: modern U.S. 'child of cool, pure water'
Kristin: (Kirsten, Kirstin, Krysta) Scandinavian 'Christian'
Lala (*LAH-lah*): Slovak 'tulip'
Lara: Latin 'famous'; Russian form of Larissa, from Greek 'cheerful'
Lavinia: (Lavenia, Lavina, French Lavinne) Latin 'cleansed,' 'woman of Latium' (religious city near Rome)
Leandra: Greek (feminine of Leander) 'lioness-like'
Leila: Arabic 'dark beauty'
Leilani (*lay-LAHN-ee*): Hawaiian 'heavenly child'
Leola: Teutonic 'dear'
Leonora: (Lenora, Lenore, Leonore) variant of Eleanor=Greek Helen 'light'
Leticia: (Letitia) Latin, now often Spanish 'joyous'
Lila: Hindi 'capriciousness of fate'; Persian 'lilac'; Polish, short for Leopoldine 'defender of the people'
Lilybet: Cornish form of Elizabeth 'God's promise'
Livana (*lee-VAH-nuh*): (Levana) Hebrew 'moon,' 'white'
Lola: (diminutive of Lolita) Spanish form of Carol 'strong woman'
Lorna: Old English 'lost'; Latin (also Lara, Laureen, Laurel, Lauren, Lora, Loren, Loretta) 'laurel, victory'
Lucerne: (Lucerna) Latin 'circle of light'
Lucita (*loo-SEE-tah*): Spanish '(Mary of the) Light'
Luz (*LOOS*): also Spanish '(Mary of the) Light'
Lydia: Greek 'girl from Lydia,' 'cultured person'
Magda (*MAHG-dah*): (Magdalene, Spanish Madalena) Greek 'woman from Magdala'
Mahalia: (Mahala: *mah-HAH-luh*): Hebrew 'woman, feminine tenderness'
Mara (*MAH-ruh*): variant of Hebrew Mary 'bitter'
Marcella: (Marcelle, Marcelline) Latin (feminine of Marcellus) 'hammer,' also said to be Teutonic 'intelligent contestant'
Margita: variant of Greek Margaret 'pearl'
Marta: variant of Aramaic Martha 'lady of the house, mistress'
Mavis: (Mavia) Celtic 'singing thrush'
Meghan: (Megan) Celtic 'strong'; Latin 'great'
Melina: Latin 'sweet as honey'
Melody: (Melodie) Greek 'song, beautiful music'
Melvina: (Melva) Latin 'sweet friend,' 'sweet wine'
Merrie: (Merry) English 'joyful'

Milada (*MIL-uh-duh*): Czech 'my love'
Millicent: (Melicent, Mellicent, Millie) Latin 'sweet singer'; Teutonic
  'good worker'
Minna: (Minnie) Teutonic 'loving memories'
Mira (*MEE-rah*): modern Israeli for Miriam 'exalted'; sometimes
  considered a form of Mary
Miranda: Latin 'admirable, to be wondered at'
Mona: Latin 'solitary': Teutonic 'lonely, far away'; North American
  Indian 'gathering the seed of the jimson weed'
Monica: Latin 'wise counselor'
Morna: (Myrna) Celtic 'tender beloved'
Nadia (*nah-DEE-uh*): Russian 'hope'
Nadine: Russian 'hope'; Greek 'charming'
Nanette: (Nanetta) Hebrew 'little graceful one'
Natasha: Russian 'born on Christmas'
Nelia (*NELL-ee-yuh*): Spanish shortening of Cornelia 'queenly,
  womanly, enduring'
Nerissa: Greek 'daughter of the sea'
Nola: (Nolana) Latin 'little bell'
Odele: (Odell, Odelette) Greek 'melody, song'
Olena (*oh-LAY-nah*): (Alena) Russian, from Greek 'light'
Olga: Russian 'holy'
Olinda: (Linda) Teutonic 'gentle'
Olivia: (Oliva, Olive) Latin 'olive' (a symbol of peace)
Onida (*oh-NEE-dah*): North American Indian 'the looked-for one, the
  desired'
Oriana: Celtic 'golden, dawning'
Pepita (*pep-EE-ta*): Spanish from Hebrew 'she shall add, she shall be
  fruitful'
Philantha: Greek 'she loves flowers'
Philippa: Greek (feminine of Phillip) 'lover of horses'
Phoebe (*FEE-bee*): (Phebe) Greek 'the moon goddess' (=Diana,
  Diane), 'brilliant'
Pierrette: French (feminine of Pierre=Peter) 'little steadfast one'
Pilar: (*pee-LAR*): Spanish 'pillar, foundation'; refers to Mary as the
  foundation of the church
Portia: Latin 'harbor, gateway'
Ramona: (Mona, Raymonde) Spanish or Teutonic (feminine of Ramon
  or Raymond) 'protector'
Rana: (Ranee, Rani) Hindustani 'queenly, royal'
Ranita: modern Israeli 'joyful song'
Regina: (Regine) Latin 'queenly'
Renee (*reh-NAY*): French 'reborn'
Risa: modern U.S. from Latin 'laughter'
Roderica: (Rica) Teutonic (feminine of Roderick) 'ruler, princess'
Rosabel: Latin 'beautiful rose'
Rosaleen: (Rosalie, Rosalind, Roselind, Rosina) Irish 'little rose'; Latin
  'pretty rose'

Rowena: Celtic 'white-bosomed, white-clad, lighthaired'
Roxanne: (Roxana, Roxane, Roxene, Roxie) Persian 'the new dawning'
Sabina: (Bina, Savina) Latin 'girl of the Sabines'
Sabrina: from the name of an Anglo-Saxon princess
Sanura: (suh-NOO-ruh): Swahili 'like a kitten'
Selena: (Selene, Selina) Greek 'moonlight becomes you'
Serena: Latin 'girl with the tranquil heart'
Sigrid: Scandinavian 'beautiful conqueror'
Simone: (Simona, Simonetta) Hebrew (feminine of Simon) 'hearing
    gladly, obedient'
Sonia: (Sona, Sonya) Greek 'the wise one'
Tabitha: Aramaic 'the gazelle,' 'the graceful girl'
Talia (tuh-LEE-uh): (Talya) Hebrew 'the gentle dew from heaven'
Tamar (tuh-MAR): (Tamara, Tammie) Hebrew 'the palm tree'
Tania: (Tanya) Russian 'the fairy queen'
Thalia: Greek 'luxuriant blossoms'. In classical mythology, Thalia was
    the muse of comedy and was also said to be one of the three Graces.
Theodora: (Thea, Theda, Theo) Greek (feminine of Theodore) 'God's
    gift'
Tilda: (short for Matilda) Teutonic 'battle maiden'
Timmi: (Timi, Timmy) modern U.S. from Hebrew Timothea 'she fears
    God'
Tonya: (Tony, Tonia) Russian, from Latin Antonia (feminine of
    Antony) 'inestimable, beyond price'
Truda: Polish from Teutonic 'spear maiden'
Una: (Ona, Oona) Latin 'unity, everything in one'; Hopi 'memory'
Undine: Latin 'of the waves'
Valda: Teutonic 'battle heroine'
Valentina: (Valencia, Valerie, Valeria, Velora) Latin 'strong and
    healthy'
Vanessa: (Vanni) Greek 'butterfly.' Used by Jonathan Swift in his
    letters to Esther Vanhomrigh
Velda: Teutonic 'wise'
Verda: Latin 'young, fresh, virginal'
Verna: (Vernita) Latin 'spring-born, vernal'
Viviana: (Vivian, Vivienne) Latin 'full of life'
Wanda: Teutonic, Slavic 'shepherdess, wandering one'
Wenona (wen-O-nuh): North American Indian 'firstborn daughter'
Wilda: Anglo-Saxon 'untamed'
Wilhelmina: (Mina, Velma, Wilma) Teutonic (feminine of Wilhelm,
    William) 'helmet, protector'
Willa: Teutonic 'resolute, firm'
Wilva: Teutonic 'determined'
Winifred: Teutonic 'friend of peace'
Yolanda: (Yolande, Yolante) Greek 'violet,' 'modest or shy'
Yvette: (Yvonne) French, Teutonic 'carrier of the bow, archer'
Zada (ZAY-duh or ZAH-duh): Syrian 'the lucky'

Zara: (Zarah, variant of Sarah) Arabic 'brightness in the east,' 'princess'
Zelda: (short for Griselda) Teutonic 'unconquerable heroine'
Zora: (Zorah, Zorana, Zorina) Latin 'aurora＝dawn'
Zuleika: Arabic 'fair and bright'

The Old Men Remember

When you and I were young, Maggie.

Who is Sylvia, what is she,
that all the swains adore her?

Nita, Juanita, ask thy soul why we must part—
Oh my darling, oh my darling,
Oh my darling Clementine—
lean thou on my heart.

My Bonnie lies over the ocean,
My Bonnie lies over the sea:
Sweet Leilani, heavenly flower,
Where Hilo Hattie does the Hilo hop,
Mademoiselle from Armentières,
You funny little Gigi,
Charmaine,
Lilli Marlene,
Oh bring back my Chloe to me.

How do you solve a problem like Maria?
Sweet Marie, come to me,
Maria Alena, Marianne,
All day, all night, Marian;
Though Mary is a grand old name,
and I loved Mary in the morning,
They call the wind Maria.

La vie en Rose:
Mexicali Rose, stop crying,
Honeysuckle Rose,
Rosemarie, I love you,
Sweet Rosie O'Grady, Rose of Tralee,
All my wild Irish Roses,
San Antonio Rose, Rosie the riveter,
Cracklin' Rosie.

Sunny,
Stella by starlight
Estrellita.

Once in love with Amy—
I dreamed with my arms around Linda,
or Michelle, *ma belle*.
I dreamed of Jeanie with the light brown hair.
Jeannine, I dream of lilac time,
Dolores, Dolly (you're still glowin'),
Ida, Sweet as apple cider,
Dinah, is there anyone finer,
Georgy girl,
Thoroughly modern Millie,

Nina, pretty ballerina,
Ravishing Ruby
—but always in love with Amy.

If you knew Susie like I knew Susie—
Wake up, little Susie. Wake up, Peggy Sue.
Lay down, Sally. Long tall Sally.
Wait till the sun shines, Nellie.
(It was from Aunt Dinah's quilting party
I was seeing Nellie home.)

Nola.
What Lola wanted, Lola got.

I lost my heart at the stage door canteen
—uh, something about Eileen.
I'll see you home again, Kathleen.
Good night, Irene.

Every little breeze seems to whisper Louise,
but poke salad Annie, sweet Betsy from Pike,
Mame, Annie Laurie, sweet Alice I like.

Frankie and Johnny were sweethearts—
Oh Genevieve, I'd have given the world.
Tangerine, with lips as red as flame.
You picked a fine time to leave me, Lucille.

Goodnight, ladies. Goodnight, ladies.
Do you remember, too?

❦ 2
Choosing Names for Boys

The Most Popular Names for English and Welsh Boys (since 1925)

According to Leslie Dunkling's *First Names First*, in England and Wales from 1925 through 1981 the name John fell from 1st to 33rd. David, 36th in 1925, had become the most popular by 1950, remained in the top ten, and was 2nd in 1981. Michael, for more than a quarter century the most popular boys' name in the United States, was 4th in England and Wales in 1950, 6th in 1965, 11th in 1975, and 10th in 1981. Other changes in rank include these:

Name	1925	1950	1981
William	2	16	41
George	3	34	below 50
James	4	17	8
Ronald	5	32	below 50
Robert	6	6	14
Kenneth	7	27	below 50
Frederick	8	47	below 50
Thomas	9	36	23
Albert	10	below 50	below 50
Andrew	below 50	28	1
Daniel	below 50	below 50	3
Christopher	below 50	14	4
Stephen	below 50	7	5

Name	1925	1950	1981
Matthew	below 50	below 50	6
Paul	below 50	8	7
Mark	below 50	below 50	9
Michael	below 50	4	10

From One Pierre to Another

The friends of young Pierre Fox of San Francisco kept making fun of his given name. His father, who had chosen it, was dead, and Pierre had no idea why a name so unusual in the United States had been selected for him. Learning that the governor of Delaware was also a Pierre, the boy wrote to him asking whether he liked the name and if he could suggest a good nickname for Pierre. Here is the governor's reply:

June 23, 1982

Dear Pierre:

Thanks for taking the time to write to me about your name. My family taught me to be proud of my name, and you should be proud of yours, too. "Pierre" is a great name that goes way back in history, and you and I are lucky enough to be among the few people in the country who have it.

I can think of many other people named Pierre who are famous. Pierre Trudeau is the prime minister of Canada; Pierre Curie was a famous scientist; Pierre Auguste Renoir was a famous painter. And don't forget all those famous hockey players named Pierre.

My ancestors were French, and my namesake lived in France before the 1800s. Perhaps you have some French ancestors too, and that's why your dad chose your name.

My father's name is Pierre, and I have a son named Pierre. My son is twenty-two years old and very proud of his name. As for nicknames, I am called Pete, and that might be a good nickname for you.

You bet I will be your friend. There aren't many of us "Pierres" around, so we better stick together.

Your friend,
Pierre S. du Pont

The governor might have suggested another appropriate nickname—Rocky, because Pierre, Peter, Pietro, and their equivalents mean 'rock'. One of the few puns in the New Testament is based on that fact. In Matthew 16:18, Jesus is reported as saying, "Thou art Peter, and upon this rock I will build my church."

Outdoorsy Names, Indoorsy Names

If a baby boy is named Jack or Sam instead of Theodore or Elbert, is the choice of name likely to influence his fortune?

William G. Gaffney (*Names,* March 1971) thinks that "names can influence character, personality, and occupation; and that (therefore) a parent can determine, or at least help to determine, his child's career by the *kind* of name he bestows."

As evidence Gaffney cites his study of U.S. Army officers' names—not the names of West Pointers, but of those whose backgrounds and abilities had made it possible for them to work their way up through Officers Candidate Schools or by battlefield promotion. These men, much more frequently than in the general population, had simple names on their birth certificates—Jack, Tom, Bud, Bob, Sam, and the like—not John, Thomas, etc., and not Egbert or Lancaster, either.

His second study was of male college teachers. Very few Jacks or Buds, etc., were found there. Academic types (and presumably other indoor types), much more often than the law of averages would predict, had names such as Grove, Theodore, Lucius, Rodney, Prosser, Elbert, Wymberly, Linville, or Fordyce. "Children with unusual names tend to become bookish early in life and perhaps as a direct consequence, frequently end up as professors," Gaffney says.

He concludes that to a considerable extent a boy's name dictates his future. There may be some truth in the conclusion, but we also have to remember that family background may be even more important. Parents who name a boy Sam and parents who name theirs Linville probably have different life-styles, different heritages, different educational levels (and hence different degrees of bookishness), and different aspirations. These factors affect first the choice of name and thereafter the boy's whole life.

The Bowen Theory of Executive Advancement

"An incredibly large proportion of the U.S. business leaders have very unusual first names. In fact, men with unusual names seem to rise to the front ranks of management out of all proportion to their numbers."

So Stephen N. Bowen (or S. Newton Bowen) said in 1973 when he was Director of Corporate Public Relations for TRW Inc., one of the nation's largest corporations. Bowen based his theory on a close look at the rosters of 1,000 companies.

Suppose, he said, that William Brown and T. Armstrong Ashburton are vying for a vice presidency. "What will you bet that nine times out of ten Ashburton gets the nod? Obviously, he has an edge, a distinctive handle that separates him from the pack."

Bowen admitted that an occasional George, Bill, Bob, or Dick gets to or near the top. But in company after company, he said, top executives had less common names.

Cessna Aircraft—Dwayne, Delbert, Virgil, Pierre, Derby, Max
Brown Foreman Distillers Corp.—Robinson, Rodman, Peyton, Mason, Owsley Frazier, Owsley Brown II
Officers of various financial institutions—Gaylord, Freeman, Montgomery, Dorsey, Marriner Eccles, Pope Brook, True Davis

An initial instead of a first name is often effective, too. Bowen referred to O. Pendleton Thomas, I. John Billera, and J. Paul Getty. Repetition of the same initial isn't bad, either: W. W. Keller, H. H. Wetzel, and "R. R. . . . does wonders for President Smith of Smith's Transfer Corp. But for ringing redundancy, my favorite is the chairman of Norman, Craig, and Kummel: Norman B. Norman."

The use of Junior or even Jr. is questionable, maybe even when a son is expected to inherit a company or a presidency.

Suppose that you are about to choose a name for a son (Bowen didn't consider daughters) and that family background suggests he is likely to go into business. What should you name him?

Bowen suggested that you look at a list of forenames of the sort often appended to desk dictionaries. "Try names like Basil, Derek, Garth, Royal, Sterling, Yale, or even Zane. Each of those has a commanding aura to it almost guaranteed to make personnel managers snap to attention."

Bowen didn't mention what is sometimes another excellent choice for a first or middle name: the mother's maiden name. In all likelihood, Armstrong in T. Armstrong Ashburton was little Tommy's mother's name. (By the way, what's a nickname for Armstrong? Army?)

Not a Sissy Name

In an Arizona gubernatorial primary, the first name of the incumbent (and eventual winner) was Bruce. One of his opponents attained a new low in mud-slinging by suggesting that that name was effeminate: "It surprises me that a state like Arizona, home of macho men, would ever elect a governor named Bruce."

A little knowledge of history might have helped him. The name gets its popularity from the Scottish national hero, Robert the Bruce or Robert de Bruce (1274–1329), who near Bannockburn on June 23–24, 1314, brilliantly outmaneuvered the English even though his Scots were outnumbered more than three to one. He drove out the English and as a result succeeded in establishing an independent Scottish monarchy that lasted almost three hundred years. In 1964, 650 years after that battle, Queen Elizabeth II of England renewed his memory by unveiling an equestrian statue of him at Bannock-burn.

Incidentally, the Arizona Bruce, whose last name is Babbitt, in 1988 made an unsuccessful run for the Democratic nomination for president.

Not *Junior*!

Some people believe that *Jr.* suggests sissiness. Here are a few of the thousands of names that could be cited to prove the contrary (adapted from a much longer list in *Beyond Jennifer and Jason* by Rosenkrantz and Satran). Seldom, however, is a grown man known as Junior, because the name suggests youthfulness and because many men do not want to live in the shadows of their fathers.

Ferdinand Lewis Alcindor, Jr.
  (He changed his name to
  Kareem Abdul-Jabbar.)
Arthur Ashe, Jr.
Marlon Brando, Jr.
William F. Buckley, Jr.
James Francis Cagney, Jr.
  (Better known as Jimmy)
James Earl Carter, Jr. (Jimmy)
James Scott Connors, Jr. (Jim)

William H. Cosby, Jr. (Bill)
Clinton Eastwood, Jr. (Clint)
Alexander M. Haig, Jr.
Harold Rowe Holbrook, Jr. (Hal)
Walter Stacy Keach, Jr. (Stacy)
Thomas P. O'Neill, Jr. (Tip)
Charles Robert Redford, Jr.
  (Robert)
Kurt Vonnegut, Jr.
Hank Williams, Jr.

Ask for Him by His Right Name

A stranger in a Scottish village wanted to find Alexander White. He met a young woman and asked her,

"Cou'd you tell me fa'r 'where' Sanny Fite lives?"

"Filk 'which' Sanny Fite?"

"Muckle 'big' Sanny Fite."

"Filk muckle Sanny Fite?"

"Muckle lang 'tall' Sanny Fite."

"Filk muckle lang Sanny Fite?"

"Muckle lang gleyed 'squint-eyed' Sanny Fite," shouted the stranger.

"Oh! It's Goup-the-lift 'stare-at-the-sky' y'are seeking," cried the girl, "and fat the deavil dinna ye speer for 'and why the devil didn't you ask for' the man by his richt name at ance?"

If You Have a Hundred Sons

An old Arabic saying is "If you have a hundred sons, call them all Muhammad." A prolific Arab and his several wives and many concubines would thus presumably be paying great homage to the Prophet.

Whether any Arab ever followed this advice literally is unknown. But a Scot did as well as he could in a similar attempt.

Many Scots in the early eighteenth century were resentful because a Stuart was no longer on the throne of Great Britain. James Francis Edward Stuart (1688–1766), son of the deposed King James II, and later the king's grandson, Charles Edward Louis Philip Casimir Stuart (1720–1788), became known in turn in England as "The Pretender." The latter, Charles Edward, was widely called by the Scots "Bonnie Prince Charlie." In Scotland these Stuarts were considered the legitimate rulers, and battles, such as the famous one at Culloden Moor, were fought in their behalf.

One fervent Scot, whose wife bore him 14 sons, named each of them Charles Edward, in honor of the bonnie prince.

100 Traditional-Modern Names for Boys

To qualify for this list, a name must be centuries old but still in use today in the United States, Canada, and the British Isles.

Common variants are included for some names. The generally accepted meanings are in single quotes. (Some meanings are in dispute.) Note that men's given names often connoted leadership, guardianship, military prowess, or religion, but now may not do so.

Adam: Hebrew 'man of earth, red earth'
Albert: (Bert, Delbert) Teutonic 'noble and bright'
Alexander: (Alec, Alex, Sandor, Sasha) Greek 'protector of people'
Alfred: (Alfredo) English 'wise adviser'
Allan: (a variant of Alan, Alain, Alano, Allen) Celtic 'cheerful,
    pleasant, attractive'
Andrew: (Andre, Andreas, Andres) Greek 'manly, brave'
Anthony: (Antoine, Anton, Antony, Tony) Latin 'praiseworthy'
Arthur: (Artur, Arturo) Celtic 'strong, noble'
Benjamin: (Ben) Hebrew 'son of my right hand'
Brian: (Bryan, Bryant) Celtic 'powerful, great leader'
Calvin: (Calvert) Latin 'bald'
Cary: (Carey, sometimes a variant of Charles) Teutonic 'beloved'
Charles: (Carl, Carlo, Carlos, Carol, Cary, Charlot, Karl, Karoly)
    Teutonic 'noble-spirited man, robust'
Christopher: (Chris, Kris) Greek 'Christ-bearing'
Clarence: (Clare) Latin 'bright, clear'
Clifford: (Cliff) English 'from the ford by the cliff'
Conrad: (Conrado, Konrad) Teutonic 'wise or brave counsel'
Daniel: (Dan, Danilo, Dannie) Hebrew 'God will judge'
David: (Dave, Davey, Davis, Davy) Hebrew 'beloved'
Dennis: (Denis, Denys, Dion) Greek 'wine connoisseur'
Derek: (Derrick, Dirk) Teutonic 'ruler of the people'
Donald: (Bogdan, Don, Danil, Donaldo, Pascual) Celtic 'proud or great
    chief'
Douglas: Celtic 'dark stranger,' 'dweller beside the dark water'
Earl: (Earle, Erle, Errol) Teutonic 'intelligent'; English 'a nobleman'
Edgar: English 'lucky spear,' 'fortunate warrior'
Edmund: (Edmon, Edmond, Edmondo, Edmundo) Teutonic 'fortunate
    protector'
Edward: (Eddy, Eduardo, Edvardo) Teutonic 'guardian of property'
Elmer: (Aylmer) English: 'famous, noble'
Ernest: (Arno, Earnest, Ernesto, Ernot) Teutonic 'serious'
Erwin: (Ervin, Irvin, Irving, Irwin, Marvin, Mervin) Teutonic 'sailor
    friend'
Ethan: Hebrew 'firm, steadfast'
Eugene: (Eugenio, Gene) Greek 'well-born'
Everett: (Eberhard, Everardo, Everhard, Everitt) Teutonic 'courageous,
    strong as a boar'
Ferdinand: (Ferdinando, Fernand) Teutonic 'venturesome'
Francis: (Francesco, Francisco, Frank, Franz) Teutonic 'free,' 'French'
Frederick: (Fred, Frederic, Fredric, Fredrick, Fritz) Teutonic 'peaceful
    chief'
Gabriel: (Gavril) Hebrew 'God is my strength'

George: (Georg, Georges, Jorge, Jurgen) Greek 'farmer, rural'
Gerald: (Geraldo, Gerry, Jerrold, Jerry) Teutonic 'mighty spearman'
Gilbert: (Gilberto, Gilpin, Wilfred, Wilbur) Teutonic 'bright promise'
Glenn: (Glen) Teutonic 'glen, dale, valley'
Gordon: Scottish 'hilly estate'
Gregory: (Greg, Gregg, Gregorio) Greek 'watchful'
Harold: (Harald, Haraldo) Teutonic 'leader, champion, great warrior'
Henry: (Enrico, Enrique, Harry, Heinrich, Heinz, Hendrik) Teutonic
    'ruler of the home'
Herbert: (Bert, Erberto, Hilberto, Herberto) Teutonic 'bright warrior'
Homer: Greek 'pledge'
Hugh: (Hugo) Teutonic 'intellectual'
Isaac: (Isaak, Isak, Itzhak, Izaak) Hebrew 'laughing'
Jacob: (Hamish, Jacques, Jacques, James) Hebrew 'the supplanter'
Jason: Greek 'the healer, the atoner'
Jeffrey: (variant of Geoffrey; Godfrey, Jeff, Jeffry) Teutonic 'peace with
    God'
Jeremy: (variant of Jeremiah; Jeremias) Hebrew 'exalted by God'
Jerome: (Geronimo, Hiram, Jerry) Greek 'holy name'
Joel: Hebrew 'the Lord is God,' 'strong of will'
John: (Giovanni, Hans, Ivan, Jean, Jehan, Johan, Jonas, Juan, Zane)
    Hebrew 'God's gracious gift'
Jonathan: Hebrew 'gift of God'
Joseph: (Giuseppe, Jose, Josef, Pepe) Hebrew 'God will increase him'
Kenneth: (Innocencio) Celtic 'handsome'
Lawrence: (Lauren, Laurence, Loren, Lorenz, Lorenzo) Latin 'laurel,
    crowned with laurel'
Leonard: (Leo, Leon, Leonardo, Leonhard, Lionel) Latin 'a lion, brave
    as a lion'
Lester: English, from Leicester 'bright'
Louis: (Clovis, Lewis, Ludwig, Luigi, Luis) Teutonic 'famous in war'
Luther: (Lothar) Teutonic 'renowned warrior'
Martin: (Marcel, Marco, Marley, Martino, Martius) Latin 'martial, like
    Mars'
Matthew: (Mathew, Mathias, Mathiau, Mateo, Matteo) Hebrew 'God's
    gift'
Melvin: (Malvin) Celtic 'chief'
Michael: (Michal, Michel, Mitchell) Hebrew 'godly'
Milton: English 'from the mill town'
Morris: (Maurice) Latin 'Moorish, dark'
Nathan: (Nathaniel, Nathanael, Natan) Hebrew 'gift of God'
Nicholas: (Klaus, Niccolo, Nicholl, Nicolai, Nicolas, Nicolo, Nikita,
    Niklos, Niles) Greek 'victor for the people'
Noah: Hebrew 'rest, peace, comfort'
Norman: (Normand, Norris) Teutonic 'man from Normandy or the
    North'
Oliver: (Oliverio, Olivier, Oliviero) Latin 'olive branch, peace'

Orville: French 'of the golden town'
Oscar: (Oskar) English 'spear of God'
Patrick: (Paddy, Patrice, Patricio, Patrizio) Latin 'patrician, noble, wealthy'
Peter: (Parnell, Peder, Pedro, Pierre, Pierrot, Pietro, Piotr) Greek 'rock, stone, boulder'
Philip: (Felipe, Filip, Phillip) Greek 'lover of horses'
Ralph: (Rafael, Ralf, Randolph, Rodolpho, Rolfe, Rudolf, Rudolpho) Teutonic 'house wolf'
Raymond: (Ramon, Raimondo, Raymund, Ray, Raymundo) Teutonic 'wise protector'
Rex: (Regis) Latin 'king, kingly'
Richard: (Dick, Ricardo, Riccardo, Rico, Riqui) Teutonic 'strong warrior, firm and powerful'
Robert: (Roberto, Robin, Ruperto) Teutonic 'bright fame'
Roger: (Hodge, Rodger, Rogerio, Ruggero) Teutonic 'famous warrior'
Ronald: (Renaldo, Ronaldo) Teutonic 'powerful adviser'
Russell: (Roserio) Teutonic 'red, red-haired,' 'like a fox'
Samuel: (Salvatore) Hebrew 'message from God, name of God'
Sidney: (Sydney) Greek, French 'of St. Denys' (but in honor of Sir Philip Sidney)
Stanley: (Estanislao, Stanislao, Stanislas, Stanleigh) 'pride of the camp'
Terry: (Terence, Terencio, Terrence) Teutonic 'popular ruler'
Theodore: (Feodor, Teodor, Teodoro) Greek 'gift of God'
Thomas: (Masaccio, Thom, Thoma, Tomas, Tomasso) Aramaic or Hebrew 'a twin'; Phoenician 'the sun god'
Victor: (Vicente, Vick, Victorio, Viktor, Vincent, Vincenzo, Vito, Vittorio) Latin 'conqueror'
Walter: (Gautier, Gualberto, Vladimir, Waldemar, Walther) Teutonic 'army commander'
Warren: Teutonic 'park-keeper, game warden, friendly protector'
William: (Guglielmo, Guillaume, Vasili, Wilhelm, Willis) Teutonic 'helmet, resolute protector'

250 Slightly Offbeat Names for Boys

The names in this list were chosen in the same manner as the girls' names on pages 18–25. Excluded are the most conventional names such as John and William, currently very popular names such as Jason and Christopher, and seemingly far-out names such as Ablu and Guyapi.

Included are a few old-fashioned names that perhaps deserve renewed popularity, such as August and Orville, a variety of rather infrequently used but attractive names such as Baird and Emlyn, and other names such as Ahmad and Casimir now popular among certain segments of the population.

Where appropriate, some of the alternative forms or approximate synonyms are listed. A few pronunciations are given, although these may vary with individuals or national subgroups. The usual national or linguistic origin is shown, but sometimes a name may also be derived from other sources and perhaps have different meanings. Note that many masculine given names are taken from surnames and place names, and for that reason do not supposedly describe or characterize, as do most feminine names.

Abel: Hebrew 'breath'
Adair: Celtic 'ford at the oak tree,' a descendant of Edgar 'lucky spear'
Addison: English descendant of Adam 'red earth'
Adel: (Adal) Teutonic 'noble'
Adrian: (Adrien, Spanish Adriano) Latin 'from Adria' (an ancient town in central Italy)
Ahmad (*AH-mahd*): (Ahmed) Arabic 'highly praised'
Alain (*ah-LANE*): French variant of Alan; Celtic 'handsome, cheerful'
Alano (*ah-LAH-no*): Spanish version of Alan; Celtic 'handsome, cheerful'
Alban: (Alben, Albin) Latin 'white, dawn's early light'
Alden: (Aldin) Anglo-Saxon 'old friend'
Aldous: (Aldis) Teutonic 'old, wise'
Alek: (Alik; Russian variant of Alexander) Greek 'he helps people'
Alger: Teutonic 'old spear, experienced spear, elf spear'
Alistair: (Alastair, Allister; variant of Alexander) Greek 'he helps people'
Angelo: (Angel) Greek 'messenger with good news, angelic'
Anson: Anglo-Saxon 'son of Ann'
Arden: (Ardin) Latin 'eager, fervent, sincere'
Ardmore: Latin and Teutonic 'more ardent, more fervent'
Armand: (Armando, Armin, Armond, Ormond; Russian Arman (*ar-MAHN*) Latin, Teutonic 'armed, protective'
Arvin: Teutonic 'friend of the people'
Ashley: Anglo-Saxon 'ash tree grove'
August: (Augustine, Augustus, Austin) Latin 'imperial, exalted, revered'
Averill: (Averil, French Avril) French 'born in April'; Teutonic 'boar battle.' Also from an English place name, Haverhill 'oat hill.'
Avery: (Aubrey; sometimes a variant of Averil) Anglo-Saxon 'ruler of the elves'
Baird: Celtic 'bard, minstrel'
Baldwin: Teutonic 'noble or bold friend'
Barnabas: (Barnaby) Hebrew, Aramaic 'consoling son, son of prophecy'
Barton: Anglo-Saxon 'he holds the land.' Also a place name.
Beldon: (Belden) Anglo-Saxon 'on the hill'

Bellamy: Latin 'beautiful friend'
Bennett: (Benedict, Bennet) Latin 'blessed'
Benton: Anglo-Saxon, a place name of uncertain meaning
Berggren: (Bergren) Scandinavian 'mountain branch.' Bergen or Bergin
   is 'hill or mountain dweller.'
Bertram: (Bartram) Teutonic 'bright raven,' 'he shall be famous'
Blair: Teutonic, Celtic 'boy from the plains'
Blake: Teutonic. May mean either 'dark' or 'light'
Bond: English, Icelandic 'he stays with the soil'
Boris: Slavic 'fighter, stranger'
Bowen: Welsh 'son of Owen "warrior" '
Bradford: Anglo-Saxon 'from the broad ford'
Brendan: (Brandon, Brendon, Brennan) Scandinavian, but not
   uncommon in Ireland 'aflame, inspirational'
Brice: (Bryce) Celtic 'awake, ambitious'
Burgess: (Burges) Anglo-Saxon 'from the town or borough'
Burke: (Burk) Teutonic 'fortress, stronghold'
Burton: (Berton) Anglo-Saxon 'village near a fort'
Byron: English 'from the cottage.' Often named for the poet George
   Gordon, Lord Byron.
Carlos: Spanish form of Charles 'manly'
Carmichael: Celtic 'Michael's stronghold'
Carvel: Manx (The Isle of Man) 'a song'
Casimir: Slavic 'he proclaims peace'
Cedric: Celtic 'chieftain'
Chalmer: (Chalmers) Teutonic 'head of a household, chamberlain'
Chandler: English 'candlemaker, he provides light'
Charlton: (Carleton, Carlton, Charleton) Anglo-Saxon 'from Charles's
   homestead'
Clay: Teutonic 'of the earth, mortal'
Clement: (Clemence) Latin 'merciful, kind'
Clive: (Cleve) from an English surname; also Teutonic 'cliff'
Clovis: from a medieval French ruler, from whose name Louis is also
   derived; also Teutonic 'famous warrior'
Colin: (Cole) sometimes shortened from Nicholas; also Celtic 'young
   and virile'
Conroy: Celtic 'persistent'
Corbin: Latin 'the raven'
Coryell: Greek 'helmeted, ready for battle'
Crispian: (Crispin) Latin 'curly-haired'
Crispus: from Crispus Attucks, first man killed in American Revolution
Culver: English 'dove, peace-loving'
Dag (*DAHG*): Scandinavian 'day, brightness'
Dallas: Celtic, from a Scottish place
Damek (*DAHM-ek*): Czech form of Adam 'man of the red earth'
Damian: (Damien) Greek 'taming, he makes people gentle'
Dana: (Dane) Scandinavian 'a Dane'; also short for Hebrew Daniel
   'judged by God'

Dante (*DAHN-tee* or *DAHN-tay*; sometimes anglicized to *DAN-tee*):
   from the name of the medieval Italian poet; Latin 'lasting'
Delmar: (Delmer) Latin 'of the sea'
Desmond: French 'of the world, sophisticated'; also an Irish surname
   'one from South Munster'
Dexter: Latin 'right-handed, dexterous'
Donovan: Celtic 'dark warrior'
Doran: Greek 'a gift'; Celtic 'a stranger'
Dorian: Greek, uncertain meaning
Dougal: (Doyle, Dugald) Celtic 'dark stranger'
Drew: English shortening of Hebrew Andrew 'manly'
Drummond: Celtic 'he lives on the hilltop'
Duncan: Celtic 'swarthy chief'
Durward: Teutonic 'unfailing guard'
Edson: (Edison) English 'son of Ed'
Einar (*I-nar*): (Danish Ejnar) Scandinavian 'nonconformist, he thinks
   for himself'
Eldred: (Eldrid) Teutonic 'battle counselor'
Ellery: Teutonic 'the alder tree'
Ellsworth: (Elsworth) Anglo-Saxon place name 'Elli's place'
Elmo: Latin, from Greek 'friendly, lovable'
Elwin: (Elwyn, Wynn) Anglo-Saxon 'godly friend'
Emlyn: Welsh 'waterfall'
Emory: (Emery, Italian Amerigo—for whom America was named)
   Teutonic 'work, rule'
Errol: usually a variant of English Earl 'nobleman'; sometimes Latin
   'wandering'
Esmond: English 'protected by God's grace'
Ethan: Hebrew 'steadfast, strong and reliable'
Eustace (*YOO-stus*): Greek 'productive'
Evan (*EE-vuhn or EH-vuhn*): Welsh form of John 'God is gracious'
Everard: Teutonic 'always true,' 'strong as a wild boar'
Fabian: (Fabiano) Latin from Fabius, a dilatory general; hence implies
   'procrastinating, indecisive'; original meaning 'bean grower'
Fairfax: English 'light-haired'
Felipe (*feh-LEE-peh*): Spanish for Greek Phillip 'lover of horses'
Fergus: Gaelic 'strong man'
Flavian: Latin Flavius 'yellow-haired'
Fletcher: English surname 'arrow-maker'
Florian: Latin 'flowering'
Fulton: English place name 'poultry farm'
Gabriel: Hebrew 'hero of God, God gives him strength'
Garrick: Teutonic (English) place name and surname (a leading
   eighteenth-century actor) 'Gara's place'
Gaspar: (Caspar, Casper, Gaspard, Jasper, Kaspar, Kasper) Spanish
   from Persian 'master of treasure'
Gavin: (Galvin) variant of Celtic Gawain 'white hawk'

Giles: Greek, Latin shield-bearer,' 'young goat'
Glendon: Celtic 'from the shady valley'
Godfrey: Teutonic 'divinely peaceful'
Goodwin: (Godwin) English 'good friend, god's friend'
Graham: Celtic 'from the gray home'
Granville: French 'large estate'
Gregor: (Gregorio, Gregory, Grigor) Greek 'vigilant'
Griffith: (Griffin) Welsh 'fierce lord,' 'red-haired, ruddy'
Grover: English surname 'one who lives in or near a grove'
Gunnar (GOO-nahr): (Gunther) Scandinavian 'warrior'
Gustave: (Gustaf, Gustavus) Scandinavian 'noble staff, God's staff'
Guthrie: Celtic 'war hero,' or Celtic place name 'where the wind blows
    free'
Hale: Anglo-Saxon 'in good health'; also an English place name and
    surname 'nook, corner'; also Hawaiian (pronounced HAH-lee) for
    Harold 'army ruler'
Hamilton: English place name and surname (sometimes spelled
    Hambleton) 'grassy hill'
Hanley: English place name and surname 'high meadow'; Irish 'warrior'
Hartwell: English place name 'deer's spring, where the deer drink'
Hassan: Arabic 'handsome'
Hendrik: (Enrico, Hendrick, Henri) Dutch variant of Henry 'ruler of
    the home'
Heywood: English place name 'high or enclosed wood'
Hilliard: Teutonic 'war guard'; most often from the English surname
    'enclosure on a hill'
Holbrook: English surname 'stream in the valley'
Houston: Scottish surname 'Hugh's town'
Igor: (Inge, Ingmar) Scandinavian, Slavic 'hero'
Ingmar: (Ingemar) Scandinavian 'well-known son'
Ingram: (Ingraham) from the English surname based on Scandinavian
    Ing, a mythical hero 'Ing's raven'
Ivar (EE-vahr): (Ives, Ivor, Yves) Scandinavian 'archer with a yew bow'
Jacinto (Hah-SEEN-toh): Spanish from Greek 'purple, hyacinth'
Jared: Hebrew 'descendant, the inheritor'
Jasper: (Casper, Gaspar, Kasper) English from Persian 'master of
    treasure'
Javier (hahv-ee-AIR): (Xavier) Arabic 'bright'; Spanish (Basque) 'he has
    a new home'
Jens (JENZ, or Scandinavian YENS): Scandinavian form of John 'God
    is gracious'
Jeremy: (Jeremiah, Jerry) Hebrew 'exalted by God'
Joel: Hebrew 'the Lord is God'
Johan: Scandinavian form of John 'God is gracious'
Jonas: Hebrew 'the dove, peace'; Lithuanian form of John 'God is
    gracious'
Jorge (HOHR-heh): Spanish equivalent of George 'farmer'

Julian (*JOO-lee-uhn*, or Spanish *HOO-lee-AHN*): from Latin Julius
  'youthful, downy-cheeked'
Junius: Latin 'forever young'
Justin: (Justus) English from Latin 'the just'
Kendall: English place name 'valley of the Kent River'
Kendrick: Anglo-Saxon 'royal rule'
Kenyon: English place name 'Einion's mound'; also from Celtic Fingin
  'light-haired'
Kerry: Celtic 'dark'; English 'ship captain'
Kester: Dutch place name; sometimes a form of Greek Christopher
  'Christ-bearer'
Kimball: English place name 'royal hill'
Konane (*ko-NAH-nee*): Hawaiian 'bright moonlight'
Kyle: English, Scottish 'strait, firth, narrow waterway'
Lambert: Teutonic 'his country's light'
Lance: short for Latin Lancelot (Launcelot) 'he who serves'
Landon: Anglo-Saxon 'from the long hill'
Langley: Anglo-Saxon 'from the long meadow or wood'
Lars: Scandinavian form of Lawrence 'laurel, victory'
Leander: Greek 'like a lion'
Lionel: French 'little lion'
Llewellyn: Welsh 'lionlike, lightning'
Lorant (*LOH-rawnt*): Hungarian, from Latin 'laurel, victory'
Lucien: (Lucian) French, from Latin Lucius 'light'; a name sometimes
  given to a child born at dawn
Madison: English from Hebrew Matthew 'God's light.' In U.S.
  sometimes from President James Madison.
Malcolm: Scottish 'follower of St. Columba' "dove"
Manfred: Teutonic 'man of peace'
Manuel (*mah-noo-EL*): (Emmanuel) Spanish 'God be with us'
Mayer: (Meyer, Myer) Teutonic 'farmer'
Maynard: Teutonic 'strong and steady'
Merton: Anglo-Saxon 'from the place by the sea'
Merwyn: (Mervin, Merwin) Celtic 'friend of the sea'
Morgan: Welsh 'sea-dweller'
Morley: English place name 'wood by a marsh'
Murray: Scottish 'one from the sea,' or the place Moray 'beside the sea'
Neville: French place name 'new town'
Newton: English and Scottish place name and surname 'new town'
Nigel (*NIGH-jul*): Greek, Latin 'dark'
Noel: French from Latin 'Christmas, Christmas carol'
Nolan: Celtic 'famous, noble'
Norbert: Teutonic 'brightness of the north'
Oakley: Anglo-Saxon 'oak tree grove'
Odell: Teutonic 'prosperous'; English place name 'woad hill'
Ogden: (Ogdon) Anglo-Saxon 'oak valley'
Olaf: name of several Scandinavian kings 'ancestral relic'

Orlando: (Roland, Spanish Roldan) Italian, Spanish 'from the famous land'

Ormond: (Ormand) Irish place name; also Teutonic 'protector'

Osmond: (Osmont, Osmund) Teutonic 'divine protector'

Palmer: English 'palm-carrying crusader'

Parker: English surname 'keeper of a park, gamekeeper'

Pavel (*PAH-vyel*): Slavic for Paul 'small'

Pembroke: Welsh place name 'headland'

Porter: English from Latin 'gatekeeper,' 'one who carries goods'

Prentice: (Prentiss) English and French, from Latin 'learner, apprentice'

Prescott: English place name 'priest's cottage'

Preston: English place name and surname 'priest's place'

Raoul: French form of Teutonic Ralph, Randolph 'protection, wolf'

Raphael: Hebrew 'God heals'

Redmond: Teutonic 'adviser, protector'

Rico (*REE-coh*): Spanish, Italian shortening of Enrico; Teutonic Heinrich or Henry 'ruler of the home'

Roald (*ROO-ahld*): Scandinavian 'famous ruler'

Roderick: (Roderic, Spanish and Portuguese Rodrigo) Teutonic 'rich in fame'

Roscoe: Teutonic 'from the deer forest'; also an English place name

Rupert: (Ruppert; variant of Robert) Teutonic 'bright fame'

Sandor: (Sander, Sanders) Slavic, Hungarian form of Greek Alexander 'he helps people'

Schuyler: Dutch 'scholar, teacher'

Sean (*SHAWN*): (Shane, Shawn) Celtic form of John 'God is gracious'

Selby: (Shelby) English place name and surname 'place of willows or copse'

Sherman: English surname 'shearer of wool'

Sherwin: Teutonic 'swift runner' (literally 'cutting the wind'); Anglo-Saxon 'bright friend'

Sherwood: English place name 'shire forest'

Siegfried (*SEEG-freed*): (Siegfrid, Sigfrid, Sigvard) Teutonic 'glorious peace'

Sigurd (*SEE-gerd*): Scandinavian 'victorious guardian'

Sinclair: (St. Clair) Scottish, English from French place name 'bright, clear'

Slade: English 'child of the valley'

Stanford: (Stafford) English place name 'stony ford'

Sumner: English, French 'summoner,' a minor official who summoned people to appear in court

Sylvester: (Silas, Silvan, Silvester, Sylvan, Sylvander) English from Latin 'forest dweller'

Terrill: (Terrell) Teutonic 'descended from Thor the powerful'

Thor: Scandinavian king of the gods

Thoreau (*thuh-ROH*): usually from the nature writer and pacifist Henry David Thoreau, based on a French form of Theodore 'gift of God'

Thornton: English place name 'thorny place'

Tomas (Spanish *toh-MAHS*; Slavic *TOH-mahs*): (Thom, Thomas) Greek, Aramaic 'a twin'

Townsend: English surname 'from the edge of the town'

Travis: (Travers) English surname 'crossroads'

Tristram: (Tristan) Celtic, Latin 'sad face, sorrowful'

Tyrone: Celtic, meaning uncertain

Upton: English place name 'town or village on the hill'

Vaughn (*VAWN*): (Vaughan) Celtic 'little'

Veryl: (Verald, Verrill) Teutonic 'manly'

Walden: (Waldo) English place name 'forested valley'; Teutonic Wald 'forest'

Welby: English place name 'farm by a spring'

Whitney: Teutonic 'from the white island'; English place name and surname 'white island'

Wilfred: (Wilfrid) Teutonic 'determined peacemaker'

Winfield: Teutonic 'friend of the soil'; English place name, Wingfield 'place for grazing'

Winston: English place name and surname 'Winec's or Wine's home'

Winthrop: English place name and surname 'Wina's farm,' (possibly) 'friendly village'

Woodburn: English place name and surname 'stream in the forest'

Woodley: English place name 'wooded meadow, wooded flat area'

Wylie: (Wiley) English place name with various meanings, including that of the Wiley River 'tricky.' As a personal name, may be interpreted as 'clever, resourceful'

Xavier: Arabic 'bright'

Yale: English 'from a secluded place'

York: English place name 'where the yew trees grow'

Zale: Greek 'power of the sea'

Zane: Rare English form of John 'God is gracious'

❦ 3
Fads and Fancies in Bestowing (or Inflicting) Names

Children's Names in the Southwest

The given names of the 857 children in an elementary school that we'll call Saguaro are fairly representative of the Southwest in general. The school is in Mesa, AZ, in which the total population mix (mainly white and Mexican-American) approximates that of the Southwest as a whole. The names of these school children of 1990, then, are presumably fairly representative of the region, although some schools might show great differences.

Most Popular Given Names in Saguaro School, 1990

Name	Number	Percentage of Sample
BOYS		
Michael	29	6.13
Jason	22	4.65
Christopher	19	4.02
Joshua	18	3.81
John	14	2.96
Matthew	11	2.33
Andrew	10	2.11
Jonathan	9	1.90
Justin	9	1.90

43

Name	Number	Percentage of Sample
Robert	9	1.90
Ryan	9	1.90

GIRLS

Name	Number	Percentage of Sample
Nicole	12	3.13
Christine	11	2.86
Melissa	11	2.86
Jessica	10	2.60
Jennifer	9	2.34
Sarah	8	2.08
Stephanie	8	2.08
Amber	6	1.56
Crystal	6	1.56
Heather	6	1.56
Lisa	6	1.56

The highest-ranking names in Saguaro School are not greatly different from the most popular children's names in other parts of the country. Biblical influence (Michael, Christopher, Joshua, John, Andrew, Matthew, Jonathan, Christine, Sarah) is still considerable, as it has been for centuries, although John, Mary, and a few others are slipping. Michael is almost a coast-to-coast favorite. The non-biblical Brandon, Jason, Justin, Ryan, and most of the girls's names listed all have had nationwide increases in popularity—some, no doubt, influenced by Hollywood and the names of soap opera characters.

In Saguaro the 473 boys share 199 *different* names, so on average each name is held by 2.38 boys. A girl there is considerably more likely to be the only one in the school who has a certain name. The 384 girls share 239 different names, an average of only 1.61 for each name.

The numbers in the previous list include close variant spellings of names, but not distant variants such as Khriss (which perhaps is derived from Christopher). Variants included in these counts are Kristopher (2), Kristoffer, John, Josh, Josue, Mychael, Sara (3), Nichole (2), Nikole, Christina (3), Cristina, and Kristina (2).

Some of the given names in Saguaro School are highly individualized, as they often are in other places. A variant sometimes results from a simple misspelling, but more often from a parent's desire for individuality or to indulge a preference for one form over another. A name that seems "odd" to some people may be a touch of rebellion against the sameness (in fast food restaurants, for instance) that American life often demands.

Girls' names tend to be more distinctive than boys' names. Some Saguaro parents have named their daughters Tawny, Lachelle, Chucketta, Loribeth, Lamista, Bree, Kariana, Mykia, Saraiah (Sarah?), Taryn, Kaleena, and Lexie; one boy is Johanthan, another Jarom. We may wonder why one couple named their son Chauvin.

For an area with a fairly large Hispanic population, the number of given names that are *probably* Spanish is surprisingly small. The only boys' names likely to be Spanish are Adalberto, Angel, Angelo, Armando, Jesus, Jose (one each), and Manuel (2). The girls' names of this sort are only slightly more numerous: Angela, Annamaria, Carina, Catalina, Consuelo, Elena, Josefina, Laurisa, Maria, and Marina.

Where are all the Albertos, Alfonsos, Alfredos, Antonios, Armandos, Benitas, Carloses, Carmens, Danielos, Doroteas, Enriques, Ernestos, Fabianos, Fernandos, Franciscas, Gabriellas, Gracias, Ineses, Isabelitas, Javiers, Jorges, Julios, Luzes, and on through the alphabet of familiar Spanish (sometimes Portuguese or Italian) names? The answer may be that almost all of these children were born in the United States, and that some of their parents were either already citizens or moving toward citizenship. Some parents may believe that the thorough Americanization of their children may be eased and accelerated if at least one of their names is "American." Often the Garcias or the Hernandezes are willing to give up a small but conspicuous part of their Spanish heritage by choosing children's names that do not call attention to that heritage. They are not ashamed—and obviously should not be—of their own names, and they seldom change their surnames. However, in selecting their children's names, they may demonstrate a wish to flow into the mainstream.

So in Saguaro School an Espinosa child may be named Samantha; an Estrada, Tanya or Frankilee; a Costello, Megan; a Mercado, Jennifer; a Villalobos, Michael. A Gonzalez may bear the unlikely name Siobhan.

Although no examples appear in Saguaro School, it should be noted that in some parts of the country Hispanic given names are being chosen—perhaps increasingly, though statistics are missing—by non-Hispanic parents. Carmens, for example, are not uncommon in families named Jackson or Maxwell. As Hispanic names become better known, they are likely to increase in popularity even among Americans with such backgrounds as German, Scandinavian, Greek, or east European. In the melting pot or salad bowl that is the United States, names also become assimilated.

The Ups and Downs of *Jane*, and the Rise and Fall of *Irene*

It's no secret that the popularity of a given name may change markedly in a few years. Fads in names are just as ordinary in the British Isles as in the United States.

A graph representing the changing fortunes of Jane in England and Wales would be composed of hills and valleys. The following figures, from the official Index of Births, represent the number of girls in 100 who were given the name Jane in the year indicated. For instance, in 1850, 4.29 girls in 100 were named Jane. (Statisticians don't worry about counting .29 of a girl.)

1850	1875	1900	1925	1950	1960	1970	1975
4.29	2.34	0.96	1.48	0.76	1.27	0.95	0.38

Irene's pattern is different—a steep rise followed by an abrupt and continuing fall:

1875	1900	1925	1950	1960	1970
0.022	0.31	2.38	0.74	0.16	0.04

The figures for Irene illustrate dramatically how some namings are affected greatly by current events. Two influences converged on Irene. Vernon and Irene Castle (he was English, she American) were a renowned team who popularized such dances as "Grizzly Bear" and "Texas Tommy." The duo were as famous in the teens of this century as Astaire and Rogers were later on. Irene's bobbed hair started a 1920s fashion trend (considered immoral by some), and her lithe, slender body inspired both envy and emulation. No one can estimate how many babies were named Irene because of her.

The second influence was quite different. In the mid-twenties, a few years after World War I ended, hopes were high for a lasting peace. Irene was the Greek goddess of peace. (Our word *irenic* 'peaceful' came from her.) Her name was known to many educated people, and some parents chose it because they, too, longed for a peaceful world for their newborn daughters. The combined effect of Irene Castle and the Greek goddess was too strong to resist.

But Irene Castle's name faded, although she lived until 1969, and Hitler, Mussolini, and Hirohito dashed hopes for peace. By 1950 only 0.74 percent of British girls were given the name, and by 1975 it had almost disappeared.

Were You Born in the 1950s?

If you or any of your friends were born in the early or middle 1950s, you probably finished high school in 1970 or thereabouts and perhaps graduated from college in the mid-1970s. You may find it interesting to reminisce about the names that you and your high school or college classmates were given at birth and to compare those with the names discussed here.

Leslie Dunkling obtained access to the 1975 graduation lists of universities in 36 states. In *First Names First*, he published the top 20 girls' names and the top 20 boys' names in each of those states. The holders of most of those names were born in about 1953. The following conclusions are not stated by Dunkling, but are deduced from his lists.

Girls

1. Mary was the most common girls' name. It ranked or tied for first in 19 of the 36 states and was in the top 10 in every one. Its lowest rank (9th) was in Utah. Its composite average ranking was 2.00 (meaning its average position of popularity was an even second place).

2. Deborah was also in the top 20 in all the states, and was first in Illinois, Kansas, Louisiana, Maryland, Massachusetts, Mississippi, Ohio, Texas, and West Virginia. Its lowest rank (11th) was in Utah. Composite rank: 2.89. The high rank may be explained in part by the great popularity of Debbie Reynolds in the 1950s.

3. Susan was first in California, Connecticut, Florida, New York, and Vermont, but only 19th in Texas. Composite rank: 3.67.

4. Linda was another name in the top 20 in all states, ranking first in Nevada. Its lowest rank was 19th in Louisiana. Composite rank: 5.77.

5. Catherine was the only other name to rank first in any state (North Carolina), but was not in the top 20 in Indiana and Mississippi. Composite rank: 10.67.

6. Patricia earned the fifth best composite average (5.67), and scored in all 36 states, but had no first places. It ranked second, however, in Nevada, New Mexico, Oklahoma, and Pennsylvania.

7. Barbara was not in the top 20, but came in second in Michigan and New York. Composite rank: 6.81.

These additional names were in the top 20 in half or more of the states: Ann(e), Carol(e), Cynthia, Dian(n)e, Elizabeth, Janet, Karen, Margaret, Nancy, Pamela, and Sandra.

Boys

1. Among the boys listed by Dunkling, John was an easy winner, as it has been in the majority of counts over several hundred years. It ranked first in 15 of the 36 states, and only in New York did it rank as low as fifth. Composite rank: 1.94.

2, 3. Robert and James fought it out for second, with Robert winning in Florida, Illinois, Nevada, New York, Ohio, Oregon, and Washington. James led in three more states than Robert did: Arkansas, Georgia, Louisiana, Mississippi, Missouri, New Mexico, Pennsylvania, Tennessee, Virginia, and Wisconsin. (Note the heavy vote for James in Southern states—attributable in part to the South's love for such combinations as Jim Bob or Jimmy Ray.) Robert, with more seconds and thirds, won the composite average, 3.14 to 3.22.

4, 5. Michael, the winner in Michigan, came in fourth. David won in two states, Iowa and Massachusetts, but was behind Michael in the composite, 5.06 to 4.58.

The next four places went to William, Richard, Thomas, and Mark. Others that ranked in the top 20 in over half of the states were Charles, Daniel, Dennis, Donald, Gary, Jeffrey, and Ronald.

The Troubles of Job

In the church register of St. Helen, Bishopsgate (England), dated September 1611, this touching little story is told:

> Job rakt-out-of-the-asshes, being borne the last of August in the lane going to Sir John Spencer's back-gate, and there laide in a heape of sea-cole asshes, was baptized the ffirst day of September following, and dyed the next day after.

(See Job 2:8:". . . and he [Job] sat down among the ashes.")

Not All Scots Are Named *Angus*

According to comedians and some television programs, Angus MacPherson or Fergus MacTavish is the prototypical name of Scotsmen, just as all Irishmen were once supposedly called Pat O'Brien or Mike Murphy.

Tain't so. There once may have been more Anguses than today, but even in 1935 the name ranked only 35th in Scotland. By 1958 it had vanished from the top 50, and now it appears only occasionally.

When a Scot enters a London pub, the regulars probably will soon be calling him Jock. That's just a friendly nickname for any Scot who ventures into England, just as in New York City any male taxicab patron is likely to be called Mac by the driver.

Most of the Scottish given names are indistinguishable from English names. The men are typically John, James, William, David, and the like, although James is relatively more frequent north of the border. Further down the list, it is true, we can find Ian, Gordon, Graham, Alistair, Duncan (as in *Macbeth*), and Malcolm (also in *Macbeth*).

Scotswomen's names, too, can hardly be distinguished from Englishwomen's: Margaret (very frequent), Mary, Linda, and the like. Agnes is probably Scottish rather than English, and Lesley is a more probable spelling than the androgynous Leslie of England and the United States. Moira, Lorna, Audrey, Lindsay, and Robina also appear fairly often in Glasgow, but not very frequently in, say, Gloucester or Galveston.

Many Scottish given names are identical with Irish, for example, Eamon, Brendan, Bridie, and Sioban. Irish Sean also appears, especially as Shaun or Shane. James may be replaced by the equivalent Hamish or Seamus. Incidentally, the rather rare Angus may be feminized to the even rarer Angustina.

This Hopens the Door to Hother Possibilities

An early onomatist, the British Charles Bardsley, enjoyed telling this story:

> A child was brought to the font for baptism. "What name?" asked the parson. "John" was the reply. "Anything else?" "John *honly*," said the godparent, putting in an "h" where it was not needed. "John Honly, I baptize thee . . ." continued the clergyman.
> The child was entered with the double name.

Does She Have a Good Right Uppercut?

It's not hard to determine the special interest of Brea Brown, an Englishman, who in 1974 gave his newborn daughter these names: Maria Sullivan Corbett Fitzsimmons Jeffries Hart Burns Johnson Willard Dempsey Tunney Schmeling Sharkey Carnera Baer Braddock Louis Charles Walcott Marciano Patterson Johansson Liston Clay Frazier Foreman. (Clay was Muhammad Ali's birthname.) If she had been born later, Brown also might have included Spinks (Leon or brother Michael), Tate, Weaver, Coetzee, Tyson, Douglas, and Holyfield, as well as about a dozen others in years when the heavyweight title was in dispute. Those names would include the redoubtable but not well-remembered James (Bonecrusher) Smith.

Numbering One's Children

In some ancient Roman families at least some of the sons were given numbers to indicate their order of birth. The fifth son, Quintus, was often given a number, perhaps because at that point some families had exhausted their supply of favorite names. Sextus, Septimus, and Octavius may have been based on paternal boastfulness.

If the Romans had been consistent, they could have named ten sons Primus, Secundus, Tertius, Quartus, Quintus, Sextus, Septimus, Octavius, Novus, and Decimus.

In modern times there is much less numbering, especially when birthrates fall. However, a former heavyweight boxing champion, the Italian Primo 'first' Carnera, had a younger brother named Secondo. In English, Quentin, derived from Quintus, is the most likely choice, and some parents who don't know Latin have used it for a firstborn. There's a rather rare feminine version of it, Quintilla. Octavius and the feminine Octavia are now rare, but were still fairly common a hundred or so years ago. Primus, Secundus, and Septimus are listed in some books of forenames, but are rarely used.

The Wild Poppy

Asked why she had named her twins Morphine and Opium, a young mother explained: "Well, I read in a paper that morphine and opium is products of a wild poppy. The poppy of these younguns was jist about as wild a man as I've ever knowed."

In another community, a girl who was her family's great hope and joy went away to college, promising that she would come back with a diploma. Instead, she came back pregnant. When a baby girl was born, of course she was named Diploma.

That was perhaps a better name than the two bestowed on the offspring of another girl who had gone astray and then gone back home. She called her twins Saffilis and Gonora. (Sodom and Gomora were the choices of still another young woman.)

And who knows what was in the minds of the couple who called *their* twins Max and Climax?

News Affects Naming

In the years after William the Conqueror and his Norman followers defeated the English at the Battle of Hastings in 1066, William became one of the most popular names for infant boys.

The tendency to choose names related to current or recent events has existed ever since. Bill Schemmel of Decatur, GA, wrote a brief article for *Harper's* about names chosen for children born in a large Atlanta hospital in the 1960s and 1970s.

The presidency of John F. Kennedy, Schemmel reported, led not unexpectedly to many John Fitzgeralds and also to a Gerald Fitzgerald and a Joan F. Kennedy; Jacqueline's name was somewhat echoed by Jacka Lyon and Jackalette. The Kennedy assassination had unfortunate onomastic results such as Lee Harvey, Ozzwald Fitzgerald, Rotunda Cortege, and Flame Eternal. The marriage of the former Mrs. Kennedy to Aristotle Onassis led to many Aristotles, Athenas, and Olympias, as well as to an Airy Onassa and Jackie Canasta.

A 1967 peace discussion between President Lyndon Baines Johnson of the United States and Aleksei Kosygin of the USSR brought a flurry of peace-hopeful names, including Linden Alex, Banes Alexander, and Alexi Banes, as well as Alexa for some girls.

The hurricane Camille, in 1968, caused a temporary run on that name, according to Schemmel. And Watergate aroused so much interest in everyone involved that such combinations as Rodino Talmadge (for two prominent participants in the hearing) were made up. Perhaps the strangest name was in recollection of presidential adviser John Ehrlichmann. A little Atlanta girl was names Earlic Ann Mann.

Whatever Happened to Six-Toed Pete?

Bob Riedy, an Arizonan, in radio broadcasts about "the old days," used to bemoan the passing of picturesque nicknames, especially those that focused on physical imperfections. "When the scene was young," he said, "we had robust monickers like 'Big Nose Kate,' 'Johnny behind the Deuce,' " 'Three-finger Brown,' 'Six-Toed Pete,' and 'Peg-leg Smith'." Now we settle for a commonplace substitute like "Tex."

"'Cherry Creek Red,' " said Riedy, "would no more have answered to his given name, Bernard, than admit to drinking sarsaparilla. 'The Cuban Queen' would have scratched the eyes out of anyone who addressed her as Amelia, and 'Lefty' Hankins would have killed to protect the secret of his given name, Buford."

Riedy moralized, "We have lost some vital ingredients of Americana during the process of civilization."

How Many Johns Aren't Named *John?*

A publication of the U.S. Immigration and Naturalization Service, *Foreign Versions, Variations, and Diminutives of English Names,* lists about 125 variants of *John* used in 18 languages. Among the possibly unexpected ones are Zane, Janko or Janicko or Janeczek or Jankielek, Ioannis, Giannes, Juhani, Hannu, Ansis, Ivashka and Ivasenko, Vanechka and Vanyushko, Jovan, Yochanan, and Juanitocho.

Better known are Evan, Jan, Johann(es), Jean, Hans, Janos, Giovanni, Jonas, Juan, Vanya, and Ivan. Note that the Russian Ivan Ivanov has a name with exactly the same meaning as John Johnson.

There are close to 90 or 100 variations of Joseph, and about as many of Alexander, Andrew, Anton, August, Basil, Francis or Frank, George, Gregory, Jacob, Michael, Paul, Peter, Stephen, Walter, or William.

Among women's given names, Mary or its equivalent Maria is apparently the champion, with over 200 versions and diminutives, but Ann and Anna and their alternatives come close. Other multiform feminine names include Anastasia, Barbara, Catherine or Katherine, Dorothy, Eleanor and Ellen and Helen, Elizabeth, Irene, Jane or Joan or Jeanne (among the feminine equivalents of John), Josephine, Lillian, Margaret, Rosa or Rose, Sophia, Stephanie, and Theresa, each of which appears in well over 60 versions.

Did Anybody Confuse Him with General Electric?

"My grandmother hated nicknames. When my father, whom she had named Leslie, began to be called 'Les' by his boyhood friends, she was greatly upset. She thought she was safe in naming the next boy Guernsey Eliphalet Luther.

"Her strategy didn't work. His friends gave him a nickname, too—'Doc.' And since he intensely disliked being Guernsey Eliphalet, he always used just his initials, G.E., in signing checks and other papers." (Contributed by Frederic Luther)

Ya Gotta Have a Middle Name, See

In the U.S. armed forces, everyone is assumed to have no fewer than three names. If there is no middle name or initial, that fact is noted in parentheses (NMI). Sometimes rookies, seeing NMI as part of another man's name, may say, "You gotta helluva funny middle name. Dya call it Nummy, or what?"

When an initial is shown on one's birth certificate instead of a name, the word (*only*) is placed after it by the armed forces. So Captain Harry S Truman was officially Harry S (only) Truman.

Rhode Island de Lafayette?

Benjamin Franklin, on learning that a child had been born to the Marquis and Marquise de Lafayette, wrote a letter of congratulation. He suggested that they plan to have 13 children in all, to be named for the 13 American colonies. He said, "Miss Virginia, Miss Carolina, and Miss Georgia will sound prettily enough for the Girls, but Massachusetts and Connecticut are too harsh for the Boys, unless they were to be Savages."

Some of the others—Delaware, New Hampshire, New Jersey, New York, and Rhode Island—might be a little awkward, too.

Think of a President
Whose Initials Were H.U.G.

Hiram Ulysses Grant was the baptismal name of the infant who would grow up to be the victorious Civil War general and the 18th president of the United States.

The young Hiram feared that his initials would lead to much teasing by his West Point fellows, but the appointing congressman inadvertently did him a favor. Hiram's mother's maiden name was Simpson, and the congressman nominated Ulysses Simpson Grant to the military academy.

Question: Which initials would be better vote-getters, U.S.G. or H.U.G.?

Naming among Primitive Tribes

Pliny, an ancient Roman naturalist, said that in the Atlas mountains of northwest Africa there were tribes of *anonymi* 'people without names.' As late as the early twentieth century, other tribes of *anonymi* were reported in relatively isolated parts of the world. In sparsely settled areas where customs of naming had not developed and where everyone knew everyone else intimately, there was perhaps no feeling that one had to address anyone in a particular way. (Similarly, it is said, some husbands and wives even in socially advanced countries never use each others' names in dialogue. In many an Irish play of this century, the head of the family is referred to only as "himself," or when appropriate as "herself" or "yourself.")

The naming practices of primitive tribes in the nineteenth and twentieth centuries have varied greatly. In some tribes names are bestowed at birth, but in others naming may be delayed until puberty or some other significant milestone, or until a time when signs seem especially propitious. Up to a century ago, some African tribes apparently called each newborn son "gun," each girl "hoe," and delayed attaching more specific names for several years. In some places a child might be named for circumstances existing at the time of birth—names equivalent to Big Rain, Dry Weather, Hungry Time, or Victory Dance. Thus the names of several children could constitute an abbreviated history of the family unit or the tribe.

According to British onomatist C.L. Ewen, it was not always the parents who chose a child's name. The tribal chief might have that privilege, or possibly a medicine man or his equivalent, or a council of elders.

The most general custom among primitive tribes was to give a child the name of a deceased ancestor, but any descriptive word that might indicate sex, order of birth, race, office, physical feature, god, historical fact, or a more fanciful concept, served the purpose of a distinguishing label.

Practices in naming often were intertwined with superstition. Some names were never to be spoken, or were not made known (even to the bearer) until adulthood. Some names, if used properly, might be regarded as protection against injury or witchcraft. In certain tribes, a name could not be knowingly reused. The Ojibway Indians, it is said, considered it dangerous to speak the names of their own husbands and wives.

Instead of being relatively permanent, the name of some primitives changed. Ewen gives as examples Waiyau boys whose names changed at puberty, Wangata men whose names changed when their first child was born (a proof of potency), and the Kwakiutl Indians of British Columbia whose names changed with the coming of winter or summer. Some Inuit on becoming old would take new names, hoping that the change would result in renewed strength. Other Native Americans would take over the name of a dead person to assure that person's immortality. In some places, each significant event in one's life would bring a new name, so that an old and honored person might have eight or ten names.

Africans imported to the Americas as slaves came from many tribes, and what seems to be the same name might have a different meaning in each language. Ordinarily, the African names appeared to be one, two, or three syllables, and to refer to common things in the people's lives—articles of clothing, trees or smaller plants, places, parts of the body, or tribal customs—or to abstractions such as friendship or surprise. (A 120-page "Dictionary of African Origins" is included in N. N. Puckett and M. Heller's *Black Names in America*.)

Most noteworthy is that, with possibly a few exceptions, the primitive names were not hereditary and therefore were not family names. Each individual was given his or her own name, which only rarely was passed on to a son or daughter. So there was no equivalent of, say, the Hunter family or the Fisher family.

Some ancient personal names, not necessarily from primitive tribes, were very long and might consist of elements that made the word equal to a complete sentence. Ewen gives a Babylonian example that would be translated "O Ashur, the Lord of heaven and earth, give him life," an early Japanese name consisting of 54 "letters," and a Basque name that meant 'the lower field of the high hill of Azpicuelha,' as well as a seemingly pessimistic Sanskrit name that meant 'disease, pain, grief, and misfortune'—perhaps an attempt to ward off such calamities.

How About Liberty, Equality, and Fraternity?

In England in the mid-nineteenth century, a boy was christened And Charity. Why? He had two sisters, named Faith, Hope.

Androgynous Names

In a *New Yorker* story by Elizabeth Tallent, the major character, an elderly scientist, is thinking about his daughter-in-law, with whom he has a love-hate relationship. Her given name is Ashley. "Even her name, he sometimes thinks, is simply one more aspect of the androgyny in which young women camouflage themselves nowadays."

Androgyny means 'having both female and male characteristics in the same body.' Hermaphrodites are androgynous, and Sunday supplements and even the sports pages sometimes carry stories about transsexuals, whose external sexual characteristics have been altered by surgery. Physiologists tell us that qualities of both sexes are present in every living being, so that to a greater or lesser extent every person is androgynous.

It is doubtful, however, that any deep awareness of androgyny is in the minds of parents who name an infant Ashley, Beryl, Gerry, or the like. A conversation like this may take place:

Parent 1: If it's a girl, I sorta like the name Ashley. It's a little unusual though.
Parent 2: Yeah, that's not bad. And your cousin Ashley would be pleased, wouldn't she?
Parent 1: I suppose so, although she once told me that people can't tell from the name whether she's a man or a woman. Some men do have that name, she said. She mentioned a famous professor, Ashley Montagu.
Parent 2: Oh, well, professors!
Parent 1: I think it's kinda cute for a girl, myself.
Parent 2: OK with me. What's a good middle name to go with it?

Whatever the reason, names that do not clearly indicate a child's sex seem to be much more common in America today than ever before. The feminist movement may be part of the explanation, abetted by approaches toward equality in the workplace, athletics, and the home. The trend toward reduced emphasis on gender differences shows up also in such things as increased feminine initiatives in dating, and its follow-ups, in unisex haircuts, and in the wearing of slacks by both sexes. Today we may not be able to tell on sight whether an approaching stranger is male or female, and after we hear the given name we still may not be sure.

Things were different in the old days. Think, for example, of our early presidents and their first ladies: George and Martha, John and Abigail, Thomas and Martha, James and Dolley, James and

Elizabeth. Only one in each pair wore the pants, and the names left no doubt about which it was. Maybe in the future we'll have presidential couples names Gerry and Kerry, or Beryl and Shelley, even Frankie and Johnny, and who can be sure which one will be the male?

But maybe not. Some people assert that individuals with equivocating names seldom reach high positions in any profession—not even in entertainment, although one rock music man who calls himself Alice Cooper has gone both far and far out.

Today's birth announcement lists have many names similar to the following, with indistinguishable or at least uncertain gender. Usually, it is true, Frances still signifies a girl, Francis a boy. Marian used to be a girl, Marion a boy, but today both names are used for both sexes. Terry is probably but not assuredly a boy, and a "cute" spelling such as Terri, Terrie, and Teri is more likely to represent a girl.

Ashley (-ly)
Bert (-i,-y)
Beryl
Billie (-y)
Bobbie (-y)
Brook (e, -s)
Carol(e), Carrol(l)
Cary (-ey)
Chris, Kris
Evelyn
Frankie (-y)
Gale, Gail
Gerry (-ie), Jerry

Jackie (-y)
Jan
Joe, Jo
Joyce
Karen (-in)
Kelly (-ey)
Kerry (-i, -ie)
Kim
Kit
Lavern(e)
Lee, Lea, Leigh
Leslie, Lesley

Lyle
Lynn(e)
Marian, Marion
Marty (-ie)
Merl(e), Myrl(e)
Nick (-ie), Nikki
Paige, Page
Pat
Shelley (-y)
Shirley
Stacey (-y, -ie)
Terry (-i, -ie), Teri
Tracy (-ie)

No Mo' Children

A married couple, according to an old joke, had three children, named Eeny, Meeny, and Miney. They explained, "There ain't gonna be no Moe."

❦ 4
Choosing a Name for Your Baby

20 Questions to Think About

Most parents give careful thought to choosing the first and middle name that will accompany their newborn child through infancy, childhood, and adulthood, perhaps into the graying, experience-wrinkled years that Robert Browning called "The last of life, for which the first was made." (The preceding lines are "Grow old along with me/The best is yet to be.") The names chosen should be suitable not just for the small bundle, but also for the future business-person, the future adult who may someday need, in turn, to choose names for still another generation.

In the list of questions that follows, not all will seem equally important to everyone. All, however, are questions that many parents take seriously.

1. Should the baby be named for a relative? a good friend? a celebrity? Fewer names today than in the past are chosen on these bases. When relatives' or friends' names *are* chosen, they often are middle rather than first names.

If Uncle Wilbur or Aunt Paula is very dear, naming an infant for him or her may be a deserved tribute. But consider this anecdote related by Audrey K. Duchert in the magazine *Names*:

> In 1884, a daughter was born to the Charles Hemenways of North Leverett, Massachusetts, and was named Ruby Marion.

A neighbor inquired, "Charles, why didn't you name her Hep-sabeth, after your mother?" He replied, "I loved my mother, but I love my daughter, too, and I wouldn't wish such a name on her."

Remember, too, that if you name the child for Aunt Paula, Aunt Corinne may feel hurt. And if you name her or him for your best friend—well, friendships have been known to break up.

Some babies are named for movie stars or other well-known people. There's nothing wrong with that, although the star's name and fame may fade quickly, and the use of the name may prove only a fad.

2. Should you choose a name that is now "in"?
Fads do exist in naming. In one decade, for example, David and Kevin for boys and Karen and Jennifer for girls may be "in," but a decade or so later, both may be largely replaced by new favorites.

Do you want your child five or six years from now to be one of four Davids or five Jennifers in a class, or do you prefer a name that, while not necessarily unique, does distinguish your child from most of the others? Or, on the contrary, do you consider a name better if it suggests that the child really "belongs" with the others, even to the extent of an identical given name?

3. Should you choose a name that is highly un-usual? Maybe somewhere you encounter the name Girisa (*gee-REE-shuh*), originally Hindi as an alternative name for the god Siva, meaning 'mountain lord,' and used in parts of India for boys as well as girls. You like its exoticism and the grandeur of its lordly deno-tation.

Ask yourself whether most people could pronounce it and spell it, and whether it matters that they probably couldn't. The name certainly has the advantage of being a conversational icebreaker. How important is that? If your little girl grows up to be a staid person, will Girisa be a suitable name?

4. How may the name affect the child's future?
No definitive studies have been made of the effect a name may have on a person's life, but on page 29 of this book you will find reports on two studies, one saying that boys named Jack, Bud, and the like usually grow up to be outdoorsy, he-man types, and the other saying that men with names such as Rodman Carew Michaelson have a better than average chance of becoming tycoons.

5. Does the name conform with your religious preferences? Some Jewish families like to honor a well-liked but deceased family member; others use names of the living, but rarely those of parents. Sometimes a name beginning with the same letter as that of the honoree's name is considered sufficient. Many Jewish children are given a Hebrew name as well as a name in the language of their country.

Roman Catholic families are expected to use the name of a canonized saint as either the first or middle name; since the number of saints is large, there are seldom problems.

A Catholic is unlikely to name a son Luther, Calvin, or Wesley, and non-ecumenical Protestants may avoid a name that suggests a denomination other than their own. Many biblical names are appropriate for both the Jewish faith and the various Christian faiths. (See the lists starting on pages 14 and 22.) Parents who adhere to none of the organized religions may want to avoid names that suggest anything pertaining to specific faiths.

6. Is the name suitable for both a child and an older person? Tina may sound fine for a 6-pound bundle of joy, but less appropriate for the 160-pound woman she may become. Stacy and Tracy have a young, ungrandmotherly sound.

On the other hand, some names sound too old for a little child. Some people say that no one under 40 should be called Edna or Maud, and some say that Nathaniel is a name befitting only an old man (although its meaning is 'gift of God').

Admittedly, such classification of names as "young" or "old" is a highly personal, subjective matter and may depend largely on people we know who have a particular name.

7. Is the name merely "cute"? Names like Ima and Iva are generally to be avoided, as in Ima Rose and Iva Thorn. Also unsound is any name that combines cutely with the surname—Ruby Redd or Roxie Stone, for instance.

8. If the surname is simple and common, are the other names also rather simple and common? This does not mean that if the surname is Brown the child's first name must be William or Mary, but some people hear a jarring or anticlimactic note in Throckmorton McAllister Brown or Hilary Ermentrude Brown. Some, however, argue that something rather spectacular is needed to offset the plainness of Brown. Still others prefer moderately uncommon names with the ordinary surname—maybe Roger Edmund Brown or Marilyn Lucille Brown.

9. Is the name appropriate to the ancestry? Some Polish people, for instance, like to choose names that bear at least a hint of the child's Polish heritage—not necessarily Stanislas but perhaps Stanley. Some folks wear their heritage very proudly and want it to be reflected in their children's names, as was true of an Illinois Irish family whose children were Terence, Deirdre, Colleen, and Patrick, and who at last report were expecting either a Michael or a Kathleen.

If the first and second names seem to indicate a heritage different from that of the surname, some people may be confused by the mixed signals: Giovanni Domingo Schmidt, for instance. On the other hand, parents with differing ancestral backgrounds may want to select given names that at least suggest the mother's background. Often the middle name may serve that purpose: William Antonio Schmidt, possibly.

10. Is the name too alliterative? Richard Reed Rathburn and Katherine Kelda Keefe? Most people wouldn't want so much repetition of the same sound.

11. Is the meaning of the name one that you believe appropriate? Several books available in most libraries give definitions of names, as do supplements to some dictionaries; a few hundred are given here on pages 14–17 and 32–35. Although many people are barely aware that names *have* meanings, choices may be affected when the definitions become known. For example, one strongly feminist couple decided against Henry when they found that it means 'ruler of the home,' and some pacifist parents ruled out a few dozen boys' names that had military connotations. And if two couples who named their daughters Lesbia and Gomora had been better informed, they might not have made those choices. Dolores, a beautiful name, has been rejected by some couples who found it means 'lady of sorrows.'

A bookish couple decided in favor of Cuthbert when they found it means 'brilliant wisdom,' and another couple, wishful for their daughter's success in life, chose Eunice because its meaning is 'joyously triumphant.'

12. Are the first and middle names sufficiently different? One couple named their daughter Helen Elaine—very pretty; but Helen and Elaine are really the same name. Others of the 60 or more in the Helen group include Eleanor, Ellen, Alena, Lena, Leonora, and (hard to believe) the Russian Olenko and Galinochka. Obviously, there is no law against such duplication, but carried to an extreme it could lead to a name such as Robert Roberto Roberti.

13. Does the rhythm of the three names (and of the first and last name alone) please you? Some people dislike two names of one syllable each, like Kent Clark (although Superman Clark Kent did all right). Samuel Taylor Coleridge's poetic ears were offended by a two-syllable name with the accent on the second syllable, like Adele or Eugene. "Never take an iambus as a Christian name," he advised in recommending Edith and Rotha as the two best names for girls. Actually, it is two iambics in succession that would displease many people: Maureen Malone, for example.

There's no complete agreement about which onomastic rhythms are most attractive, and it is certainly true that euphonious vowel and consonant combinations can often overcome possibly unpleasant rhythms. In general, people who compile books about given names recommend unequal numbers of syllables in the names. For instance, with a one-syllable surname a two- or three-syllable given name may be best: Conrad Lake, Roberta Mead; with a two-syllable surname a one- or three-syllable given name: Grace Keller, Rosamund Leclaire; with a surname of three or more syllables, a one- or two-syllable given name: Ray Gallagher, Nancy Rutherford. But attractive exceptions to these principles do exist.

14. Does the middle name have a function? The middle name may have a family or religious connection, as suggested previously. Often it may be the mother's maiden name or some other name associated with her family.

It can become a future alternative to the first name, which the child may in later years want to use instead of the first name. For example, a boy named Robert Leighton Correll, after being known to teachers and fellow students as Robert or Bob for over 20 years, decided that for the purposes of his profession R. Leighton Correll would provide an air of distinction that was not present in Robert L. Correll.

15. What is the nickname likely to be? Do you like it? Although it is impossible to predict for certain what nickname other children will give a boy or girl, the odds are that it will be one of the conventional ones: Ed for Edward or Edgar, Liz or Betty for Elizabeth, and so on. To some extent, then, parents control what the nickname will be. Ideally, it should be a nickname that will sound attractive in conjunction with the last name. One unfortunate boy, whose last name was Dick, was christened Richard, for which Dick is a nickname. He was thus Dick Dick, which became Tick Tick, Tick Tock, and other variants. His schoolmates' fun became even greater when one of them went to a zoo and discovered a small African antelope called a dik-dik.

One of Dick's classmates was a girl named Ariadne, who was first nicknamed Airy, then Windy.

16. Does the name indicate gender clearly? A television actress named Michael Learned has had to insist that *Miss* be placed before her name in the list of credits. When one sees such names as Jan, Merl(e), Beryl, Joyce, or Robin, one cannot be sure whether the bearer is female or male.

Maybe in an age in which many people are working for a leveling-off of sex differentiation, everybody should be named Robin, Jan, etc. But if parents decide to give a child such a name, the choice should be a carefully reasoned one.

17. Is the name easy enough to pronounce and to spell? A girl named Ursula had to tell people repeatedly that her name was to be pronounced *UR-suh-luh*, not *ur-SOO-luh*. And our friend Ariadne found that almost none of her classmates and not all of her teachers could spell her name.

18. If you believe in numerology, are you satisfied with what the numbers tell you? The author of this book isn't a believer, partly because numerologists contradict one another. They have widely different methods of equating letters and numbers and no less different interpretations of the results. But if you are a believer, apply your favorite formula and see whether you like what it says about the numerological vibrations of the name you are considering.

19. Are both parents happy or at least satisfied with the name? The man and the woman cooperated in conception and will (it is hoped) cooperate in the child's nurture and upbringing. In a good marriage, a child can be an added cohesive force. As far as possible, nothing about the child, including the name by which he or she is called every day, should be divisive of the family.

20. Some years in the future, when the child asks, "Why did you name me _____?" will you be able to give a good, clear answer?

❦ PART II

The Names We Inherit

🍎 5
The Names That Most of Us Answer To

"Say, Just Vott fer Kind uf Names Are Dos?"

Lebanon Valley College, in Annville, PA, nestles near the heart of the Pennsylvania German (miscalled "Dutch") country. Its teams are the Flying Dutchmen. Womelsdorf and Hershey—good German names—are not far away, and the ridges of the Blue Mountains, which resemble many in Germany, parallel the valley. Stanley F. Imboden, Class of '55, revisited the campus and a nearby cemetery late in the 1980s. In the college's alumni magazine, he wrote about what he saw.

In the cemetery, "a few steps north of my alma mater," he said, he looked at the names on the stones and wondered, "Say, just vott fer kind uf names are dos?

"Vell, let me see vonce. Aftosmes, Light, Fields, Struble, Fencil, Beyerle, McGill, Finkelstein, Marquette, Yeakel, Carmean, Retreivi, Uchida, Radanovic, Sorrentino, Kelly, Smith and, I guess, Imboden, too. By golly, they're all Lebanon Valley names! All American names!"

All-American names.

The 100 Most Common American Surnames

In 1974 the Social Security Administration (SSA) compiled a list of American surnames for which they had ten thousand or more files each. (There is no more recent compilation.) The bureau found it had 3,169 names on the list—presumably the most common American surnames. The top one hundred are given here, with the number of occurrences of each.

Because the SSA's computer recorded only the first six letters of each name on the list, letters given here in parentheses have been added to indicate the most common additional letters.

1. Smith	2,382,509	33. Baker	412,676
2. Johnso(n)	1,807,263	34. Richar(ds) (dson)	409,262
3. Willia(ms) (mson)	1,568,939	35. Lee	409,068
4. Brown	1,362,910	36. Scott	408,439
5. Jones	1,331,205	37. Green	406,989
6. Miller	1,131,205	38. Adams	406,841
7. Davis	1,047,848	39. Mitche(ll)	371,434
8. Martin(ez) (son)	1,046,297	40. Philli(ps)	362,013
9. Anders(on) (en)	825,648	41. Campbe(ll)	361,958
10. Wilson	787,825	42. Gonzal(ez) (es)	360,994
11. Harris(on)	754,083	43. Carter	349,950
12. Taylor	696,046	44. Garcia	346,175
13. Moore	693,304	45. Evans	343,897
14. Thomas	688,054	46. Turner	329,752
15. White	636,185	47. Stewar(t) (d) (dson)	329,581
16. Thomps(on)	635,426	48. Collin(s)	324,680
17. Jackso(n)	630,003	49. Parker	322,482
18. Clark	549,107	50. Edward(s)	317,197
19. Robert(s) (son)	524,688	51. Murphy	311,337
20. Lewis	495,026	52. Cook	298,396
21. Walker	486,498	53. Rogers	298,288
22. Robins(on)	484,991	54. Griffi(n) (th) (ths)	291,862
23. Peters(on)	479,249	55. Christ(ian) (opher)	
24. Hall	471,479	(ianson) (enson)	
25. Allen	458,375	(ensen)	281,525
26. Young	455,416	56. Morgan	273,267
27. Morris(on)	455,179	57. Cooper	269,560
28. King	434,791	58. Reed	267,589
29. Wright	431,157	59. Bell	267,026
30. Nelson	421,638	60. Bailey	263,908
31. Rodrig(uez)	416,178	61. Kelly	262,701
32. Hill	414,646	62. Wood	258,422

63. Ward	257,686	82. Russel(l)	220,676
64. Cox	256,842	83. Foster	220,156
65. Lopez	254,535	84. Daniel(s) (son)	219,156
66. Steven(s) (son)	254,165	85. Hender(son)	218,715
67. Howard	248,065	86. Perez	217,801
68. Sander(s) (son)	245,440	87. Fisher	216,884
69. Bennet(t)	243,553	88. Powell	212,681
70. Brooks	242,491	89. James	212,201
71. Watson	240,219	90. Perry	211,478
72. Gray	239,604	91. Butler	210,515
73. Rivera	238,457	92. Jenkin(s) (son)	208,325
74. Nichol(s) (son)	237,129	93. Barnes	206,776
75. Hernan(dez) (des)	235,498	94. Reynol(ds)	198,326
76. Hughes	231,754	95. Patter(son)	198,205
77. Ross	231,054	96. Colema(n)	197,123
78. Myers	230,561	97. Simmon(s)	196,506
79. Sulliv(an)	239,839	98. Graham	194,096
80. Long	229,615	99. Wallac(e)	194,067
81. Price	225,893	100. Stephe(ns) (nson)	192,023

Those one hundred names account for about one-sixth of all Americans.

The Four Chief Kinds of Surnames

Suppose that you were one of the one hundred males in a typical English village in A.D. 1300. The odds would be one in five that your name was John (20 percent), and fifteen in a hundred that it was William (15 percent).

Others of your fellow villagers would be known by another name that, like John, is biblical. The approximate order of such names, according to Charles W. Bardsley, would likely be Thomas, Bartholomew, Nicholas, Philip, Simon, Peter, and Isaac.

The remaining males probably had names that, like William, became increasingly common some time after the Norman Conquest of 1066: Richard, Robert, Walter, Henry, Guy, Roger, and Baldwin.

Surnames were just beginning to come into existence in England. You were not William Somebody—just William. Your wife may have been just Emma, and thus indistinguishable from other Emmas. If someone referred to you as William or Emma, the question "William who?" or "Which Emma do you mean?" had to be asked.

To reduce the confusion, people had begun long before to add some words for further identification, and in the fourteenth century or so the procedure was becoming systematized:

> William from the dale (the place where he lived)
> William who is the son of John (the father's name)
> William the cooper (the occupation)
> William the short (a description)

These natural, almost inevitable, ways of identifying eventually turned into the four classifications into which nearly all European—and hence American—surnames fall. (Asian and African names developed various patterns of their own.)

The unimportant words in the English identifications would tend to be slurred over and then omitted in speaking:

> William dale
> William John's son
> William cooper
> William short

The capital letters now used in writing names were added later.

These were not yet family names—not until the custom arose of passing down the second name from father to children. When William Cooper's son Robert was called Robert Cooper even though he was a tailor or a fletcher, a family name came into being. When William Johnson's son Bertram was Bertram Johnson rather than Bertram Williamson, there was a family name. The son of William Dale might live on a hill instead of down in a dale, but he had a real family name if people called him, say, Peter Dale. William Short, even with that family name, might be six feet tall.

The word *surname* has become equated with *family name*—a name that can be inherited. *Sur-* means 'additional' or 'extra.' The surname is the additional name that identifies the family of the person whose name is Bertram or Bertha or whatever.

In modern America, surnames based on place names (Hill, Winchester, etc.) are the most frequent, accounting for over 40 percent of the total. Patronyms, which are usually fathers' names or other ancestral names but may be names of famous people such as Alexander or Bartholomew, make up about 30 percent. About 16 percent of our surnames are occupational (Carpenter, Mason), and about 11 or 12 percent are descriptive (Swift, Armstrong). Only 1 or 2 percent fall into other categories, and those are most often

Asian Names (Song, Tanaka) or Middle Eastern names (Ibrahim, Mustafa) that are simply transliterated from the original language.

The 50 Most Common American Surnames Based on Occupations

About one-sixth of American surnames are derived from the names of occupations that were common during the name-giving period, about six hundred to eight hundred years ago.

This list gives the top 50 most common names, in order of frequency, together with brief explanations of most.

1. **Smith**
2. **Miller**
3. **Taylor** (an old spelling of *tailor*)
4. **Clark** 'scholar, scribe, clergyman' The British pronounce *clerk* as *clark*.
5. **Walker** 'cleaner of cloth' Clothmaking was a leading cottage industry in the Middle Ages. See also Webb, Fuller, and Tucker.
6. **Wright** 'carpenter or metalworker'
7. **Baker**
8. **Carter** 'driver of a cart'
9. **Stewart** 'person in charge of a household, estate, or farm'
10. **Turner** 'worker with a lathe'
11. **Parker** 'gamekeeper,' 'person in charge of a park or hunting area'
12. **Cook**
13. **Cooper** 'maker of tubs, barrels, casks, wooden pails' Metal, then plastics, later supplanted wood and largely eliminated coopers.
14. **Bailey** (several spellings) 'administrative officer, estate manager'
15. **Ward** 'watchman, guard, keeper'
16. **Howard** (originally Heyward) 'person in charge of hedges or fences, boundary-watcher, guard against straying livestock,' sometimes 'ewe-herder,' About one-third of today's American Howards are African-American, because of the popularity of Oliver Howard, Civil War Commissioner of the Freedmen's Bureau.
17. **Myer(s)** (from German; equivalent to Meyer, Meier, Mayer, etc.) 'chief servant or overseer,' 'a farmer'
18. **Foster** (= Forester) 'warden of a forest,' 'gamekeeper'
19. **Fisher** 'person who caught fish or sold them'
20. **Butler** 'person in charge of bottled goods or wine casks,' 'maker of bottles'
21. **Hayes** 'person in charge of hedges or fences,' = Hayward, Howard, (sometimes) 'one who lived in a hedged area or near it'
22. **Schmidt** (German for Smith)

23. **Snyder** (Dutch for Taylor. Many a German Schneider changed the spelling to Snyder or Snider after coming to America.)
24. **Porter** 'gatekeeper,' 'one who carried things'
25. **Spencer** 'dispenser, custodian of a storage room' A sort of civilian quartermaster of the Middle Ages.
26. **Hoffman** (from German; several other spellings) 'owner or manager of a farm,' 'a farm worker'
27. **Webb** (= Weaver and German or English Web(b)er; Webster was a female weaver) 'weaver of cloth'
28. **Tucker** 'person who cleaned cloth or thickened it'
29. **Wagner** (also Wag(g)oner) 'one who built or drove wagons,' 'cartwright'
30. **Mason**
31. **Meyer** (See No. 17)
32. **Hunter** 'a person who hunted game'
33. **Hunt** (= Hunter)
34. **Warren** 'keeper of a game preserve' Also sometimes a place name for one who lived near a game preserve or near a rabbit hutch; sometimes a patronym for 'descendant of Warin, protection.'
35. **Gardner** (also Gardiner) 'gardener'
36. **Schultz** (German; many spellings) 'magistrate, administrator, foreman, overseer'
37. **Knight**
38. **Weaver** (See No. 27)
39. **Berry** 'servant in a manor' Also a place name for one who lived in or near a fortified place or on a hill.
40. **Chambers** (also Chamberl(a)in) 'person in charge of a royal or noble reception chamber or of the household'
41. **Carpenter** (French Carpentier) 'worker with wood'
42. **Chapman** 'peddler, tradesman'
43. **Harper** 'person who played a harp for a nobleman or at fairs, etc.'
44. **Cohen** (Hebrew; several spellings) 'rabbi or priest' (especially one said to be descended from Aaron)
45. **Fuller** 'person who cleaned cloth or thickened it'
46. **Schneider** (See No. 23)
47. **Franklin** 'a substantial landholder of medieval times, a freeholder'
48. **Zimmerman(n)** (German for Carpenter)
49. **Weber** (See No. 27)
50. **Keller** (German) 'one who worked in a place for storing food,' 'one who made women's caps or hairnets' Also a place name for 'one who came from Keller' "wine cellar."

The 50 Most Common American Surnames That Are Patronyms

Almost one-third of American surnames are patronyms, which are of two types: a name that indicates who one's father or other ancestor was, or the name of a famous person such as a biblical or historical figure.

The 50 most common American patronyms, in order, are listed here. Those with more than six letters may have alternative forms besides those given here.

1. **Johnson** 'son of John'
2. **Williams, Williamson** 'son of William'
3. **Jones** 'son of John'
4. **Davis** 'son of Davie,' a pet form of David
5. **Martin, Martinez, Martinson** 'son of Martin,' from the god Mars
6. **Anderson, Andersen** 'son of Andrew'
7. **Wilson** 'son of Will'
8. **Harris, Harrison** 'son of Harry'
9. **Thomas** 'son of Thomas'
10. **Thompson** 'son of Thomas'
11. **Jackson** 'son of Jack,' a pet form of John or sometimes Jacob
12. **Roberts, Robertson** 'son of Robert'
13. **Lewis** 'descendant of Lewis'
14. **Robinson** 'little son of Rob,' a pet form of Robert
15. **Peterson, Petersen** 'son of Peter'
16. **Allen** 'descendant of Alan' May also be a place name, from any one of several British rivers.
17. **Morris, Morrison** 'son of Morris'
18. **Rodriguez, Rodrigues** (Spanish or Portuguese) 'son of Rodrigo'
19. **Richards, Richardson** 'son of Richard'
20. **Adams** (numerous variants) 'descendant of Adam'
21. **Mitchell** 'descendant of Michael'
22. **Phillips** (numerous variants) 'descendant of Phillip'
23. **Gonzalez, Gonzales** (Spanish or Portuguese) 'son of Gonzalo'
24. **Garcia** (Spanish or Portuguese) 'descendant of Garcia' (= Gerald) May also be a place name.
25. **Evans** (Welsh) 'son of John'
26. **Collins** 'little son of Cole,' a pet form of Nicholas
27. **Edwards** 'son of Edward'
28. **Murphy** (Irish) 'descendant of Murchadh' (= sea warrior)
29. **Rogers** 'son of Roger'
30. **Griffin, Griffith, Griffiths** (Welsh) 'descendant of Griffith'
31. **Christian, Christianson, Christenson** (several variants) 'son of Christian' (= follower of Christ)
32. **Morgan** (Welsh) 'descendant of Morgan'
33. **Kelly** (Irish) 'grandson of Ceallach' (= contentious) Is usually a place name if English or Scottish.
34. **Lopez** (Spanish) 'son of Lope or Lupe' (= wolf)
35. **Stevens, Stevenson** 'son of Stephen'
36. **Sanders, Sanderson** 'son of Sander' (= Alexander)
37. **Bennett** 'little descendant of Benne,' a pet form of Benedict

38. **Watson** 'son of Wat,' a pet form of Walter
39. **Nichol, Nichols, Nicholson** 'descendant of Nicholas'
40. **Hernandez, Hernandes** (Spanish or Portuguese) 'son of Hernando'
41. **Hughes** (Welsh or English) 'son of Hugh'
42. **Sullivan** (Irish) 'grandson of Suilebhan' (dark-eyed)
43. **Price** (Welsh) 'son of Rhys'   An earlier form was ap Rhys=son of Rhys, but the *a* was dropped.
44. **Daniel, Daniels, Danielson** 'son of Daniel'
45. **Henderson** 'son of Henry'
46. **Perez, Peres** (Spanish or Portuguese) 'son of Pero' (= Pedro = Peter)
47. **Powell** (Welsh) 'son of Howell'   An earlier form was ap Howell; see No. 43.
48. **James** (Welsh or English) 'descendant of James'
49. **Perry** (Welsh) 'son of Harry' Earlier ap Harry; see No. 43.
50. **Jenkins, Jenkinson** 'little son of Jen,' pet form of John

The 25 Most Common American Surnames Describing People

About one-tenth of American surnames describe some especially notable characteristic of an ancestor who lived several hundred years ago. Most of these relate to obvious physical qualities, but a few indicate traits of mind, personality, or character.

In some instances, a person may have been thought to resemble an animal, such as a fox, and may have been called by that name. In this book, however, names derived from animals, birds, and fish are given in separate lists.

The top 25 descriptive names are listed here along with their most common meanings.

1. **Brown** 'brown-haired'
2. **White** 'light-complexioned,' sometimes 'white-haired'
3. **Young** 'a younger brother, or anyone younger than another in the family or other group,' 'young-looking'
4. **Gray** 'gray-haired'
5. **Long** 'tall'
6. **Russell** 'small and red-haired'
7. **Black** (also **Blake**) usually 'dark, swarthy, dark-haired,' sometimes the opposite 'light-complexioned, blond, pale'   Two similar Old English words, *blaec* and *blāc*, had these opposite meanings, and a name might come from either.
8. **Little** 'short, small'

9. **Reid** '(Scottish variant of Reed) 'red-haired, ruddy'
10. **Curtis** 'courtly, courteous, well-bred, elegant'
11. **Powers** 'poor man,' sometimes 'one who has taken a vow of poverty,' sometimes a respelling of a Welsh place name, Powis or Powys
12. **Klein** (German; also Kline, Cline) 'short, little'
13. **Gross** (German) 'large, heavy'
14. **Sharp** 'keen-witted, intelligent, fast-thinking'
15. **Blake** (See No. 7)
16. **Wise** 'learned, experienced, sage'
17. **Weiss** (German for White)
18. **Moody** 'brave, bold, impetuous, proud, headstrong' The modern meaning of *moody* was not applied until Shakespeare's time.
19. **Lang** (German for Long)
20. **Lloyd** (also Loyd, Lloyds; Welsh) 'brown-haired or gray-haired or brownish in complexion'
21. **Short** 'small in stature'
22. **Moreno** (Spanish, Italian) 'dark-complexioned' In its rare use as a Hebrew name, it comes from a title meaning 'Master'.
23. **Bass** 'short, fat'
24. **Golden** 'one with golden hair'   May also be derived from Golduin 'gold, friend'
25. **Savage** 'wild, fierce, uncouth'

The Most Common Surnames in Ten American Cities and in London

These rankings are based on counts in telephone directories for 1990. Since low-income families are somewhat less likely to have telephones, names of such families may be underrepresented.

Note how ranks vary between cities. Although Smith is the leader in seven (including London), it is badly beaten by Johnson in Chicago, edged out by both Williams and Johnson in Los Angeles, and preceded by nine Hispanic names in Greater Miami, where Rodriguez outscores Smith by more than two to one.

Greater Atlanta

Atlanta names conform in general to the national patterns, except that William(s)(son) recently moved ahead of Johnson.

1. Smith	5. Brown(e)	9. Wilson
2. William(s)(son)	6. Davis	10. Jackson
3. Johnson	7. Harris(on)	11. Miller
4. Jones	8 Thomas	12. Martin(son)

13. Moore	16. Anderson	19. Clark(e)
14. White	17. Thompson	20. Robert(s)(son)
15. Taylor	18. Walker	

Boston

In Boston, Murphy, Cohen, and Kell(e)y rank higher than in most other places. Just outside the top 20 are Taylor, Wilson, Peter(s)(son), King, Lewis, and Moore.

1. Smith	8. Miller	15. Anderson
2. Brown(e)	9. Lee	16. Clark(e)
3. Johnson	10. White	17. Thompson
4. Kell(e)y	11. Davis	18. Robert(s)(son)
5. Murphy	12. O'Brien	19. Thomas
6. William(s)(son)	13. Jones	20. Martin
7. Cohen (Cohan, etc.)	14. Harris(on)	

Chicago

Johnson, William(s)(son), and Smith continue to battle for first place in Chicago. All the leading names are conventionally British, despite Chicago's varied populations. However, Rodriguez, in 21st place, is poised to push out Thompson or Walker.

1. Johnson	8. Jackson	15. Moore
2. William(s)(son)	9. Miller	16. Taylor
3. Smith	10. Anderson	17. White
4. Jones	11. Thomas	18. Martin(son)
5. Brown(e)	12. Wilson	19. Walker
6. Davis	13. Lee	20. Thompson
7. Harris(on)	14. Robin(s)(son)	

Denver

Again Martinez is the only Hispanic name in Denver's top 20. (It was tenth in 1981.)

1. Smith	8. Davis	15. Harris(on)
2. Johnson	9. Wilson	16. Taylor
3. Miller	10. Peter(s)(son)	17. Clark(e)
4. Brown(e)	11. Thompson	18. Robert(s)(son)
5. Anderson	12. Martinez	19. Thomas
6. William(s)(son)	13. Martin(son)	20. White
7. Jones	14. Moore	

Indianapolis

Indianapolis's leading names, like those of Atlanta, closely resemble the national pattern. No Hispanic names are in the top 20.

1. Smith	8. Wilson	15. Thomas
2. Johnson	9. Moore	16. Anderson
3. William(s)(son)	10. Taylor	17. Martin(son)
4. Jones	11. Clark(e)	18. Robert(s)(son)
5. Brown(e)	12. Thompson	19. Jackson
6. Miller	13. Harris(on)	20. Wright
7. Davis	14. White	

Los Angeles

William(s)(son) holds a small lead, as it did nine years earlier, with Smith barely beating out Johnson for second place. The rank of Lee reflects in part the Asian presence. Seven of the top names are Hispanic, although their order has changed.

1. William(s)(son)	8. Brown(e)	15. Anderson
2. Smith	9. Martinez	16. Sanchez
3. Johnson	10. Jones	17. Jackson
4. Gonzal(ez)(es)	11. Lopez	18. Miller
5. Garcia	12. Hernandez	19. Thomas
6. Lee	13. Harris(on)	20. Moore, Taylor
7. Rodriguez	14. Davis	[tie]

Greater Memphis

The predominance of British names in most of the South is confirmed in the Greater Memphis area.

1. Smith	8. Harris(on)	15. White
2. William(s)(son)	9. Allen	16. Walker
3. Jones	10. Moore	17. Robert(s)(son)
4. Johnson	11. Clark(e)	18. Martin(son)
5. Brown(e)	12. Wilson	19. Anderson
6. Davis	13. Jackson	20. Wright
7. Taylor	14. Thomas	

Greater Miami

Of the top 20 names in Greater Miami at the end of the 1980s, 12 are Hispanic, including the top 9. (Less than a decade earlier, Smith was in the seventh spot.)

1. Rodriguez	8. Diaz	15. Brown(e)
2. Gonzal(ez)(es)	9. Lopez	16. Miller
3. Garcia	10. Smith	17. Gomez
4. Perez	11. Sanchez	18. Jones
5. Hernandez	12. William(s)(son)	19. Davis
6. Fernandez	13. Alvarez	20. Martin(son)
7. Martinez	14. Johnson	

Minneapolis

If anyone doubts that Minnesota is a state well-populated by people of Scandinavian descent, Minneapolis names ending in *-son* or *-sen* may help to prove the point. Those endings are not always Scandinavian—Johnson and Wilson, for instance, are much more often English—but the odds are still good that a -*son* or -*sen* has some Danish, Icelandic, Norwegian, or Swedish blood in his or her veins.

1. Anderson(sen)	8. Carlson(sen)	15. Davis
2. Peters(son)(sen)	9. Erickson	16. Martin(son)
3. Olson(sen)	10. Williams(son)	17. White
4. Nelson	11. Thom(p)son	18. Baker
5. Larson(sen)	12. Jones	19. Clark
6. Smith	13. Schmidt	20. Johnson
7. Miller	14. Wilson	

New York (Manhattan)

Not unexpected in Manhattan are the high rank of Lee (partly because of a large Asian population) and of several names that are generally Jewish. The big news is that during the eighties Rodriguez passed Jones and Davis, and that Garcia, Rivera, Perez, and Gonzalez are moving toward the top 20.

1. Smith	8. Green(e)	15. Robin(s)(son)
2. Brown(e)	9. Davis	16. Lewis
3. William(s)(son)	10. Jones	17. Robert(s)(son)
4. Cohen (Cohan, etc.)	11. Harris(on)	18. Martin(son)
5. Lee	12. Levin(e)	19. Thomas
6. Johnson	13. Schwartz (Schwarz, etc.)	20. Wilson
7. Rodriguez	14. Friedman(n)	

London, England

The names list for London looks very similar to those for most American cities—not surprising because of the centuries-old British base for most American surnames. The presence of Patel, usually a Hindi name, may be unexpected, but it reflects the considerable number of Indian residents. (The directory also lists many Singhs, as well as many Middle Eastern names such as Ali and Shah, though not in the top 20.)

1. Smith	8. Robert(s)(son)	15. Davies
2. Brown(e)	9. Patel	16. Morris(on)
3. Jones	10. James	17. Richard(s)(son)
4. William(s)(son)	11. Johnson	18. Lewis
5. Clark(e)	12. Wilson	19. Davis
6. Harris(on)	13. Martin(son)	20. King
7. Taylor	14. Thomas	

❦ 6
Changing Surnames

11 Reasons Why Some Americans Have Changed Their Names— or Have Had Their Names Changed for Them

Many thousands of Americans have surnames that they or their ancestors did not bring to these shores. The changes have been made both voluntarily and involuntarily for varied and sometimes individual reasons, often involving such considerations as those listed here.

1. Necessity. Toy Chan's name didn't look like Toy Chan in China, where it consisted of two rather elaborately drawn characters (logographs) that were utterly meaningless in America and obviously couldn't be printed in one of our phone books. So here it was written with Roman letters that can be sounded somewhat like the original. Toy Chan does not accurately reflect the Chinese pronunciation, but it presumably comes as close as our alphabet allows. Similarly, names written originally in Hebrew, Cyrillic, Arabic, and a number of other alphabets had to be transliterated into the one used in the United States.

Less dramatically, because most American typewriters and typesetting machinery cannot cope with the diacritical markings used above or below certain letters in several European languages, those marks usually disappeared shortly after the boat stopped at Ellis Island.

2. Inability to spell. Sometimes an immigrant could not spell his or her name in Roman letters. When a name was told to an immigration official, the official had to write it as it sounded to him—perhaps something very different from the real spelling and often, as a result of an official's attempts to "Americanize" immigrants' names for them, a name that only vaguely resembled the original, either in sound or in spelling. The new spelling—the new name—often became the official one. Similarly, an employer might misspell a name but an immigrant who was illiterate in the Roman alphabet would not know the difference.

3. Carelessness. An immigration or other official might through carelessness spell a name incorrectly or illegibly, and a timid immigrant might not object.

4. Difficulty in pronouncing or spelling a name. Some names are difficult for most Americans to spell or pronounce. Czajkowski, for example, is a Polish name that means 'where the gulls are,' so one Mr. Czajkowski changed his name to Gull. A Mr. Dzeckaeiar simplified his to Decker. The ancestors of John Sevier, Tennessee's first governor, changed the family name from Xavier. Paul Revere's father, whose name was Rivoire, changed it to Revere "so the bumpkins can pronounce it easier."

5. Disagreements with relatives. A member of a family might change his or her name—considerably or slightly—to avoid being associated with a disliked relative.

6. Desire to break with the past. America represented a new beginning, and some newcomers had no desire to retain anything that reminded them of an unhappy past.

Some criminals choose aliases to dissociate themselves from crimes they have commited, as well as to avoid detection for crimes they may commit.

7. Desire for material success. There was a widespread feeling, sometimes justified, that a "wrong" or "bad" name could prevent one from getting a job or becoming prosperous. Second- or third-generation Americans in particular might change their names to others that supposedly lacked any stigma. In a largely French-speaking part of Louisiana, a German König translated his name to Roy, a Weiss to Le Blanc, but also in Louisiana a French Roy translated his name to King. A number of Jewish actors changed to noncommittal names before going far in show business. (See page 91).

8. Fear of bad treatment. Some newcomers had fled from lands where they were mistreated and they believed, rightly or wrongly, that a change of name might avert further mistreatment here. In World War I, many German-Americans changed their names because they feared abuse and were indeed sometimes cruelly treated. (See page 85.)

9. Holding the coattails of earlier arrivals. Knowing that the French Lafayette was regarded as an American hero, some French-Americans changed their names to Lafayette.

10. Getting rid of a semantic objection. Gelbfisch 'goldfish' for no good reason seemed humorous to many Americans. Frankenstein reminded them of the creator of the monster. Some Americans blushed when they had to try to pronounce Fuchs or Lipschitz. Such names were often changed.

11. Dislike of the original name. Many Jewish people, in particular, disliked the names that may have been forced on them in Germany, Russia, or elsewhere, and eagerly altered them to something more appealing. A Mr. Ochsenschwantz 'ox tail' happily became a Mr. Freedman.

It is impossible to say which of these reasons was the most likely cause of change, but the fourth (difficulty of pronunciation or spelling) was certainly high on the list. Immigrants in general were eager to conform to what they found in their new homeland, and their children and grandchildren even more so. If a name was so unlike others that teachers, for instance, had trouble with it, it was often simplified by those who had the difficulty—a practice that would scarcely be tolerated in today's atmosphere of respect for each other's cultural heritage. One teacher, who couldn't pronounce a complicated name ending in *-witch*, told two little brothers that in her class their last name would be Holz. Their father came to see her one day and introduced himself as Mr. Holz.

Zbigniew Brzezinski

The Polish-American Zbigniew Brzezinski was an important shaper of foreign policy in Jimmy Carter's presidential administration. Said a contemporary wiseacre, "Where but in America could a man named Zbigniew Brzezinski make a name for himself without changing it?"

Shaking Off the Bad Luck

Some Indonesians, after recovering from serious illness or other severe misfortune, change their names. Presumably, the evil spirit that was responsible will be confused and unable to recognize and pursue the former victim.

America Entered the War, and the *Muellers* Became *Millers*

To blend in more easily with other Americans, many relative newcomers—usually in their first, second, or third generation here—have changed their names. For many Germans, the process accelerated in the early years of World War I, when Germany was perceived as the enemy. When, in April 1917, the United States actually entered the war, name changing speeded up still more.

One reason for changing was that German-Americans increasingly considered themselves ordinary Americans with no or few remaining close ties to their former homeland. Like everybody else, they were attending war rallies, buying Liberty Bonds, talking about a war to end war, castigating Kaiser Bill, and watching their own sons march off to be gassed in muddy trenches or pierced by jagged shrapnel.

With misguided patriotism, some other Americans—usually the relatively uneducated—began to express distrust of German-Americans, to call them Kraut and Heinie, to throw eggs at their houses, to beat up their children on the schoolground, to accuse them of spying or at least of sending money to help the Kaiser. In chauvinistic zeal, they changed the name of sauerkraut to Liberty cabbage, hamburger to Salisbury steak, weiners to hot dogs (a term first reported a few years earlier in the *Saturday Evening Post*).

Under such pressures, many Muellers or Müllers, perhaps after clinging to their name for several American generations, translated it to the cognate Miller. Schmidt translated to Smith, Weiss to White, Lang to Long. Other translation changes are illustrated by these names:

Braun to Brown	Koenig to King	Krafft to Strong
Koch to Cook	Schneider to Taylor	Schwartz to Black
Metzger to Butcher	Ziegler to Mason	Zimmerman to
Weber to Weaver	Klein to Small or	Carpenter
Jaeger to Hunter	Little	

Sometimes, instead of translating, these Americans merely changed a letter or two. Schneider, for instance, might become Snyder (a Dutch spelling); Bauer became Bower; Schaffer, Shafer; Fischer, Fisher; Stauffer, Stover; Bloch, Block; Schoen, Shane.

Occasionally, a much more drastic shift was made, especially with a long, conspicuously German name such as Meisenheimer, which might become any "American" name that struck the family's fancy. It is doubtful that name changes made any German-Americans any more or any less patriotic. And not all of them changed. The Mueller boy, the newly named Miller, and the Miller with English ancestors all died together in the bloody mud along with Carey, Scarlatti, Svensson, Jones, Latowski—and all the rest.

In 1933 Adolf Hitler became chancellor of Germany. In that year, according to Robert M. Rennick, writing in *Names*, 22 Hitler or Hittler families were listed in New York City telephone directories. Twelve years later, when the war was coming to an end, there were no such listings. It is probable that these families were harassed so much that they could not withstand the pressure. No record of what substitute names they chose has been found.

Contrary to what the disappearance of that one name suggests, by World War II the distrust of German-Americans had largely disappeared, and name changes among them were comparatively few.

Hyperpatriotism resulted even in changes of a few town names. Perhaps the best example is Brandenburg, TX, where during World War I people disliked being in a town named for a place in Germany, even though a famous concerto carried the name. To show their Americanism they renamed it Old Glory. The change seems to have resulted in little glory, fame, or growth. Its post office serves 58 rural residents and 61 boxholders.

The Rabbit Who Became an Irishman

A Czech family named Zajíc, which means 'rabbit,' came to the United States and found that no one in their largely Irish community could pronounce their name in the good old Czech way. They thought about translating the name to Rabbit, but others laughed at that. Someone suggested Hare, but an Irish neighbor recommended O'Hare as having definite advantages. So the Zajíc children, renamed O'Hare, quickly blended in with their Irish schoolmates.

The irony is that O'Hare has no connection with rabbits. It's an Irish patronym meaning 'grandson of Ir' or 'grandson of Aichear' (embittered).

The Irish won another victory with the Sýr family, whose Czech name means 'cheese.' They decided that they would like the German equivalent, Käse, but Irish acquaintances said that Käse didn't seem very American and persuaded them to choose the somewhat similar-sounding Casey. No relation to cheese, of course: Casey means 'descendant of Cattasach' (watchful).

Alterations by the Happy Tailors

There are now more than one hundred thousand Schneiders in the United States, but at least as many others whose ancestors changed that name to Snyder, Snider, or something else. Schneider is German for 'tailor'; the earliest people to hold that name were tailors.

Sometimes in Germany another name was combined with Schneider. Hoffschneider, for instance, was a farm tailor. But Scheckschneider poses a problem because Scheck has several meanings. One of those is in *"sich scheckig lachen,"* which means 'to split one's sides with laughter.' It may not be what the first Scheckschneider intended, but it's easy to picture him as a happy, roly-poly fellow slapping his thighs as he exploded into laughter.

Elmer Johnson of Florida has traced the alterations the descendants of two Scheckschneider brothers who came to Louisiana in the eighteenth century made to their name. In Louisiana and in southeast Texas, Johnson found the name spelled in about 20 different ways.

Some simply dropped a couple of *c*'s: Sheckshneider. Others chopped out more: Shexneider or Shexnyder. Some added an *l*: Shexnaildre or Chexnaildre.

Another meaning of Scheck was 'check,' and so we find Checksnyder, Checksnider, and Checksneider. Hard to explain is Cheznaidre, though maybe the *chez* is from French for "at the house of." But even the Cheznaidres' ancestors may have been those happy, roly-poly tailors of long-ago Germany.

Ten Types of Alteration in Surnames

A person changing a name in America usually has an unlimited range of selection. He or she may choose any name that has ever existed if it can be written or at least approximated in the Roman alphabet and if it does not break the current code concerning obscenity. The name may even be an invented one that perhaps no other person has ever used.

Ordinarily, though, name-changers do not go to extremes, if for no other reason than the desire that the name be pronounceable, reasonably short, and not embarrassing to its holders or the people they meet.

Most names are changed in one of these ways:

1. Transliteration from another alphabet. A Pole named Ruczynski need not change the name, because Poles use the Roman alphabet, as Americans do. But a Russian with essentially the same name must transliterate it from the Cyrillic. It will probably come out Ruczynsky, but it may not, since there is not an exact letter-for-letter correlation between Cyrillic and Roman. For example, Russian has letters pronounced like our blends *zh, ts, ch, sh, sch*; its E is pronounced *ye*, Ë is *yo*, and X is about like *kh*. Because of such differences, the same name (Tschaikovsky, for instance) may be spelled in two or more ways.

Many Asian and Arabic names obviously must be transliterated. Names in Roman alphabets that use diacritical marks with certain letters usually have those marks dropped. Composer Antonin Dvorak's surname, for instance, is written Dvořák in his native Czechoslovakia (which explains why it is pronounced *duh-VOR-zhock*).

2. Shortening.   This is probably one of the two most frequent types of change. Sometimes only a letter is dropped, as when Meyer decides he wants to be Myer. Sometimes the loss is considerable, as when four Greeks, each named Pappageorge, changed their names to Papp, Pappa, Pappas, and George. A Polish Kolodziejchuk cut back to Kolodi. Feuchtwanger became Wanger, and Dingfelder became Feld.

The surgery can occur at either end, or both: Koenigsberger may become Konig, Berger, or Berg. Rarely, the cut may be in the middle: a Kasminski became Kaski.

3. Getting rid of unusual letter combinations. In central and eastern Europe, and other countries, some letter combinations occur that are rarely found in English. These include, *cz, sz, dz, fj, hj, hl, hn,* and *tk* (at the start of a syllable). These are often reduced in the United States to a single letter, so that Swedish Hjelmstrom, for example, may be changed to Helmstrom. Or the change may be greater: one Tkach became Thatcher.

4. Making a name seem more "American." This overlaps number 3, but does not necessarily include unusual letter combinations. Hordy switches to Hardy, Hoit to Hoyt. Adamowski changes to an unquestionably American Adams.

5. Substituting.   A German shopkeeper named Meier switched to Meyer because he found that was how most of his customers and suppliers thought his name was spelled. Because a Mr. Mass didn't like Roman Catholics, he became Moss, but a worshiper in the Catholic faith got even by a complete change of name, from Parsons to Priest.

6. Lengthening.   This is rare, but for personal reasons, it sometimes occurs. A Syrian-American named Hadad, for example, changed to the more conventional spelling, Haddad. And a number of Poles who liked the *-ski* ending so frequently found in Poland, added it when they came here, although perhaps an even larger number dropped it. Some Polish Rybaks switch to Ryback. Some Czech Hrubys lengthen the name to Horuby, but probably more shorten it to Ruby.

7. Transposition of letters.   A family named Borert transposed the *b* and the first *r* to become Robert.

8. Translation. This and shortening are the two most frequent types of change. German Freund becomes Friend; French Meunier, Miller; Italian Piccolo, Small; Slavic Svec, Shoemaker; German Blumenthal, Bloomingdale.

9. Shift in pronunciation. This happens very frequently and usually without being intended. A Latino name, Perez, for instance, in the homeland is normally pronounced *PER-ez*, but in the United States most people call it *Per-EZ*. Ivan J. Kramoris had said that he prefers the accent on *Kra-*, as it would be in most Slavic languages, but that Americans automatically say *Kra-MOR-is*. Louis Adamic liked *Ah-DAH-mitch*, but Americans wavered between *AD-um-ik* and *Uh-DAM-ik*. A person named Pitz lost the battle to retain the pronunciation *Peetz*.

10. Substitution of an entirely different name. Some people, including some whose ancestors came to America long ago, simply switch their names to something else. Ernest Maass compiled a long list of names to which Cohen was changed: Brunswick, Cane, Carlton, Carsen, Clark, Cole, Collins, Cone, Cowan, Cunard, Gerard, Kelly, Kennedy, and others.

How to Change Your Name

In most states, laws do not require any set procedure for changing a name, but if you are contemplating a change, it would be wise to check first with county officials. The chances are that a large majority of changes in the United States have been made without any legal action whatever. The person or persons simply decided what name they wanted and then began using it.

The complexities of modern life, however, make it desirable to have a name change approved by a court. Information about a person now may be kept in literally hundreds of places such as credit files, armed forces files, government offices, and a host of others. Changing a name without having an official record made may increase greatly the difficulty of keeping all these records straight, or of appealing when a seeming injustice has been done. Questions concerning wills and inheritance may be almost impossible to answer without adequate records. If a faraway uncle, for instance, bequeaths a million dollars to Lucy Rable, and if she has changed her name to Melinda Orwell without having an official record made, she may have to spend a large part of the inheritance just to prove that she is Lucy Rable and the niece of the dead man.

Official change of name is simple and normally entails low or no court costs, although if the petitioner wants assistance from a lawyer, the costs may climb. Normally you simply will make an appointment with a local circuit judge and will take along evidence—preferably a birth certificate—to show who you are. In all likelihood, the judge will do no more than ascertain your present name and the desired name, and then sign a legal form endorsing the change. A talkative or curious judge may also ask the reasons for change. The request almost certainly will be approved, although (especially with persons whose knowledge of the English language and of American customs is slight) the judge may recommend further consideration. One immigrant family, for instance, thought that Siffle would be close to the sound of the name they brought from the old country, but the judge, knowing that the similarity to *syphilis* might later cause embarrassment, suggested that Siffer or Safford might be a better choice.

Whether or not a change of name is recorded officially, certain agencies need to be notified: the post office, obviously; the phone company, landlord, credit card companies, and anyone else to whom regular payments are made; and the agencies that issue drivers' licenses and keep track of voter registration. In some cases, the armed forces, a draft board, immigration officers, a parole board or parole officer, or any other official body to whom one has a legal obligation should be notified. The Social Security Administration requires notification, although it does not assign a new number.

❦ 7
Professionals Who Changed Their Names

201 Actors and Actresses: Original Names

Tell me, I pray thee, thy name.—Genesis 32:29

Walter Matuschanskayasky obviously had a good reason for changing his name. He is known today as Walter Matthau.

Decide for yourself whether each of these other actors and actresses—past and present—gained or lost by change of name.

Name changing was often dictated by movie studios, but in recent years producers have been more inclined to let would-be stars keep their natal names. If Meryl Streep (her real surname) had been born earlier, who knows what she might have been called?

Eddie Albert—Edward Albert Heimberger
Alan Alda—Alphonse D'Abruzzo
Fred Allen—John Florence Sullivan
Woody Allen—Allen Stewart Konigsberg
June Allyson—Ella Geisman
Julie Andrews—Julia Wells
Ann-Margret—Ann-Margret Olsson

George Arliss—George Augustus Andrews
James Arness—James Aurness
Beatrice Arthur—Bernice Frankel
Fred Astaire—Frederick Austerlitz
Gene Autry—Orvon Gene Autry
Lauren Bacall—Betty Joan Perske
Lucille Ball—Dianne Belmont
Anne Bancroft—Annemarie Italiano
Ethel Barrymore—Ethel Blythe

Lionel Barrymore—Lionel Blythe

Rex Bell—George F. Beldam

Jack Benny—Benjamin Kubelsky

Milton Berle—Milton Berlinger

Sarah Bernhardt—Henriette-Rosine Bernard

Vivian Blaine—Vivienne Stapleton

Janet Blair—Martha Janet Lafferty

Amanda Blake—Beverly Louise Neill

Robert Blake—Michael Gubitosi

Dirk Bogarde—Derek Jules Gaspard Niven Van Den Bogaerde

Shirley Booth—Thelma Booth Ford

George Brent—George Brendan Nolan

Fannie Brice—Fanny Borach

Charles Bronson—Charles Buchinsky

George Burns—Nathan Birnbaum

Raymond Burr—William Stacey Burr

Ellen Burstyn—Edna Rae Gillooly

Richard Burton—Richard Jenkins

Red Buttons—Aaron Chwatt

Michael Caine—Maurice Micklewhite

Dyan Cannon—Samille Diane Friesen

Judy Carne—Joyce Botterill

Diahann Carroll—Carol Diahann Johnson

Irene and Vernon Castle (dancers)—Irene Foote and Vernon Blythe

Lon Chaney, Jr.—Creighton Chaney

Cyd Charisse—Tula Finklea

Cher—Cherylyn La Piere

Claudette Colbert—Lily Claudette Chauchoin

Mike Connors—Kreker Ohanian

Gary Cooper—Frank James Cooper

Joan Crawford—Lucille Le Sueur, then Billie Cassin

Tony Curtis—Bernard Schwartz

Yvonne de Carlo—Peggy Yvonne Middleton

Ruby Dee—Ruby Ann Wallace

Sandra Dee—Alexandra Zuck

Angie Dickinson—Angeline Brown

Marlene Dietrich—Maria Magdalene Dietrich

Phyllis Diller—Phyllis Driver

Troy Donahue—Merle Johnson

Diana Dors—Diana Fluck

Kirk Douglas—Issur Danielovitch Demsky

Patty Duke—Anne Marie Duke

Dale Evans—Frances Octavia Smith

Nanette Fabray—Ruby Bernadette Nanette Fabarés

W. C. Fields—William Claude Dunkenfeld

Barry Fitzgerald—William Shields

Joan Fontaine—Joan de Havilland

Dame Margot Fonteyn (ballet)—Peggy Hookham

Redd Foxx—John Elroy Sanford

Arlene Francis—Arlene Francis Kazanjian

Kay Francis—Katherine Gibbs

Zsa Zsa Gabor—Sari Gabor

Greta Garbo—Greta Gustafsson

Ava Gardner—Lucy Johnson

John Garfield—Julius Garfinkle

Judy Garland—Frances Gumm

James Garner—James Baumgarner

Mitzi Gaynor—Francesca Mitzi Marlene de Czanyi von Gerber

Ben Gazzara—Biago Anthony Gazzara

Lillian Gish—Lillian de Guiche

Ruth Gordon—Ruth Jones

Elliot Gould—Elliot Goldstein

Stewart Granger—Jimmy Stewart (sic)

Cary Grant—Archibald Alexander Leach

Peter Graves—Peter Aurness

Lorne Greene—Lorne Green

Buddy Hackett—Leonard Hacker
Jean Harlow—Harlean Carpentier
Rex Harrison—Reginald Carey
June Havoc—Ellen Evangeline
  Hovick
Sterling Hayden—John Hamilton
Helen Hayes—Helen Hayes Brown
Susan Hayward—Edythe Marrener
Rita Hayworth—Margarita
  Cansino
Pee Wee Herman—Paul Rubenfeld
William Holden—William Beedle
Judy Holliday—Judith Tuvim
Bob Hope—Leslie Townes Hope
Hedda Hopper (columnist)—Elda
  Furry
John Houseman—Jacques
  Haussmann
Rock Hudson—b. Roy Scherer;
  took Roy Fitzgerald as legal
  name
Tab Hunter—Arthur Gelien
Walter Huston—Walter
  Houghston
Betty Hutton—Betty Thornburg
Burl Ives—Burl Icle Ivanhoe
Al Jolson—Asa Yoelson
Jennifer Jones—Phyllis Isley
Boris Karloff—William Henry Pratt
Danny Kay—David Daniel
  Kaminski
Buster Keaton—Joseph Francis
  Keaton
Dorothy Lamour—Mary Leta
  Dorothy Kaumeyer
Lassie—Pal
Sir Harry Lauder—Harry
  MacLennan
Stan Laurel—Arthur Stanley
  Jefferson
Vivien Leigh—Vivian Hartley
Jerry Lewis—Joseph Levitch
Carole Lombard—Jane Alice
  Peters
Sophia Loren—Sofia Scicolone
Myrna Loy—Myrna Williams

Shirley MacLaine—Shirley
  MacLean Beaty (sister of
  Warren Beatty)
Guy Madison—Robert Moseley
Karl Malden—Malden Sekulovich
Jayne Mansfield—Vera Jayne
  Palmer
Frederic March—Frederick Bickel
Julia Marlowe—Sarah Frances
  Frost
Dean Martin—Dino Crocetti
Walter Matthau—Walter
  Matuschanskayasky
Steve McQueen—Terrence Steven
  McQueen
Vera Miles—Vera May Ralston
Ray Milland—Reginald Truscott-
  Jones
Ann Miller—Lucille Ann Collier
Liza Minnelli—Lisa Minelli
Carmen Miranda—Maria do
  Carmo Miranda da Cunha
Marilyn Monroe—Norma Jean
  Mortenson
Yves Montand—Ivo Livi
George Montgomery—George
  Montgomery Letz
Gary Moore—Thomas Morfit
Zero Mostel—Samuel Joel Mostel
Paul Muni—Muni Weisenfreund
Pola Negri—Appollonia Chalupiec
Mabel Normand—Mabel Fortescue
Kim Novak—Marilyn Novak
Merle Oberon—Estelle Merle
  O'Brien Thompson
Margaret O'Brien—Angela Maxine
  O'Brien
Maureen O'Hara—Maureen
  FitzSimons
Jack Palance—Walter Palahnuik
Mary Pickford—Gladys Mary
  Smith
Jane Powell—Suzanne Burce
Paula Prentiss—Paula Ragusa
George Raft—George Ranft
Sally Rand—Helen Beck

Martha Raye—Margaret Tersa Yvonne O'Reed
Debbie Reynolds—Mary Frances Reynolds
Ginger Rogers—Virginia McMath
Roy Rogers—Leonard Slye
Mickey Rooney—Joe Yule, Jr.
Soupy Sales—Milton Hines
Susan Sarandon—Susan Tomaling
Telly Savalas—Aristotle Savalas
Romy Schneider—Rosemarie Albach-Retty
Lizabeth Scott—Emma Matzo
Randolph Scott—Randolph Crane
Mack Sennett (producer)— Michael Sinnott
Ann Shirley—Dawn Evelyeen Paris, then Dawn O'Day
Dinah Shore—Frances Rose Shore
Phil Silvers—Philip Silversmith
Red Skelton—Richard Skelton
Suzanne Somers—Suzanne Mahoney
Elke Sommer—Elke Schletz
Sissy Spacek—Mary Elizabeth Spacek
Kim Stanley—Patricia Kimberly Reid

Gale Storm—Josephine Cottle
Meryl Streep—Mary Louise Streep
Barry Sullivan—Patrick Barry
Max von Sydow—Carl Adolf von Sydow
Robert Taylor—Spangler Arlington Brugh
Danny Thomas—Amos Jacobs
Rip Torn—Elmore Rual Torn, Jr.
Lana Turner—Julia Jean Mildred Frances Turner
Twiggy—Lesley Hornby
Rudolph Valentino—Rodolpho Alfonzo Raffaelo Pierre Filibert Guglielmo di Valentina D'Antonguolla
Nancy Walker—Ann Myrtle Swoyer
Warner brothers (producers)— Albert, Harry, Jack, and Samuel Eichelbaum
John Wayne—Marion Michael Morrison
Tuesday Weld—Susan Ker Weld
Gene Wilder—Jerry Silberman
Shelly Winters—Shirley Schrift
Natalie Wood—Natasha Gurdin
Jane Wyman—Sarah Jane Fulks
Loretta Young—Gretchen Jung

56 Musicians and Musical Entertainers: Original Names

Tony Bennett—Anthony Benedetto
Irving Berlin—Israel Baline
Eubie Blake—James Hubert
Victor Borge—Borge Rosenbaum
Maria Callas—Maria Kalogeropolos
Ray Charles—Ray Charles Robinson
Chubby Checker—Ernest Evans
Alice Cooper—Vincent Furnier

Bobby Darin—Robert Cassotto
John Denver—Henry John Deutschendorf Jr.
Johnny Desmond—Giovanni de Simone
Dion—Dion Di Mucci
Bob Dylan—Robert Zimmerman
Duke Ellington—Edward Kennedy Ellington
"Mama" Cass Elliott—Ellen Naomi Cohen

Fabian—Fabian Anthony Forte
Freddie Fender—Baldemar Huerta
Connie Francis—Concetta Franconero
Crystal Gayle—Brenda Gayle Webb
Bobbie Gentry—Roberta Streeter
Dizzy Gillespie—John Birks Gillespie
Skitch Henderson—Lyle Russell Cedric Henderson
Hildegarde—Hildegarde Loretta Sell
Billie Holiday—Eleonora Fagan
Engelbert Humperdinck—Arnold Dorsey
Elton John—Reginald Kenneth Dwight
Tom Jones—Thomas Jones Woodward
Gypsy Rose Lee—Rose Louise Hovick
Liberace—Wladziu Liberace
Julie London—Julie Peck
Madonna—Madonna Louise Ciccone
Tony Martin—Alvin Morris
Dame Nellie Melba—Helen Porter Mitchell
Lauritz Melchior—Lebrecht Hommel
Joni Mitchell—Roberta Joan Anderson

Jelly Roll Morton—Ferdinand Joseph La Menthe
Jacques Offenbach—Jacob Eberst*
Patti Page—Clara Ann Fowler
Minnie Pearl—Sarah Ophelia Colley Cannon
Roberta Peters—Roberta Peterman
Edith Piaf—Edith Gassion
Della Reese—Deloreese Patricia Early
Artie Shaw—Abraham Isaac Arshawsky
Nina Simone—Eunice Kathleen Waymon
Ringo Starr—Richard Starkey
Cat Stevens—Steven Georgion
Connie Stevens—Concetta Ingolia
Franz von Suppé—Francisco Ezechiele Eermcegildo Suppé Demelli
Tiny Tim—Herbert Khaury
Tina Turner—Annie Mae Bullock
Conway Twitty—Harold Lloyd Jenkins
Bruno Walter—Bruno Walter Schlesinger
Muddy Waters—McKinley Morganfield
Hank Williams, Sr.—Hiram King Williams
Stevie Wonder—Steveland Morris
Tammy Wynette—Wynette Pugh

59 Sports Figures: Familiar Names and "Real" Names

Common nicknames such as Tom, Dick, and Hank are not included in this list.

---

*The Encyclopaedia Britannica explains, "He was the son of a cantor at the Cologne Synagogue, Isaac Juda Eberst, who had been born at Offenbach Am Main. The father was known as 'Der Offenbacher' (i.e., the man from Offenbach), and the composer was known only by his assumed name."

Sparky Anderson—George Anderson

The Bambino—George Herman "Babe" Ruth

Sal the Barber—Salvatore Maglie

Bear Bryant—Paul Bryant

Rick Barry—Richard Barry

The Big O—Oscar Robertson

Big Poison—Paul Waner

Big Train—Walter Johnson

Yogi Berra—Lawrence Berra

Ty Cobb—Tyrus Cobb

Crazy Legs—Elroy Hirsch

Daffy Dean—Paul Dean

Dizzy Dean—Jay Hanna Dean

Joltin' Joe Dimaggio—Joseph Dimaggio

El Cordobés—Manuel Benitez Perez

The Galloping Ghost—Harold "Red" Grange

The Gipper—George Gipp

Lefty (Goofy) Gomez—Vernon Gomez

Lefty Grove—Robert Grove

Rocky Graziano—Rocco Barbella

The Greatest—Cassius Clay (later Muhammad Ali)

Gabby Hartnett—Charles Hartnett

The Horse—Alan Ameche

Catfish Hunter—Jim Hunter

Iron Man—Henry Louis (Lou) Gehrig (also Joseph Jerome McGinnity)

Sandy Koufax—Sanford Koufax

The Lip—Leo Durocher

Little Mo—Maureen Connolly

Little Poison—Lloyd Waner

Joe Louis—Joe Louis Barrow

Connie Mack—Cornelius Alexander McGillicuddy

The Man—Stanley (Stan) Musial

Rocky Marciano—Rocco Francis Marchegiano

Pistol Pete Maravich—Peter Maravich

Nellie—Jacob Nelson Fox

Satchel Paige—Leroy Paige

Papa Bear—George Halas

Pelé—Edson Arantes do Nascimento

Boog Powell—John Powell

Betsy Rawls—Elizabeth Earle Rawls

Pee Wee Reese—Harold Reese

Branch Rickey—Wesley Branch Rickey

Sugar Ray Robinson—Ray Robinson (b. Walker Smith)

Pete Rozelle—Alvin Ray Rozelle

Bubba Smith—Charles Aaron Smith

Duke Snider—Edwin Snider

Willie Stargell—Wilver Dornell Stargell

Casey Stengel—Charles Dillon Stengel

The Stilt—Wilton (Wilt) Chamberlain

Sunny Jim—James Bottomley

Birdie Tebbetts—George R. Tebbetts

Y. A. Tittle—Yelberton Abraham Tittle

Rube Waddell—George Edward Waddell

Rube Walberg—George Elvin Walberg

Jersey Joe Walcott—Arnold Raymond Cream

The Whip—Ewell Blackwell

Hack Wilson—Lewis Robert Wilson

Cale Yarborough—William Caleb Yarborough

Yaz—Carl Yastrzemski

❦ 8
A Chapter for the Smiths, Johnsons, and Changs

Smith 2,382,509; Thatch(er) 10,001

Only 3,169 surnames represent over half of the American people. In fact, over 56 percent of all Americans will answer to one of those names. Smith, as everyone knows, heads the list. When the Social Security Administration last counted, it had in its files the earnings' records of 2,382,509 Smiths.

The next 3,168 names all had 10,000 or more of their records in the SSA files. At the bottom of this group stood Thatch, which includes such names as Thatcher, with 10,001.

The rest of the 1,286,556 SSA names are divided among the other 11 percent of the population—about 186 persons per name.

More Facts about Smiths

1. Smith County, KS, is the geographic center of the United States, and Smith Center is its county seat.

2. The first colonial American Smith family (not the first individual) was that of John Smith—the one who founded Barnstable and Sandwich, MA, early in the seventeenth century. His wife bore him 13 children. (So that's why there are so many Smiths!)

3. In England 11 baronets and 28 knights are named Smith, although that name is usually hidden behind some more high-sounding facade, such as *Smythe* or a hyphenated name.

4. Five American colleges have Smith as part of their name.

5. Three first ladies were Smiths: Abigail Smith Adams, Margaret McKall Smith Taylor, and Rosalynn Smith Carter.

6. Unusual given names of Smiths:
Five Eighths Smith
William McKinley Louisiana Levee Bust Smith (born during a flood)
Major Smith
Minor Smith
Bright Smith
Orange Smith
Icycle Smith
Loyal Lodge No. 296 Knights of Pythias Ponca City Oklahoma Smith
Omega Smith (the end)

7. One John Smith boasted that when he was a bachelor, he had a fan club that girls and women of his community formed. It was, of course, called the Pocahontas Club.

8. A Jim Smith Society meets in Las Vegas. (Guess what the criterion for membership is.)

9. In 1978, according to Elsdon Smith, 1.0144 percent of Americans were named Smith. He estimated a total of 2,180,960 of them at that time. Add in variants such as Smythe or Smid and the total rises to 2,378,440. Add to that the names such as Kowal and Haddad, which are synonymous with Smith, and the total becomes (conservatively) 4,736,350.

10. Let's translate Elsdon Smith's figures into visual terms. Imagine that all 2,180,960 "real" Smiths join hands and form a circle with its center in Smith County, KS. The circle will reach central Nebraska on the north and the Oklahoma line on the south. To the west the Smiths stand not far from the streets of Denver, and to the east they are near Topeka.

Next, imagine the center of the human circle to be in Albany, NY. The line of Smiths now emcompasses Philadelphia, New York

City, Boston, Rochester, and Harrisburg, all of Connecticut, Rhode Island, Massachusetts, and New Jersey, and most of New Hampshire, Vermont, and New York, and about a third of Pennsylvania. A couple of hundred thousand other Smiths in the circle have to let go of their neighbors' hands and paddle around in the Atlantic.

A similar Johnson circle would have a radius about three fourths as long, and one composed of Williamses and Williamsons would be a little over five eighths as long, with the Brown and Jones radii somewhat shorter than that.

11. The 1990 *Guinness Book of World Records* reports that in England and Wales the number of "nationally insured" Smiths is 659,050, including 10,102 "plain" John Smiths and 19,502 persons named John plus middle-name-or-initial plus Smith. If one includes the uninsured Smiths, the total rises to more than 800,000.

What Does a *Sexsmith* Do with a *Sexauer*?

Sexsmith sounds like a urologist or a gynecologist, but that origin appears unlikely. A variant is Sixsmith, which suggests that this smith must have come from Sixte, a place in France. Elsdon Smith, however, suggests that the original Sixsmith may have made small (six-inch?) daggers or swords. A guess that Sexsmith made sextants and other navigational instruments is dubious, for the word *sextant* was invented after the name-giving period.

Sexauer (variant Sexaur) is easier. He or she came from Sexau, a place in Germany.

(Inevitably, such names lend themselves to jokes. "Do you have a Sexauer in this office?" "No but we get long coffee breaks.")

Some Hog Farmers Yell "Hooey"

William Sooy Smith, a contracting engineer, got tired of being a Smith. He wanted a name that would be not only uncommon but even unique.

One day he had a burst of inspiration. He decided to combine his middle and last names. He became William Sooysmith.

H. Allen Smith, who told the story in *People Named Smith*, says that the change didn't improve things a great deal, because "Sooy is a cry used in calling hogs."

Legitimatizing Accidental Smiths

Abraham Lincoln used to tell a story about an Illinois justice of the peace whose commission and seal had not yet arrived. He married one impatient couple anyway and gave them this receipt:

> State of Illinois
> Peoria County
> To all the world Greeting. Know ye that John Smith and Peggy Myres is hereby certified to go together and do as all folks does, anywhere inside coperas precinct, and when my commission comes I am to marry em good and date em back to kivver accidents.

Could There Be a *Jones* Spinoff?

TNSDUNSPHI. Maybe that set of letters doesn't look very exciting, but it covers a gripe that thousands of persons may echo.

The letters stand for The National Society to Discourage Use of the Name Smith for Purposes of Hypothetical Illustration. You know the sort of thing: "There were these two people, see—we'll call 'em Smith and Jones—and they. . . ."

The organization began in 1942 when Glenn E. Smith, a graduate student at the University of Minnesota, became annoyed because in many class sessions a professor would say something like, "Now we'll look at a typical taxpayer. Call him John Smith."

So Glenn Smith founded TNSDUNSPHI, raised a few dollars from a few Smiths to publicize it, and soon found himself presiding over a rather flourishing organization.

It is especially appropriate that Glenn E. Smith was the founder. According to H. Allen Smith, Glenn's father was, of course, a Smith, and his mother's maiden name was Smith, so all four of his grandparents were Smiths and so were at least four of his great-grandparents, to say nothing of unnumbered uncles, aunts, and cousins.

Imagine That All the Johnsons Gathered in Manhattan

Only Smiths outnumber Johnsons in the United States.

If all the nominal sons and daughters of John in America and Europe were to assemble on Manhattan island, some of them might either have to get their feet wet in the Hudson or the East River or crowd the bridges to the other boroughs.

To begin with, there would be some two million Johnsons from the United States. The British Isles would add a few hundred thousand more. The Johnstons, supplemented by a few Johnstones, would add another couple of hundred thousand.

Jones also means 'son of John'; about 1,400,000 live in the United States alone. Many of the 600,000 Jacksons trace their ancestry to Jack, a nickname for John, although in some cases for Jacob or James. Evans is a Welsh form of John, and there are over a third of a million Evanses in the United States, plus a few Heavenses. There are also many less common British forms of Johnson, such as John, Johns, Johnikin, Johnigan, Jonson, Ja(y)nes, Jenks, Jenkins(on), Jenner, Jennings, Jennison, and Littlejohn.

So far we haven't introduce the descendants of John in or from continental Europe. The Scandinavians gave us Hansen and Hanson and their variants, as well as some Jons(s)ons. Johansons, Jensens. Germany has Johann(es) and some forms with Hans such as Hansel or Hanschmidt 'the John who is a smith' or Henson, as well as such unlikely looking forms as Gentzen, Geschke, and Ham(m)an(n). The Dutch have Jan(t)sen and some other forms: the Italians, Di Giovanni and various combinations with Gian- such as the Giannini who started the Bank of America, as well as Ianni and diminutives such as Iannello; the Spanish, Ibañez; the Greeks, Gianakakis, Gian(n)op(o)ulos, and Ionnides.

Eastern Europe is overrun with the sons of John. Ivan is a frequent beginning, as in Ivan(ov) (ovic) (ow) (cich) (auskas). Russian Ivan Ivanov is only a disguise for John Johnson, and publisher William Jovanovich, with a Yugoslavian name, is really plain old Bill Johnson. Jan begins maybe a hundred east European variants, such as Polish Janowski or Janiszewski, or Lithuanian Jankauskas, or Hungarian Janosfi. Polish Jasinski goes back to Jas, a nickname for Jan, which means John. The Romanians may spell the name Jonescu or Jonesku, or sometimes Ionescu or Enesco. A Lithuanian whose ancestral name may have been Jonynas or Jonnitis once turned up as a fine American pro quarterback named Unitas.

Still other descendants of John, if they convened with the rest in Manhattan, would swell its population even more. By that time some of them would be taking over New Jersey.

The Most Common Name in the World

No, it's not Smith, Johnson, or any you're likely to think of immediately.

It's Chang, now transliterated as Zhang, estimated in 1990 by the Guinness people as numbering 104 million persons, from 9.7 to 12.1 percent of all Chinese.

❦ 9
Surnames and Genealogy

Knowledge of Names:
A Tool for the Genealogist

"I was trying to trace my family tree," a young woman we'll call Iris Faulkner said recently, "and I got back as far as my great-great-grandparents, but then I was lost. I just couldn't find anything more about any Faulkners in the area, and I couldn't find out where they came from. Suddenly, like magic, they were just there."

Iris was helped by a friend, Ray, who was better versed in genealogy. He asked her whether she had searched the records of the late eighteenth century for possibly varied spellings of Faulkner.

"Well," Iris said, "I looked for Falkner, and Faukner, and I did find some Faukeners, but they weren't connected to us."

Ray pulled from his shelves a book that listed American surnames of 1790. It showed 13 spellings of Faulkner in use at that time.

"My guess," Ray said, "is that there may be a clue in one of these other spellings—most likely Falconer, which is, as you probably know, the meaning of the name. If you can trace it back far enough—and admittedly that can be difficult—you'll probably find that in the Middle Ages in England some remote ancestor of yours trained falcons and used them in hunting small game."

Ray proved partly right, partly wrong. The variant that Iris found to be the name of her eighteenth-century forebears was Falkener, not Falconer, but the source and the meaning were what Ray said.

Names are necessarily the focus of much—probably most—of the work of the genealogist, whether amateur or professional. Some newspapers run regular columns of genealogical inquiry, typically consisting of entries requesting help from anyone knowing about the holders of a certain name in the comparatively recent or possibly more remote past. Here are a couple of representative entries:

> Who were parents of Stella HUNTER who m. George CARSON? They were at Heltonville, Lawrence County, in 1876. Want parents, marriage date, place, correspondence with descendants of Christely HELLENBURG, HILDENBORG, HILGENBORG, HELLENBORG 1810 Virginia/Tennessee and Mary HOUSHOUR. Known children: Eliza b. about 1851; John b. 1853 m. Lucy A. HANSON Feb. 21, 1872, Monroe County, Ind.; Elizabeth b. about 1860; Mary Catherine b. 1863; Andrew (Jack?) JACKSON, b. about 1843 m. Sarah J. HOUSHOUR Feb. 21, 1867, Lawrence County, Ind.

Information about long-dead people is often hidden in musty records in places such as courthouses and churches, or in research that other genealogists have performed in the past. The Church of Latter Day Saints (Mormons) in Salt Lake City houses the most extensive collection of American genealogical information available anywhere; it is not confined to members of that faith. Canadians have done considerable genealogical work, as have scholars in all parts of the British Isles and in most European nations. When a search needs to be continued abroad, the various national genealogical societies often can be helpful in supplying leads.

Many public libraries, including some in small towns, also have fairly extensive genealogical collections, usually with emphasis on past residents of the immediate area. An especially good collection is that of the New York Public Library (Fifth Avenue at Forty-Second Street), whose librarians, well trained in genealogy, can be very helpful to patrons.

A good source of printed information is the Genealogical Publishing Company, 10001 North Calvert Street, Baltimore, MD 21202. It specializes in reprints of books and other materials. A recent catalog has over one hundred pages, with descriptions of about ten books, etc., on each page. From those hundreds of publications, here are some representative titles:

Americans of Royal Descent
Emigrants from England, 1773–1776
Passengers Who Arrived in the United States, Sept., 1821-Dec.,
  1823 (427 pages)
Southern Families, Vol. XV. (Allred, Anderson, Delafield, Etheridge, Hayes-Hays, Jernigan, Matthews, Rose, Tate, and other families are covered.)
Wallingford, Connecticut, Early Families
Emigrants to Pennsylvania, 1641–1819

Information about marriage notices, baptism, deaths, and wills is contained in other publications.

The serious tracer of American families almost always eventually searches in foreign sources—whether in person or through printed materials. Again, much guide material is available. For example, two volumes by Margaret D. Falley, *Ancestral Research, Irish and Scotch-Irish*, give details about the major Irish repositories; dates of coverage of material on specific families; and (in Volume Two) a bibliography of family histories, pedigrees, and source materials published in books and periodicals, and including parish, town, and county histories, church records, and summaries of family data.

Names! The more the genealogist knows about names, the more successful the investigation may be. Always the search is based on names, but glimpses of the people whom the names represent are not infrequent. In almost everyone's family, there are likely to be found civic leaders and highwaymen, women who brought up large families after losing husbands, maiden ladies or prostitutes, workers in occupations now almost vanished, soldiers or sailors who died young or became colonels or sea captains, illegitimate as well as legitimate children—each person (except possibly infants) with a name, a life, a story that transcends the brief notice in an old church or on a hard-to-decipher tombstone.

In Thomas Gray's still-familiar words, written in the eighteenth century,

Beneath those rugged elms, the yew-tree's shade,
  Where heaves the turf in many a mouldering heap,
Each in his narrow cell forever laid,
  The rude forefathers of the hamlet sleep,
  Their name, their years, spelt by the unlettered Muse,
  The place of fame and elegy supply.

The modern genealogist sometimes provides the missing elegy.

Headaches for a Genealogist

In the Middle Ages, two brothers or other near relatives sometimes had exactly the same name. Genealogists can run into a wall in attempting to determine which of two thirteenth-century Fulk fitz Wains was really the ancestor they sought, or which Robert Helias de Say, or which John le Strange. Then there was John Matravers, who by different wives had sons named John, and the younger of those had two sons named John.

In France such a problem was usually avoided. A younger brother of Jehan 'John' was sometimes named Jehannot 'little John,' and sometimes a second Guillaume 'William' was named Guillot 'little William.'

The duplication of names occasionally extended to girls. The will of a sixteenth-century Englishman, Thomas Reade, refers to "my daughter Katheryn the younger" and "my eldest daughter Katheryn."

Not Everybody Pronounces *Enroughty* as *Darby* (or, Ain't Genealogy Fun?)

After H. L. Mencken's *The American Language* appeared in 1919, his office received many letters adding to its store of information. One F. W. Sydnor told of the confusion caused in Henrico County, Virginia, by a duplication of names. Mencken incorporated the story in his *American Language: Supplement II* in 1948.

> The records show one *Darby Enroughty* (pronounced *En-ruff-tee*) to have been living near Four-Mile creek in 1690. He had a son named *John* and one named *Darby*. Later there were two *John Enroughtys* living in the same locality, cousins, whose name was frequently found in the records. Double Christian names were rarely used in those days, and it became necessary to distinguish between the two *Johns*. *John Enroughty*, the son of *John*, was known by his Christian name, but *John* the son of *Darby Enroughty*, was designated *John Enroughty the son of Darby, John Enroughty of Darby*, and at least once as *John Darby*. The *Enroughtys* of Henrico and those known as *Darby* (real

name *Enroughty*) are all descendants of *Darby Enroughty*. Those bearing the name *Enroughty* are the descendants of his son *John*, and those bearing the name of *Darby* are the descendants of his son *Darby*.

All clear?

The Celts in the American South

A historical note for genealogists in the South:

Most histories of the southern United States say or imply that most of its white people are of English stock, while granting that there is a French pocket in Louisiana, that here or there are some towns or counties with more than a scattering of people of German or other European background, and that in recent times many people of Spanish heritage have entered Florida. The conventional view about the Englishness of the South was expressed by one historian in 1976, who said that the South is "the biggest single WASP nest this side of the Atlantic."

Grady McWhiney and Forrest McDonald (writing in the journal *Names*) challenged such statements about the dominance of early settlement by the English and the consequent degree of Englishness. Using sophisticated methods of name analysis, they demonstrate that the highest percentage of white Southerners before the Civil War period were descended from people in the *Celtic* areas of the British Isles: Ireland, Scotland, Wales, and the English counties closest to those areas (fringe counties with a high proportion of Celts).

The authors conclude that in 1790 or thereabouts "the further south and west from Philadelphia, the more Celtic the population: In the Upper South, Celts and Englishmen each constituted about two-fifths of the population; in the Carolinas more than half the population were Celtic, and Celts outnumbered Englishmen five to three."

They go on: "Celts completely dominated the frontier from Pennsylvania southward, where they constituted three-fifths to nearly one hundred percent of the total population. [For example,] In the North Carolina tidewater districts, from 39 percent of the population in Edmonton to 48 percent in Newbern were Celts, but in the upland interior they constituted 63 percent of the population in the Fayette district and almost 100 percent in the Hillsborough district."

Relatively few Europeans emigrated to the South after 1790 or 1800. As a result, by 1850 "the Celtic portion of the southern white population stabilized at 50 percent or slightly less, the English stabilized at about a third of the total; the remainder were largely of German, French, or Spanish origin."

Today, all other European nations are still represented only scantily in the South. Most modern Southern whites are descended from people who arrived in 1800 or earlier. If McWhiney's and McDonald's careful research is accurate, not far from half of those ancestors came from Scottish, Irish, Welsh, or other Celtic backgrounds.

Some family genealogists who have automatically assumed that their Southern ancestors were English may want to look at the possibility of Celtic roots.

How to Find the Meaning of a Surname

The best source of surnominal meanings is *New Dictionary of American Family Names* by Elsdon C. Smith. Smith briefly defines and gives the nationality of some 20,000 names, including all the most common names and many that are unusual. However, even that book can include fewer than 2 percent of the more than a million American surnames; a treatment of all the names would require many volumes and would be prohibitively expensive.

If Smith does not appear to list the name you are interested in, look to see whether he may have placed it under any possible variant spelling. Next, check a dictionary of the language that the name probably comes from. If it is an occupational name, a descriptive, or a general place name such as Lake, the dictionary should help.

If you think it may be the name of a specific place, consult a detailed map of the country—if possible, one that includes the names of rather small towns, as a good road map does. Many uncommon German names, for instance, are taken from town names or names of specific mountains or other physical features. If you suspect that the name is a patronym, you may find (especially among Slavic names) that it is a variant spelling of the name of a saint or other famous person. Saint Basil, for instance, shows up in such varied forms as Vasely, Wasielawski, and Vasilevich; Alexander, as Lesko, Oleksandrenko, Sandor.

With Italian and Slavic names, watch especially for nicknames and shortened forms. For instance, among Italian names, although the equivalent of Anthony may be Antonelli or a variant, it also may be Tonelli or a variant of that; Francisco sometimes appears as Cisco, Ciscolo, or Ciccone; Jacob is almost unrecognizable as Giacomo, Chiapetta, Como, and Mazzucci; Nicholas may show up as Colonna, and Thomas as Massi or a variant.

Further hints may be found in this book—for example, the information about diminutives (page 111) or about affixes that mean 'son of' (below). Two other sources are Elsdon Smith's *American Surnames* and J. N. Hook's *Family Names: How Our Surnames Came to America.*

How to Recognize
Everybody's Little Boy

Over 30 percent of American surnames have the meaning of 'son of,' 'grandson of,' or 'descendant of,' and very frequently such patronyms are signaled by a prefix or a suffix. Often the ancestral background of a name can easily be determined from the affix. The following clues are generally accurate indicators, although the fact that people sometimes have changed their names to those representative of other nationalities creates some exceptions.

acs, as in Lukacs 'descendant of Luke': Hungarian
aitis, onis, us in Petraitis or Petronis 'son of Peter': Lithuanian
ak, as in Michalak, sometimes spelled *ack* in the United States 'descendant of Michael': Polish.
akis, akos, as in Petrakis, Petrakos 'descendant of Peter': Greek
ap or *Up*, as in ap Richard or Upjohn 'son of Richard' 'son of John': Welsh. Now rare, having been reduced to *P*, as in Powell, or *B*, as in Bowen.
chuk as in Klemchuk 'descendant of Clement': Ukrainian
czyk, czak, as in Rybarczyk 'son of the fisherman,' Matczak 'son of Matthew': Polish
D,' De, Di, as in D'Angelo 'son of the angel,' De Stefano 'son of Stephen,' Di Bernardo 'son of Bernard': Italian. In French or Spanish names, *De* usually indicates a place rather than a person.

ek, ik, as in Janicek, Janik 'descendant of John': Polish
enko, inko, as in Pavlenko, Paolinko 'son of Paul': Ukrainian
es, as in Lopes 'son of Lope or Lupe': Portuguese. Sometimes may be
   Spanish.
escu, as in Antonescu 'descendant of Anthony': Romanian. Sometimes
   spelled *esco.*
ez, as in Martinez 'son of Martin': Spanish. Occasionally *az* or *es* in a
   variant.
Fitz as in Fitzsimmons 'son of Simon': Irish or English
Mac, Mc, M', Me, as in MacNeil, McNeil, M'Neely, Meneely 'son of
   Neil or of Conghal': Scottish or Irish. See also page 130.
O', as in O'Dea 'grandson of Deoghadh': Irish
off, ov, as in Petroff or Petrov 'son of Peter': Russian, sometimes
   Bulgarian
ovic, as in Jankovic 'son of John': Yugoslavian. Often dropped or
   changed to *ovich* in the United States. The *o* may be missing or
   substituted for.
ovich, as in Grigorovich 'son of Gregory': Russian, sometimes
   Yugoslavian. The *o* may be another vowel, or missing.
ovici, as in Grigorovici 'son of Gregory': Yugoslavian (Serbian)
poulos, as in Antonopoulos 'descendant of Anthony': Greek. Often
   appears as a variant or *os.*
s, as in Evans 'son of John': Welsh. Appears often in English names,
   too.
sen, as in Svensen 'son of Sven': Norwegian or Danish
son, as in Swedish Swanson 'son of Swan,' Swedish or Norwegian Olson
   (also Olsen in Norway) 'son of Ole or Olaf,' English Williamson
   'son of William.' Sometimes shortened to *s.*
vicius, as in Matulevicius 'descendant of Matthew': Lithuanian
wiak, wicz, as in Bartowiak 'son of Bartholomew,' Adamowicz 'son of
   Adam': Polish. Often respelled as *vits* or *witz.*

Diminutives also often carry the suggestion of 'little son of.' See the
following article.

Thank Heaven for Little Ones

A young Italian mother was caressing her infant. "Ah,
Pietro mio," she cooed. "Piccolo Pietro. Petri mio. Petrelli mio. Te
amo, Petrelli."

It was probably in such a way that diminutives began—pet
names that mean 'little.' They are often based on the father's name;
perhaps little Pietro's father was also Pietro. But sometimes the
source is a pet form of the name, as Petri is of Pietro, or sometimes
it is merely the infant's name with a diminutive ending.

In English, Jenkinson, Jenkins, and Jenks are interesting examples of diminutives. Jen is a nickname for John; -kin is an English (originally Low German) diminutive ending; and -son or the -s in Jenkins and Jenks means 'son of.' So each of the three names means 'little son of John.' Wilkinson, Wilkins, and Wilks are parallel names: 'little son of Will.' The diminutive -kin appears in many other names, such as Watkins 'little son of Walter,' Elkin 'little Elie or Elias,' and Larkin 'little Lawrence.'

Another English diminutive is -cock, as in the name of Gordon Johncock 'little John,' a prominent auto race driver; Hitchcock or Hedgecock is 'little Hitch,' a nickname for Richard. In the form -cocks or -cox the meaning 'son of' is added, so Wilcox is 'little son of Will.'

The endings -ie, -y, and -ey are sometimes diminutives, as in Willie or Will(e)y, but are not reliable indicators, since often they mean 'island,' as in Hardie or Hardy, or (with *l*) 'a meadow,' as in Fairlie or Fairley.

Many English surnames were borrowed from the French after the Norman Conquest. If you see an English name ending in -eau, -el(le, -et(te), or -on, or in the double diminutive -elin, -elet, -inet, or -elot, the odds are that it was originally a French name. Examples of some of these, from either English or French, are Watteau, Mallet(t)(te), Marriott, Hamon, Michelet or Michelin, and Philpott, referring respectively to little Vatier, Mal, Mary, home, Michel, and Philip.

The most distinctive of the several Irish diminutives are -an and especially -gan. Ryan and Nolan, for example, go back to Celtic words meaning 'little king' and 'little noble one.' The ending -gan appears in scores of names such as Finnegan 'little fair one' and Milligan 'little bald one.'

The Germans most often use -ke (to which the English -kin is related): Gehrke 'little spear-wielder,' Lemke 'little Lem or Lampo.' Less frequent is -lein as in Heinlein 'little Heinrich'; the ending may be written as -len. Sometimes -isch appears: Janisch 'little John.'

The Dutch may use -ke, too, as well as -je: Lutje 'little folk' and Henke 'little hedged place.'

Lithuanian diminutives include -ikas, -ulis, and -kus, as in Jonikas and Janulis, both of which mean 'little John,' and Butkus 'little Butkintas.' Onomatists who saw the gigantic all-pro Dick Butkus playing defense for the Chicago Bears doubted the appropriateness of the name.

The Italians are the greatest lovers of diminutives. All these endings appear again and again: *-etti* and *-etto*; *-ello*, *-ella*, *-elli*, and the Neapolitan *-illo*; *-ini* and *-ino*; *-occo*, *-ucci*, and *-uzzo*. A few examples: Martinelli 'little Martin,' Morello or Moretti 'little Amore' or 'little dark one,' Parillo 'little treasure,' Paolino or Paolini 'little Paul,' Piccini 'little man,' Masucci 'little Thomas.'

The opposite of a diminutive is an augmentative—much more rare. In Italian, *-one* is often an augmentative. For example, Petrone or Petroni(o) is 'big Pietro,' and Capone supposedly has a big head.

❦ 10
Some Jewish Family Names

Zvonko Rode's "Fifteen Sources of Jewish Family Names"

1. Biblical names: Abraham, Aaron, etc.

2. Derivation from biblical names: Sacks (from Isaac), Lewin (from Levi)

3. Translations of biblical names: Baruch 'blessed' sometimes becomes Benedict or Selig. Ephraim (associated with fish) might become Fisch(el), Rybowitz, Karp, Hecht 'pike,' Heilbut 'halibut,' Lax, or Lox.

4. Hebrew names with German or Yiddish endings: David could become Tevele, and Simon might become Schimmel or Suskind. (Elsdon Smith, however, mentions no Jewish connection with the last two names.)

5. Similarities to Hebrew names: Gabriel might become Gebert or Gebhardt; Jacob could be Koppelmann.

6. Names indicating place (especially numerous): Bachrach (a town), Bing (from Bingen), Birnbaum (a town), Halpern (Heilbronn), Hirschberg (town), Schoenfeld (town), Steinberg (town), Tannhauser 'one who lived in a forest house.'

7. Countries: Schwab (from Schwaben, Swabia), Hess (German), Österreicher (Austrian), Welish, Reuss(er) (Russian), Turk

8. House signs: Adler 'eagle,' Blum 'flower,' Engel 'angel,' Nussbaum 'nut tree'

9. Patronyms: Bendavid 'son of David,' Isaacson, Mendelsohn, Abramowicz, Jacobovitz

10. Trades and occupations: Cantor, Goldschmidt, Koch 'cook,' Steiner 'mason,' Ta(e)nzer 'dancer, juggler'

11. Descriptions: Kraus 'curly,' Rothbard 'red beard,' Jaffe 'beautiful,' Zadik 'just'

12. Nicknames: Graf, Kaiser, Koenig

13. Arbitrary (probably imposed): Kanarienvogel 'canary bird,' Mausehund 'mouse dog,' Raubvogel 'predatory bird,' Regenbogen 'rainbow,' Cohnreich 'rich Cohen' (priest)

14. Acronyms: Zak (from *zera kedoshim* 'the seed of martyrs'). See the following article.

15. Changed names: Silver from Silberberg 'silver mountain,' Wilson from Weichselbaum 'cherry tree,' Winston from Weinstein (a mountain's name), Wolf from Wolkowicz 'son of Wolf'

Rode gives many additional examples. Note that Jews and Gentiles use many of the same names.

Names That Are Acronyms

Acronymic names are based on the initial letters of two or more words. The Hebrew alphabet has no vowels; vowel sounds are indicated by a system of dots and lines placed below or above the letters.

Two illustrations of acronyms: *ben* Rabbi Nachman 'son of Rabbi Nachmann' → *Baran*; *zera* Kedoshim 'the ancestor of martyrs' → *Zak*.

Here are other examples, but it must be remembered that some of these names (Bach, for instance), more frequently come from other sources.

Beth *Chadash* (a book title) → Bach
ben Reb Tzabok → Baratz
ben Reb David → Bard, Barth, Bradt, Bardowicz
ben Reb Moshe Shmuel → Barmash
ben Shimson→Basch
Chatan Reb Pinkhas 'son-in-law of Pinkhas' → Charap
dayan umelitz 'judge and defender' → Dym
kohen tzedek 'priest of righteousness' → Katz
moreh tzedek 'teacher of righteousness → Metz
Rabbi Moshe ben Maimon → Rambam
Shabbetai Cohen → Schach
sheyibye leorekh yamin tovim 'may he live long and good days' →
    Schalit

Unusual Ways to Select Surnames

Instead of being named for a place, a person, an occupation, personal appearance or other characteristics, some people get their surnames in ways that seem odd.

During the late eighteenth and early nineteenth centuries, in parts of what is now Germany, laws were passed requiring all Jews without surnames to adopt them. France's Napoleon and Russia's Tsar Alexander issued edicts to the same effect. Some Jews were unwilling and suspicious of the rulers' motives, but governments insisted. For a fee, a Jew could buy an attractive name such as Diamant, Saphire, Rosenthal 'rose valley,' or Grünberg 'green mountain.' Those who refused to pay, or could not, might be told that their names were to be Eselkopf 'donkey head,' Verderber 'wrecker,' Schmalz 'grease,' Drachenblutt 'dragon blood,' Saumagen 'sow belly,' or Wanzenknicker 'louse cracker.' Needless to say, most such names have been changed since that time.

Biblical names were often forbidden, but many Jews dared to adopt them anyway. For that reason, thousands of Jews are named Abraham, Abram, Abramowicz, and the like. Some Jews opened their Bibles randomly and picked the first name they saw. Benzion Kaganoff (*A Dictionary of Jewish Names*) tells of a rabbi who opened the prayer book and assigned the first word on a page as the name of one family in his congregation, the second word to a second family, and so on, until all had surnames. In some German-controlled parts of Hungary, Jews were arbitrarily assigned one of four names: Weiss, Schwartz, Gross, or Klein. A few Jews chose names popular in the literature of the time; Kaganoff gives Sternberg and Morgenthau as examples.

Some Native Americans, too, were forced to choose surnames. Ordinarily they or an Indian agent translated a nickname; in that way came Running Deer, Lone Wolf, Red Cloud, and similar names, but also some derisive names such as Fool Head, Crooked Nose, or Cowardly Fox. H. L. Mencken (*The American Language, Supplement Two*) says that one agent mistranslated Young Man Whose Very Horses Are Feared into Young Man Afraid of His Horse. Other names referred to bodily functions or parts not mentioned in most American names.

Chinese legend says that all Chinese names—there seem to be no more than a thousand of them—are derived from an ancient poem, "The Families of a Hundred Houses." As a result, literally millions of unrelated people may be named Chang, Chin, Li, or other common names.

Similarly, Korea has but few names. Gary Jennings (*Personalities of Language*) tells a story of an American officer who during the Korean war said to his Korean friend, "Let's get the hell out of here, Kim," and two thirds of the company started to run away.

Jennings asserts more seriously that the few Chickahominy Indians surviving in Virginia are all named Bradley. "The name commemorates either the popularity or the fecundity of an early English colonial, a runaway indentured servant, who joined and married into the tribe."

❦ 11
Names of African-Americans

Names of Slaves

African-American slaves were each given, as a rule, a very common English name. Among 972 names of male slaves recorded between 1619 and 1799, Newbell Niles Puckett, a scholar of African-American history and author of *Black Names in America*, found these to be the leaders:

Jack (57)	Caesar (21)	Frank (16)
Tom (47)	Dick (20)	Charles (15)
Harry (34)	John (18)	Joe (14)
Sam (30)	Robin (18)	Prince (14)
Will (23)		

Much further down the list came names surviving from Africa, most often with only one or two representatives among the 972 in the sample. These included, for instance, Anque, Bumbo, Jobah, Quamana, Taynay, and Yearie.

The names of women slaves followed a similar pattern. Here are the most common of their names in a sample of 603:

Bet (38)	Betty (15)	Nan (13)
Mary (22)	Sarah (15)	Peg (12)
Jane (18)	Phillis (14)	Sary (12)
Hanna (16)		

Some of the women, too, were still called by African names such as Abah, Bilah, Comba, Dibb, Juba, Kauchee, Mima, and Sena.

In both sexes, a higher proportion of African names might have survived if Africans had all spoken essentially the same language. But there are hundreds of African languages; the 90 million people in the Bantu group alone, for instance, speak more than two hundred different languages. The slaves were not all brought from the same part of Africa and consequently often could not understand one another. They were therefore likely to call their fellows by the names they heard the owners or foremen use for them.

In French-speaking Louisiana, slave names reflected the dominant language and so were generally different from those in the English colonies. There the names were often François, Jean, Pierre, and Leon for men, and Manon, Delphine, Marie Louise, Celeste, and Eugenie for women. Spanish areas had male slaves with names such as Francisco, Pedro, and Antonio, and females named Maria, Isabella, and Juana.

Names Adopted by Free African-Americans

While they were enslaved, African-Americans almost always had just one name, but when they became free they immediately chose surnames while usually (not always) keeping the given names they had been accustomed to. When retained, a given name was generally changed to its full form: Thomas, not Tom; Elizabeth, not Bet. Jack was no longer among the leaders.

Hundreds of free African-Americans fought in the American Revolution. They included, in the Fourth Connecticut Regiment, these surnames, among others:

Freeman (the most popular)	Rogers	Liberty
	Ball	Phillips
Johnson	Caesar	Rhodes
Brown	Jackson	Vassall
Greene		

After the Civil War a few of the newly freed men and women took the name of a former master—possibly sometimes out of affection, other times simply because the name was familiar and handy. In general, though, they tried to conform to the customs of the land in which they were then (at least on paper) completely free men and women. One of the customs, it seemed, was for most people to have one of two hundred to three hundred especially common names. The extent to which the former slaves chose these common "white" names for themselves is shown in this list of the top 15 names among African-Americans of Augusta, GA, in 1877:

1. Williams (2)
2. Jones (4)
3. Johnson (3)
4. Smith (1)
5. Jackson
6. Thomas
7. Brown (5)
8. Walker (11)
9. Davis (6)
10. Green
11. Robinson
12. Scott
13. Harris
14. Turner
15. Anderson

(The number in parentheses shows the rank of the same name, when available, among Augusta's whites in the same year.)

Eight Stems from *Roots*

Alex Haley's famous *Roots* detailed the tracing of his ancestry back to Africa. The following events are among those that occurred during its amazing reception after publication and again after episodes based on it were presented on television—one of the most successful series in television history.

1. On February 18, 1977, "Kunta Kinte Reid, a 7-pound, 11-ounce baby boy, was born to John and Nefhertiti Reid in Harlem Hospital." His mother was quoted as saying, "Like Kunta Kinte [the main character in *Roots*], he should be free, and he should be somebody and know that he is somebody."

2. In that same month, 19 other babies born in New York City were named Kunta Kinte or Kizzy (Kunta Kinte's daughter). There were also 15 such names reported from Los Angeles, 10 from Detroit, and 8 from Atlanta, as well as a male and female pair of twins in Cleveland.

3. Travel agencies in March 1977 reported "a virtual explosion of American interest in travel to Africa," especially via Air Afrique. Some agencies started special "Roots" tours that went to Senegal and included time in Jaffure, Gambia, where Kunta Kinte was born.

4. Although Doubleday published *Roots*, other houses moved to share the wealth. Random House, for instance, reissued *Generations*, concerning family histories, and published a book of selections related to the theme of *Roots*, with Haley as a consultant. Random House and Miami-Dade Junior College cooperated in a *Roots*-based project with tapes, films, books, and courses—bought immediately by 150 institutions.

5. Scholars conducted interviews with slaves' descendants who still lived in the relatively isolated Sea Islands off the coast of South Carolina and Georgia.

6. The Carnegie Foundation underwrote a Madison High School (Brooklyn) program to fight ethnic tensions, and other schools and colleges started programs similar in purpose, with or without foundation support.

7. David Duke, director of the Knights of the Ku Klux Klan at the time—whose race for the senate in 1990 received national attention—asked the ABC-TV network, which put on the televised *Roots*, for equal time to respond to its "vicious malignment of whites." His request was denied.

8. Usually in the Genealogy Room of the New York Public Library most of the chairs had been vacant, but on some occasions A.R. (After *Roots*) a seat was hard to find.

❦ 12
Names from the British Isles

Those Good Old English Names

In searching through records kept by English courts and other official bodies—records mainly from the thirteenth and fourteenth centuries—C. L'Estrange Ewen found many surnames he considered amusing. He reported these, and more serious stuff, in his *History of Surnames in the British Isles*.

We may wonder whether W. Cockesbrayn of Sussex was very smart. Geoffrey Drinkedregges of Lincolnshire must have been very thirsty. J. Fivepeni was apparently less lucky than Hugh Findesilver.

Perhaps Hackewude's axe was dull. We can rejoice with Edward Havejoy, and perhaps with Richard Hotgo, but we must be sorry for J. Rotenhering of Yorkshire and George Shotbolte of Essex. We've probably all known someone like C. Smartknave and Thom. Swetemouth.

Here are others from Ewen's list to pique interest and curiosity:

W. Barlicorn
Hy. Blancfrunt
J. Brasskettle
Maudlyn Brickbatt
J. Bullimore
Rob. Buttermouth
Rich. Catskin
Rich. Cokeye

Hugh Doggetail
J. Domesoft
Thom. Drinkmilk
J. Drunken
Mary Eightacres
Alan Evilchild
Anne Godhelpe (or
    Godhelpe Anne)

Serle Gotokirke
Rob. Hanging
W. Harepyn
Sarra Hopshort
Mary Isbroke
Rich. Lateboy
Harvey Leapingwell
Geoff. Lickefinger

121

Rob. Litelbodi
J. Litelskill
Maud Lusshefish
Rog. Milksoppe
Rich. Nettelbed
W. Oldflessh
J. Onehand
Alice Peckechese
Rich. Pitchfork
Grace Pluckrose

J. Pokepot
J. Ratellebagge
Rich. Ringgebelle
Geo. Sawhell
Hen. Scapetrough
J. Shepewassh
Rob. Silverspon
W. Smalwryter
Ann Speerpoint
Aug'tine Spurnewater

W. Strokelady
W. Stykkefyshe
_____ Sweatinbed
Jacob Tiplady
Hen. Tukbacon
J. Underdonne
Walt. Wanderbug
J. Waytelove
Rob. Witheskirtes

Ewen says, "No attempt will be made by the writer to determine origin, meaning, or classification of these examples, which will be left entirely to the reader." A wise decision!

Titles of Respect

"These men that you have selected for the grand jury," Judge Doddridge of the Huntingdon, England, Assizes complained to his sheriff, "are not of a rank suitable to serve His Majesty's court in this year of our Lord 1619."

So the sheriff, a man of good humor, picked a new grand jury, headed by Maximilian King. He read his new list aloud to the judge, like this:

Maximilian   KING of Toseland
Henry   PRINCE of
   Godmanchester
George   DUKE of Domersham
William   MARQUIS of
   Stukely
Edmund   EARL of Hartford
Richard   BARON of Bythorn
Stephen   POPE of Newton
Humphrey   CARDINAL of
   Kimbolton
Robert   LORD of Waresley

William   ABBOTT of Stukeley
Robert   BARON of St. Neots
William   DEAN of Old Weston
John   ARCHDEACON of
   Paxton
Peter   ESQUIRE of Easton
Edward   FRYER of Ellington
Henry   MONK of Stukeley
George   GENTLEMAN of
   Spaldwick
George   PRIEST of Graffham
Richard   DEACON of Catworth

People with many of these same surnames were still living in or near Huntingdon two centuries later. At least one of them, Maximilian King, had exactly the same name as his distant ancestor.

Can You Read This Man's Name?

(a) *[signature]*

(b) *[signature]*

(c) *[signature]*

(d) *[signature]*

(e) *[signature]*

(f) *[signature]*

We don't know how the world's greatest dramatist spelled his name. All the authenticated surviving signatures are shown here. (Many forgeries have been uncovered.) Shakespeare's signatures are about as decipherable as those that some modern business people append to their letters.

The blurry appearance of most of the signatures can be explained in part by abuse that the original documents have endured.

Shakespeare signed his will in three places, and those signatures (*d*, *e*, and *f* above) were long on unprotected public display. Charles Hamilton (*In Search of Shakespeare: A Reconnaissance into the Poet's Life and Handwriting*) commented, "What Shakespeare's six signatures looked like originally—with every minuscule stroke of his goose quill—we will never know because the documents are now faded and damaged. . . . Until recently, a casual visitor could have his way with [the original of the will] upon payment of a modest will-inspection charge. For a shilling he could rub his greasy fingers over the very places where the great poet put his quill, or even kiss the signatures with wet, passionate lips."

The signatures do seem to show that the playwright did not spell his name "Shakespeare." His contemporaries often did, though. That's what printers put on the title pages of most of his plays issued singly (the quartos), and also on the famous posthumous collection known as the First Folio (1623). And his friend Ben Jonson wrote "Shakespeare" at least once and "Shake-Speare" another time.

Other sources, including various business and legal records, show these variations in his name:

Shagspere	Shackespere	Shaxspere
Shakspere	Shakespere	Shackespeare
Shake-speare	Shakspeare	Shackspere
Shakespear		

In 1930 a scholar found a total of 93 early and late variants. Why so many? Mainly because in Elizabethan and Jacobean times spelling was not yet standardized. People still spelled almost as they chose; the same person might spell the same word in different ways; and there was no adequate dictionary to turn to. (Printed books were still rather rare.)

What, then, is the "right" spelling of the dramatist's name? "Shakespeare" has the support of tradition as well as wide usage when the writer was still alive. But some handwriting experts, including Hamilton, say that the six signatures look like Shackper (*a*), Shakspear (*b*), Shakspea (*c*), Shackspere (*d*), Shakspere (*e*), and by me William Shakspeare (*f*). Both "Shakespeare" and "Shakspere" can be found in modern scholarly writing.

How Do You Pronounce *Purcell,* *Maurice,* and *Doran?*

In England and Ireland, the first syllable of names like the following is usually stressed, but American usage moves the stress to the end.

	British	American
Bernard	*BUR-nerd*	*ber-NARD*
Burnett	*BUR-nut*	*ber-NET*
Costello	*COS-tuh-lo*	*cos-TEL-o*
Gerard	*JURD*	*juh-RARD*
Jacoby	*JAC-uh-bee*	*juh-KO-bee*
Mahony	*MAY-uh-nee*	*muh-HO-nee*
Maurice	*MOR-us*	*muh-REES*
Moran	*MOR-un*	*mo-RAN*
Savile	*SAV-ul*	*suh-VILL*
Waddell	*WAD-ul*	*wuh-DELL*

British Hyphenated Names

The British custom of using hyphenated names, observed mainly by prominent, estate-owning families, has never really caught on in the United States, although some years ago H. L. Mencken (*The American Language, Supplement Two*) did discover a Congressman named Horace Seely-Brown. Some married women have retained their maiden names, as when Louise Rae Clark became Louise Rae Clark-Simmons. Much more often, however, a modern American woman who wishes to retain her name for business, professional, or other reasons simply does not adopt her husband's name. Mrs. Simmons may still be known as Ms. Clark. (See also pages 275–276.)

In Britain the heir to money from the female side of a family was sometimes required, by prior consent or by the terms of a will, to adopt the female family name. Sometimes the male family name was then dropped, but in the nineteenth century the custom arose of using both names, with a hyphen between. Winston Churchill, for instance, was really Winston Spencer-Churchill.

The names sometimes became ungainly. A Wellesley-Pole eventually became Pole-Tylney-Long-Wellesley. H. L. Mencken commented on two other names:

The name of Vice-Admiral the Hon. Sir Reginald Aylmer Ran-
furly *Plunkett-Ernie-Erle-Drax*, K.C.B., D.S.O., R.N. . . . would
ruin him in the United States. So would that of Walter Thomas
James Scrymsoure-Steuart-Fothringham, a Scotch magnate.

Elsdon Smith (*American Surnames*) points out another problem, that of alphabetizing. Librarians, he says, cannot decide whether
author Bulwer-Lytton belongs in the Bs or the Ls.

Some Church-Related Surnames

In the Middle Ages, plays often were performed on street
corners, sometimes on large wagons pulled from one intersection to
another to serve as stages. Characters were varied and sometimes
represented churchmen such as abbots, bishops, or the pope himself.
When surnames were being selected, an actor sometimes chose the
name of a character he had portrayed. Some of the names in the
following list arose from that practice.

Occasionally, a name like King, Queen, Prince, or Proffitt
(prophet) was bestowed because of roles bearing such names. Sometimes, however, people took the name Bishop or King because they
were servants to persons of high rank or members of their entourage,
maybe soldiers who protected them. Others were given the name as
a nickname—flatteringly if the person seemed princely, kingly, highly
religious, and so on, but possibly satirically or derisively.

Names such as Abbey, Church, or Temple were often given
because the person lived close to such a structure or worked in it
or had some other connection with it.

What happened in England also happened in other European
countries. Only a few of the non-English equivalents are given here.

Abbate, Abt 'abbot' (Italian,
   German)
Abbey
Abbott
Angel
Angelo, D'Angelo, and variants
   'angel' (Italian, Greek)
Baptist(e), Bat(t)ista 'one who
   baptizes' (English, French,
   Italian, Spanish)

Bishop
Brothers
Can(n)on
Cantor(e), Kanter, Kantor 'cantor,
   lead singer in a synagogue or
   cathedral' (English, Italian,
   German)
Chap(p)el(l)
Chaplin 'chaplain, one in charge
   of a chapel'

Church (Scottish Kirk)
Clark(e), sometimes Clerk(e) often 'clergyman,' sometimes 'scribe or recorder'
Cleary 'clerk' (Irish)
Cohen, Cohn, Cohan, Cone (other variants) 'priest' (Hebrew)
Converse 'convert'
Cross
Crozier 'one who carries a cross or bishop's staff or crook'
Cruz 'cross' (Spanish, Portuguese)
Deacon
De Santis 'holy man' (Spanish, Portuguese)
Dominiak, Domingo, Domingues, Dominguez, Dominick, Dominique, Dominovich, etc. 'one born on the Lord's day' (Polish, Portuguese, Spanish, Italian, French, Yugoslavian, etc.)
Durward 'doorkeeper in a religious house, palace'
Friar
Holliman 'holy man'
Kagan(ovich) (off) 'rabbi' (Polish, Russian)

Kirch(en) (ner) (off) 'church, churchyard' (German)
Lord (more likely a nobleman rather than God)
McNabb 'son of an abbot' (Scottish)
Monk(s), Munk 'monk'
Nunn 'nun'
Pagan(o) (i) (ini) 'an irreligious person' (Italian, Spanish)
Papa, Pappas 'priest' (Italian, Greek)
Parish
Parson(s) (also sometimes derived from Peter)
Pfaff, Prete 'priest or other religious functionary' (German, Italian)
Primmer 'official at the first canonical hour'
Prior
Rector
Sermon(er)
Sexton
Shepherd (several spellings, including German Scheaffer)
Temple
Vicar(e), Viker(y) 'substitute for a priest or other functionary' (Italian Vicari)

By Their Clans You Shall Know Them

Although some Scots made their way to what is now the United States during the seventeenth century, many more came in the eighteenth, at a rate ranging from a few hundred to a few thousand a year, often because of troubles with their Irish neighbors or English tax collectors. Included among the emigrants were many "Scotch-Irish," a term that is usually shorthand for Lowland Scots who had earlier been moved into northeast Ireland by British King James I (himself a Scot).

The next article concerns the names borne by the major clans, as reported in the anonymous *The Scottish Tartans*. These clans called the Highlands their home, and many but not all of their members, whether leaders or followers, blood-related or not, used the clan name as surname.

The list of clans that follows includes the approximate number of Americans who bore each clan name in 1974 (figures supplied by the Social Security Administration). For several reasons, however, the figures cannot be trusted to indicate the actual number of, say, Gordons or MacGregors in the United States who are of Scottish descent: (1) SSA counts were based on only the first six letters of a name, so that Morrises and Morrisons, for example, are lumped together; (2) *Mac* and *Mc* spellings are not differentiated; (3) many people have changed their names, either to or from Scottish; (4) some Scottish, Irish, and English names are identical (the best-known Kennedy was of Irish descent, but the same name has designated a Scottish clan for several centuries). A name without a number indicates that fewer than 10,000 Americans bear that name.

Brodie
Bruce 53,017
Buchanan 68,432
Cameron 54,533
Campbell 361,958
Chisholm 13,116
Colquhoun c. 10,000
Crawford 160,150
Cumming 101,664
Cunningham 136,559
Davidson 105,716
Douglas 107,290
Drummond 17,321
Dundas
Elliott 145,675
Erskine
Farquharson
Ferguson 144,751
Forbes 32,283
Fraser 27,036
Gordon 159,580
Graham 194,096
Grant 128,122
Gunn 23,473
Hamilton 191,883
Hay 18,120
Home
Innes

Johnston 149,030
Kennedy 174,909
Kerr 47,125
Lamont 12,251
Macalester 29,317
MacAlpine
MacArthur 12,843
Macaulay 28,277
MacBean
Macbeth
MacDonald 57,682
MacDougall 18,566
MacDuff 13,153
MacEwan
MacFarlane 54,941
MacFie
MacGillivray
MacGregor 16,105
MacInnes
McIntyre 11,389
Mackay 10,538
Mackenzie 18,295
MacKinley 24,647
Mackinnon 98,162
Mackintosh 39,153
MacLachlan
MacLaine 18,648
McLaren

MacLean 41,464

MacLennon

MacLeod 31,120

Macmillan 71,703

MacNab

MacNaughton

McNeill 54,211

MacNicol

MacPherson 34,791

McQuarrie

MacQueen 19,360

Macrae 18,081

McTavish

Malcolm

Matheson 15,129

Maxwell 65,670

Menzies

Morrison 455,179

Munro

Murray 185,068

Ogilvie

Ramsey 75,026

Robertson c. 100,000

Rose 144,357

Ross 231,054

Scott 408,439

Sinclair 25,436

Skene

Stewart 329,581

Sutherland 32,400

Urquhart

Is That Name Scottish or Irish?

A Gordon family in Buffalo always confidently asserted that the name and the ancestral Gordons were Scottish. However, when one of them made a careful genealogical study, she found out that those particular Gordons came from Dublin.

Like Gordon, a number of other names cannot be definitely classified as Scottish or Irish. Campbell and Blair, for instance, are usually thought to be Scottish, but thousands of Americans of Irish ancestry proudly bear those names.

A study that appeared as the "Annual Report of the American Historical Association for 1931" classified 45 names as follows. (M' here signifies both *Mc* and *Mac*.)

> *Class I:* Practically no Irish use recorded: M'Leod, Munro, M'Pherson, M'Kinnon, M'Laren, Robertson, M'Intosh, Sutherland, M'Kenzie, Bruce, M'Gregor, Cameron, Fraser, Duncan, Ritchie, Ross, Buchanan
>
> *Class II:* Substantial Irish usage: Christie, M'Donald, Donaldson, Ramsay, Robb, M'Farlane, M'Intyre, Morrison, Murdoch, Tait, Rankin, Baxter, Jamieson, Forsyth
>
> *Class III:* Names with original numbers in Ireland approaching or exceeding those in Scotland: Ferguson, Campbell, Findlay, Black, Gordon, M'Dougall (with M'Dowell), Moffatt, Maxwell, Blair, Craig, Orr, Cummings, Boyd, Cunningham

Incidentally, although some people say that *Mac* always shows Scottish and *Mc* indicates Irish ancestry, the generalization is not correct. Elsdon Smith, one of America's leading onomatists, has written in *American Surnames*: "The Scots used the Gaelic *Mac* but not the O. Both the Irish and the Scots contract the prefix into Mc and M'. Such contractions are without special significance, notwithstanding some authorities who have affirmed that *Mac* is Irish and *Mc* is Scottish, and others who have declared just the opposite."

Historically, almost all Irish names were prefixed by the Gaelic equivalent of O 'grandson of' or *Mac* (shared by Scots), which may be interpreted as either 'grandson of' or 'son of.' In many, though, the prefix gradually vanished.

The majority of both Irish and Scottish names recall a distant ancestor, often especially famous for military prowess, strength, or a prized dark, glowering appearance. The transliterations of some of the Gaelic forms may look both imposing and unpronounceable. Murchadh 'sea warrior' doesn't look bad; it became Murphy. Somehow Dubhfhflann 'dark Flann' emerged as Dowling, and a 'little red Flann' sowed the seeds of countless Flanigans. Flaithbheartach 'bright ruler' is now the much simpler Flaherty. Eachmharcach 'tamer of horses' is now McCaffrey, and Cionadh 'born in fire' is the ancestor of many McKinneys or Kinneys.

The ancestor of Hearn or O'Hearn(e) may have been Odhar 'pale little fellow,' but today's men with that name may prefer an alternate lineage, from Earadh 'fearless' or Eachthighearn 'lord of the horses.' If a modern Kell(e)y is more contentious than someone else, he may blame his forefather Ceallach 'quarrelsome.'

❦ 13
The National Origins of Some of Our Surnames

54 Name Endings That May Reveal National Origin

This list may help if you are curious about the nationality or the meaning of a surname. Some of the items are true suffixes, others (especially in German and Scandinavian names) are words that are frequently combined with others.

Additional endings are treated in the articles on *son of* (page 110) and diminutives (page 111).

accio: Italian 'bad'; Boccaccio 'bad or ugly mouth'
buch, -baugh: German 'brook'; Steinbach 'stony brook'
baum: German 'tree'; Greenbaum 'green tree'
beck: Swedish, Norwegian 'brook'; Harbeck 'rabbit brook'
berg: German, Scandinavian 'mountain'; Lundberg 'grove, mountain'
bert: German, French 'bright'; Robert 'fame, bright'
berto, -berti: Italian form of *-bert*; Roberto
brecht: German form of *-bert*; Albrecht, Ruprecht
blad: Swedish, Norwegian 'leaf'; Lindblad 'linden leaf'
blatt: German 'leaf'; Greenblatt 'green leaf'
bo: Norwegian 'farm'; Sudbo 'south farm'
borg: Swedish 'castle'; Swedenborg 'Swedish castle'
born: German 'stream'; Kaltenborn 'cold stream'

borough, -brough: English 'fort'; Kimbrough 'royal fort'
bury, -berry: English 'fort'; Stanbury or Standberry 'stone fort'
by: Norwegian, English 'farm or village'; Ashby 'ash tree village'
dahl: Swedish 'valley'; Ekdahl 'oak valley'
fiore: Italian 'flower'; Montefiore 'flower mountain'
ford: English 'ford, crossing'; Stanford 'stony crossing'
gard: Norwegian, Danish 'farm'; Nyga(a)rd 'new farm'
grave: English 'grove'; Hargrave (or Hargreaves, Hargrove) 'hare's grove'
gren: Swedish 'branch'; Dahlgren 'valley branch'
hardt, -hard, -hart: German 'hard, firm'; Gerhart 'firm spear'
haus: German 'house'; Neuhaus 'new house'
heim: German 'home'; Sonnheim 'sunny (or swampy) home'
holm: Swedish 'river island'; Lindholm 'linden river island'
land: English 'land,' Scandinavian 'farm, part of a farm'; Nyland 'new or
    newly cleared farmland'
leigh, -lee, -ley, -ly: English 'wood, valley, glade, meadow'; Ripley 'long,
    narrow meadow or wood'
lof, -love: Swedish 'leaf, heather'; Younglove 'young leaf'
lund: Swedish 'grove'; Asplund 'aspen grove'
man(n): English, German 'servant of'; Harriman 'servant of Harry'
mark: Swedish 'field'; Lundmark 'field in a grove'
ness: English, Scottish 'cape, headland'; Harkness 'hawk cape'
olf, -olfo, -olph: German, Italian, English 'wolf'; Rudolph, Rudolfo,
    Rudolf 'fame, wolf'
one: Italian 'large'; Capone 'large head'
ova: Russian 'daughter of'; Petrova 'daughter of Peter'
quist: Swedish 'twig'; Lindquist 'linden twig'
rop, -rup: English 'farm'; Northrop, Northrup 'north farm'
rud: Norwegian 'farm'; Stensrud 'stony farm or clearing'
ska: Russian, Czech, or Polish; feminine equivalent of *-sky* or *-ski*
ski, -sky: Russian, Czech, or Polish 'of the nature of,' 'son of,' 'from'
    (Polish spelling is usually *-ski*)
stad: Danish, Norwegian 'farm, place'; Flagstad 'windy place'
stein: German 'stone'; Finkelstein 'little bird stone' (pyrites)
strom: Swedish 'stream'; Engstrom 'meadow stream'
thal: German 'valley'; Blumenthal 'flower valley'
thorp(e): English 'farm'; Oglethorpe 'one from Odkell's farm'
ton: English 'settlement, village, town, homestead'; Paxton 'Pack's
    homestead'
ville: French 'estate'; Mandeville 'one from Mando's estate'
wahl, -vall: Swedish 'field'; Ekwahl, Ekvall 'field with oaks'
way: English 'path, road, way'; Greenway 'green path'
wich: English 'dwelling'; Greenwich 'green dwelling'
wiec: Polish 'one who (does something)'; Mysliwiec 'hunter'
win: English 'friend'; Goodwin 'good friend, God's friend'
worth: English 'homestead'; Ellingsworth 'homestead of the Ellings'
    (Ella's people)

The Ten Most Common Irish-American Surnames

1. Murphy
2. Kelly (may be Scottish or English)
3. Sullivan
4. Kennedy (often Scottish)
5. Bryant
6. Kelley (may be Scottish or English)
7. Burke
8. Riley
9. O'Brien
10. McCoy

The great majority of Irish names are patronyms, perhaps signifying loyalty to and affection for one's forebears.

The O' in many Irish names means 'grandson of' or perhaps more loosely 'descendant of'; the apostrophe is only a convention followed in writing, although it is sometimes said to represent a supposedly missing *f*. Mc, Mac, or M means 'son of.' Mac followed by G sometimes is written *Ma* as in Maguire. With M' a vowel is sometimes substituted for the apostrophe, as when M'Neely becomes Meneely.

The Ten Most Common Welsh-American Surnames

Most or all of these names are often English, even though Welsh in origin.

1. Williams
2. Jones
3. Davis
4. Thomas
5. Lewis
6. Evans
7. Rogers
8. Morgan
9. Hughes
10. Price

These ten are all among the top one hundred American surnames. Welsh names appear in such proportionately high numbers because in Wales comparatively few different names are used, with many holders of the same name. In some towns with several hundred people, maybe only 10 or 12 surnames will be found.

In earlier times, many Welsh names were prefixed by *ap* 'son of,' as in Hugh ap Howell. *Ap* was often contracted to *P* and combined with the last name, as Hugh Powell. The following are among the Welsh names derived in that way:

Parry (ap Harry)
Penry (ap Henry)
Perry (ap Harry)
Pew or Pugh (ap Hugh)
Ployd (ap Lloyd)
Price, Preece (ap Rhys)

Pritchard (ap Richard)
Probert (ap Robert)
Prosser, Prowse (ap Rosser)
Prynn (ap Rhun)
Pulliam (ap William)
Pumphrey (ap Humphrey)

In a few instances, *ap* became B: ap Owen → Bowen.

The Ten Most Common German-American Surnames

Many Schmidts have become Smiths; Schneiders are now often Snyders or Sniders; and many Fischers are Fishers. The Myer-Myers-Meyer-Meyers-Meier-etc., families have become well mixed. The following, then, is little more than a list of the spellings of German names so great in frequency that they rank high even though many early holders of the name may have changed it.

1. Myers
2. Schmidt
3. Hoffman(n)
4. Wagner (sometimes English)
5. Meyer

6. Schwarz
7. Schneider
8. Zimmerman(n)
9. Keller
10. Klein

The Ten Most Common Scandinavian-American Surnames

The spellings of some Scandinavian nationalities are combined in this list, for example, Anderson, Andersen, Andersson, Anderssen, Andresen, etc. Also, some of these—especially Anderson, Nelson, and the various forms of Christianson—are frequently English.

1. Anderson
2. Peterson
3. Nelson
4. Christianson
5. Olson

6. Hansen
7. Carlson
8. Larson
9. Erickson
10. Swanson

The Ten Most Common Italian-American Surnames

1. Russo
2. Lombardo, Lombardi
3. Romano
4. Marino
5. Lorenzo (may be Spanish)
6. Costa (may be Spanish or Portuguese)
7. Luna
8. Rossi(ni)
9. Esposito
10. Gallo

Although people of Italian descent are numerous in the United States, no Italian name fills much space in directories. Like the Irish, the Italians use a large number of surnames, with consequently few occurrences of any one name.

The Ten Most Common Hispanic-American Surnames

1. Rodriguez
2. Gonzalez
3. Garcia
4. Lopez
5. Rivera
6. Martinez
7. Hernandez
8. Perez
9. Sanchez
10. Torres

16 Noble Spanish Surnames

Here are some Spanish surnames derived from titles of royalty, nobility, government officials, and members of their entourages. Frequently, in both Spanish and other languages, a person who bears the name today does not have ancestry of high rank. However, one or more of his or her forebears may have served as followers of a noble person, may have acted the role in a play, or may have acted or looked like someone noble.

Baron 'baron'
Bascompte 'viscount'
Camerero 'chamberlain,' 'monastery worker'
Castellan 'governor of a castle'
Clavero 'keeper of the keys'
Cocinero 'cook'
Conde 'count'
Duque 'duke'
Escriba 'scribe'
Hidalgo 'lord, nobleman'

Infante 'younger son or nephew of the king,' 'young monk or nun,' 'foot soldier,' 'baby'
Marques 'marquis'
Montero 'huntsman'

Portero 'royal messenger,' 'gatekeeper'
Rey (Reyes) 'king'
Vasallo 'vassal'

Characteristics of Japanese Surnames

Most Japanese surnames consist of two parts, with meanings that may or may not seem related. These combinations were made hundreds of years ago, no doubt by people who liked the poetic effect or the connotations of the parts.

As a result, the same component may be found in either first or second position in some names, although one position may be much more common and the other very rare. Matsu 'pine,' for instance, most often comes first. Here are some examples from the Manhattan and Los Angeles phone books.

Hiramatsu 'flat, pine'
Matsuda 'pine, rice field'
Matsuhira 'pine, flat'
Matsukawa 'pine, river'
Matsumoto 'pine, origin'
Matsunaka 'pine, middle'

Matsuo 'pine, little'
Matsuoka 'pine, hill'
Matsushima 'pine, island'
Matsushita 'pine, below'
Matsuyama 'pine, mountain'
Shimatsu 'island, pine'

Knowing the meanings of even the following few components will enable you to translate hundreds of Japanese names:

are 'have'
da or *ta* 'rice field'
fuji 'wisteria'
fuku 'good fortune'
furu 'old'
gawa 'river'
guchi or *kuchi* 'mouth'
hara or *no* 'field'
hashi 'bridge'
hira 'flat'
hon 'base'
hoshi 'star'
iwa 'rock'
kami or *ue* 'upper'

marui 'round'
matsu 'pine'
mori 'forest'
mura 'village'
naka 'middle'
o 'little'
ō 'large'
oka 'hill'
saka 'slope'
shima 'island'
shita 'below'
sugu 'bell'
toyo 'plentiful'
wa 'peace'
yama 'mountain'

❦ 14
Some Other Sources of Surnames

Misleading Surnames

Some surnames don't mean what they appear to. We would naturally suppose that the ancestral Moody was a changeable and often gloomy person. But in reality Old English *mōdig*, from which the name comes, meant 'bold, brave.'

A former college student of the author was a lively young woman who moved and thought rapidly. Her name, Quick, seemed appropriate. Actually, however, when surnames were taken about seven centuries ago, it meant 'alive,' a meaning that survives in the expression "the quick and the dead."

A medieval Parson wasn't necessarily a preacher. Par was one of the nicknames for Peter, so Parson is usually the equivalent of Peters or Peterson.

The ancestor of Forget, a French name, may not have been forgetful. The name often means 'little forge' and refers to a black-smith.

Philpott has nothing to do with filling or pots. It's a diminutive of Philip 'lover of horses' and so means 'little Philip' or 'little horse-lover.'

Similarily, Coward does not refer to fearfulness or cowardice. It refers to the occupation of herding cows and so is comparable to Shepherd or Shep(p)ard.

Many names also could be listed that, although not really misleading, have historical definitions not at all in keeping with the modern image. One of the best examples is Kennedy. Thanks to President John F. Kennedy and many of his relatives, people tend to think of Kennedys as handsome folks. But in Celtic the name could mean either 'helmet head' or 'he with the ugly or misshapen head.'

Some Surnames from the Bible

Some biblical names appear in dozens of variant forms in the United States. The eponymous children of John are treated in a separate section. Here are abbreviated lists of variants of other popular names from the Old and New Testaments. Forms generally from the British Isles are listed first.

Abraham(s)(son), Abram(s)(son); Polish Abrahamowicz, Abramovitz; Russian Abramovich

Adam(s)(son), Addams, Acheson, Adcock 'little Adam,' Addison, Aiken, Aitken(s), Akins, Atkin(s)(son), Eason, Keddy, McAdam(s); Czechoslovakian Adamek; Greek Adamopoulos; Italian Adamo, Adduci; Lithuanian Adomaitis; Polish Adamczyk (ovitz)(owski); Russian Adamovich; Spanish Adan

Andrew(s), Anders(on)(en)(sson)(ssen), Andresen, Drew; Polish Andrysiak, etc.; Russian Andreyev; Spanish and Portuguese Andrade; Ukrainian Andrajenko; Yugoslavian Andrejevi

Bartholomew, Bartlett, Barth, Bartel(s), Bates, Battle (sometimes); Czechoslovakian Barta; German Bartke, Bart(o)sch; Hungarian Barto(s), Bartok; Italian Bartolini, Bartolomeo; Lithuanian Bartkus; Polish Bartkiewicz, Bartkowski, etc.; Russian Bartkowsky

Christ(ian)(ianson), (ensen), (opher), Christman, C(h)rystel, Crist, Criss, Cris(s)man, Scottish Christie or Christy; Czechoslovakian Kristof; French Christophe; German Christoph, Kris, Krist; Finnish Risto; Greek Christopoulos; Italian (de) Christoforo; Latvian Kriss; Polish Krzysztof, Krzys; Russian Christoff; Spanish Cristobal. (Kristin is a frequent Slavic form.)

Daniel(s)(son); Bulgarian Danilovic; Italian Danielo; Lithuanian Danilevicius; Polish Danielczyk, etc.; Ukrainian Danyluk, Danylenko. (English or French Dana may mean 'descendant of Daniel' or 'a person from Denmark.')

David(s)(son), Davis, Davie(s), Davison, Davey, Dawson, Dawes, Deakins, Dewey. (Dozens of Slavic variants begin with Dav- or Daw-. Day, when Welsh, usually means 'descendant of David' but if English means 'dairy worker.')

Elias(on), Eliot, Elliot(t), Ellis(on), Elkins, Welsh Bellis, Ely (sometimes)

Jacob(s)(son)(sen), Cobb(e); Armenian Hagopian; Czechoslovakian K(o)uba; French Jacob or Jacque(s); German Jacobi, Jacoby, Jakob, Jaeckel, Kob(e), Kopp(elmann); Italian Giacomo and other names with Giaco- or Iaco-, Mel(l)one (from Giacomelli), Pucci(ni)(from Iacopucci), Baca (which also may be Slavic); Polish Jakubowski, etc., Polish or Russian Kubik, etc.; Scandinavian Jacobsen, etc., Spanish Diaz or Portuguese Dias (both from Diego = Jacob), Dieguez

James(on), Jami(e)son; Spanish Santiago (from the place Santiago 'Saint James')

Jordan, Jorden, Jordon, Jurden, Judd, Judkins, Judson; Italian Giordano

Luke(s)(y), Lukas, Luck, Luck(e)y, Luc(e)y, Lucie, Lukin(s); Bulgarian Luka; French Luce (also from Louis), Lucien; German Luekin(g)(s), Lux; Hungarian Lukacs; Italian (di) Luca, Lucia(no), Lucci, etc.; Polish Lukasz, etc.; Russian Lukanovich; Spanish Lucero; Ukrainian Luchanko, Lucenko

Mathew(s)(son), Matthew(s)(son), Madison, Mat(t)son, Macy (sometimes), English or Irish Madden, Scottish or Danish Mathes(on), English or Swedish Mattson, English or French May(s); Czechoslovakian Matousek, Matus(zek)(ow); Finnish Mattinen; German Mathis, Mat(t)hies, Mattheu, Matz(kin), Theis; Italian Maffei, Matteo, Mattia(ci)(ce); Lithuanian Matul(is)(evicius); Polish Maciejeweski, Matuszuski, etc.; Scandinavian Madsen, Madson, Mathies(s)en; Russian Matkovich; Spanish Matias, Mateo(s)

Mark (in England usually refers to boundary markers, but in the forms Marks, Marcus, and Marquis generally is derived from the New Testament Mark. German or English Marx may have either derivation). The biblical origin is apparent in Czechoslovakian Markovitz; French Marceau; Greek Markopoulos; Italian Marco, Marcelli, Marcetti, etc.; Lithuanian Markevicius; Scandinavian or English Martinsen (or -son); Polish Marek, Marcinek, Markiewicz, Markowski; Portuguese or Spanish Marques; Spanish Marquez; Ukrainian Marchik, Marko. Also related by derivation to Martin, from the god Mars.

Michael(s)(son), Mitchell, Mickel(s), Mickens, Micklin, Mickey, Mickie, Mix; Bulgarian Mihailovic; Czechoslovakian Mihalek, Mic(h)al, Miskovic; Finnish Mikkonen; French Michel, Michet, Michaud, Michaux; German Michaelis; Greek Mikalonis, Miklos, Mikos, Mi(c)halopoulos, Mikalaitis; Italian Miceli, Michini, Michelini; Lithuanian Mikus; Polish Michal(ak)(ski)(czewski) (owski); Portuguese or Spanish Miguel; Scandinavian Michaelsen, Michaelson, Mikkelson, Michelsen; Yugoslavian Mikulich

Paul(l)(son)(ey), Scottish M(a)cPhail 'son of Paul'; Pavel or Paul in several continental languages; Czechoslovakian Pajko, Pav(lik)(ov)(ovic); French Polley; German Paulus, Pavlow; Greek Pavlos, Pavlatis; Italian Paoli, Paulini, Paulino; Lithuanian

Pavlauskas; Polish Pawlak, Pawlicki, Pawlowski; Russian Pavlov(ich);
Scandinavian Paulsen, Paulson, Poulson; Spanish Paula, Paulo;
Ukrainian Pavlik, Pavlenko, Pawluk; Yugoslavian Pavlovich
Peters(on), Pearson, Perkins, Pierce, Peirce, Pearse, Parnell, Parrot,
Parson(s)(sometimes), Person(s), Peary, Peery, Peer(e), Peet(e),
Parks (sometimes), Perry (sometimes), Peterkin(s), Peterman,
Peterson, Piers, Pierson, Irish Ferrick, Welsh Bearse or Bearce,
Perkins(on), Pierce, Piers, Scottish Peete, Perrie, Petry or Petrie, Piri;
Bulgarian Petkof, Petroff; Danish Ped(d)ersen, Petersen; Dutch
Peet(e), Pieter(s); French Peer(e), Perrau(d)(lt), Perret, Perrin(e),
Perron, Peyrot, Pierre, Pierrot; German Peterman(n); Greek Patrakos,
Petrakis, Petropolos, Petros; Hungarian Petofi; Icelandic Petersson;
Italian Perelli, Pieroni, Perillo, Per(r)one, Petrelli, Petri, Petrone,
Petrucci, Pieroni, Pierro, Pietro; Lithuanian Petkus, Petraitis,
Petronis; Norwegian Ped(d)ersen, Peterson, Pettersen; Polish
Bieschke, Petrowski, etc.; Portuguese Pires; Romanian Petrescu;
Russian Petroff, Petrov(ich), Petruska; Spanish Perez, Pero; Swedish
Pers(s)on(s), Peterson, Petterson
Simon(e), Simmons, Simpson, Sim(m)(s), Simeon, Simond(s), Simcock
or Simcox 'little Simon,' Sim(p)kins, Fitzsimmons, Syme(s),
Symond(s); Armenian Simonian; French Simeone, Simoneaux; Greek
Simonaitis; Italian Simone, Simonini, Simonetti; Lithuanian
Shimkus, Simaitis; Polish Sienkiewicz, Simek, Simkowski, Szymanski,
Szymczak; Russian Simeone, Sienkiewicz; Scandinavian Simonsen,
Simonson; Spanish Jiminez; Yugoslavian Simovic
Stephen(s)(son), Steven(s)(son), Steave(s), Steff(e)(en)(ens),
Stim(p)son, Stinson; many continental forms, generally starting with
Step- or Stav-, but Spanish Estep or Estevez
Thomas(sen)(son), Thom(p)son, Thom(p)sen, T(h)ompkin(s)(on),
Tomblin, Tomlinson, Tomb, Toombs, Massey or Massie (from the
second syllable), Scottish McComb, Macomber, McTavish;
Czechoslovakian Toman, Tomas(ek)(kovic); French Thomas,
Masson, Maslin, Massie; German Thoma(s), Mass; Hungarian
Tamas; Italian Masso, Massi, Tomaselli, etc.; Lithuanian Tumas;
Polish Tomczak, Tomaszewski, etc.; Spanish Tomas

Some of the other biblical figures whose names survive as surnames in one or more spellings are these:

Aaron	Gideon	Moses
Abel	Isaac	Noah
Abner	Jeremiah (Jeremy)	Reuben
Amos	Jesus	Samson
Augustus	Job	Samuel
Benjamin	Joel	Saul
Cain	Joseph	Solomon
Caspar	Lazarus	Timothy
Gabriel	Levi	Tobias

Directions in Surnames

In some surnames the major points of the compass are apparent: East, Eastern, North, Northern, South, Southern, West, Western. They are only a little less visible in many compounds, such as Easterwood, Eastham 'eastern homestead,' Easton 'east village,' Northbrook, Northcote or Northcott or Northcutt 'north cottage,' Northey 'north island,' Northrop 'northern farm,' Southcott, Southey, Southworth 'southern homestead,' Westfield, Westlake, or Weston 'west village.'

Others are less obvious: Escott 'east cottage,' Essex 'east Saxons,' Estall 'east hall,' Esterly 'eastern grove,' Esterman 'one from the east' (but if Jewish, 'husband of Esther'), Estes 'son of East,' Estridge 'east ridge,' Estwick 'eastern dairy';

Norberg (Swedish for 'north mountain'), Norbury 'northern fort,' Norbert (German for 'north, bright'), Norcott 'north cottage,' Norcross 'north cross,' Nordby (Swedish for 'north village'), Norden (Scandinavian or Dutch for 'one from the north'), Norgaard (Norwegian or Danish for 'north yard'), Norman 'northman' or 'one from Normandy,' Norrington 'northern part of the village,' Norstrom or Nordstrom (Swedish for 'north stream'), Norton 'north village';

Soder (Swedish for 'south,' often in compounds such as Soderquist 'south twig'), Sudbo (Norwegian for 'south farm'), Sudbury 'south fort,' Sudlow 'south hill,' Sussland 'southern district,' Sutcliff 'south cliff,' Sutherland 'south land,' Sutton 'south village';

Wester (Dutch for 'one from the west'), but also in various Scandinavian, German, or English compounds such as Westerberg 'western mountain,' Westerhausen 'western house,' Westerveld 'western field,' or Westerfield, Weston 'western village,' Wisham 'western homestead.'

The Human Zoo

In the Middle Ages, when surnames were generally adopted, few people could read. Signs used simple pictures instead of words to identify a place of business. One might walk down a street and perhaps see pictures of a rooster, a bush, an owl, and a lion, and children might be told, "Go to the Lion and get me some ale."

People who owned one of the businesses or who lived close to the sign often became known by the sign. William near the Lion quite easily was shortened to William Lyon (an old spelling of the word).

Most animal surnames probably arose in that way. Some, however, arose because certain people appeared to share a quality or several qualities of an animal and were thus named. Fox may have been clever and wily, German Baer as strong or as hairy as a bear, and Hare was perhaps unusually fleet. A few surnames arose because a person's occupation involved some kind of animal. Russian Soboleff, for instance, trapped sables.

Wolf, in its several spellings, is the most common name in this group. One reason is that wolves were numerous in Europe, especially in the north, and were feared and admired and often made the subject of tales. Some of these tales involved werewolves—men who supposedly could turn into wolves—an ability now called *lycanthropy*, from the Greek name for the animal.

The following names of wild animals are among those formed in one or more of the three ways mentioned above and still existent, some of them in spellings other than those given here. A few of the terms, such as Cooney for 'rabbit,' are seldom used now for the animals themselves but survive mainly as proper names.

bear: English, French Bear (sometimes); German Baer; Behr(ens), Behnke; Italian Urso; Ukrainian Vedmedenko
beaver: Czech Bobar
deer: English Deer(e), Hart or Hurt, Pritchett, Doe, Roe, Roebuck; Czech Jelinek; French Cerf; German Hersh, Hirsch; Spanish Reno; Polish Sarna
elephant: English, French Oliphant, Olivant
fox: English Fox, Colfax 'black fox'; Scottish Guptill; Czech Liska; Finnish Kettunen; German Fuchs; German or Dutch Voss; Italian Volpe; Polish Liss; Russian or Ukrainian Lys(s)
gopher: Russian Suskov
hare: English Hare, Cooney; Czech Zajicka, Krolik; German or Dutch Haas; Polish Krolik; Polish or Ukrainian Zajac; Yugoslavian Kunc
hedgehog: Czech Jeschek
lion: English or Scottish Lyon(s); English Leo; German Lo(e)we, Loewy, Lau; Spanish Leon(e)
marmot: Polish Boba(k)
marten: Czech Kunka; German Marder; Italian Martarano
otter: English Otter; Swedish Utter; Polish Wydra
sable: German Zobel; Polish Sobel, Zabel; Russian Soboleff

squirrel: German Eich(h)orn
unicorn: German Einhorn
walrus: Czech Mroz, Mrosek
wildcat: Polish Zbik
wolf: English, German Wolf(f)(e); German Wulf(f); Czech Welk, Vlk;
  Greek Lycos; Hungarian Farkas; Lithuanian Volf; Polish Volkow;
  Russian Volkov; Ukrainian Vovcenko
zebra: Polish Zebrowski

Domestic animals have their namesakes, too, although those for dogs are inexplicably rare, exceptions being Talbot, which can mean 'white hunting dog,' Doggett, which can mean 'with a head shaped like a dog's,' and Canine.

Horses, goats, and others were often portrayed on business signs, and some people had characteristics of cats or other animals, but probably most of the following names arose because of raising or tending the animals.

bull: English Bull(ock), Steer(e), Farr (may also refer to a boar or,
  when Scottish, to a place in Sutherland); German Ochs; Polish
  Bicek; Ukrainian Buhajecko. (Polish Krowa herded cows.)
cat: Czech Kocoubek; Italian Gatto(ne), Gatti
goat: English Cheever(s), Haver, Kidd; French Chevrolet, Chevrier;
  German Bock; Italian Capra; Russian Kosloff; Ukrainian and Czech
  Kozel(ka)
hog: English Hogg, Pigg(ott), Hogue, Farrow, Purcell, Sugg(s)
horse: English Steed, Stedman, Stott; French Cheval; Italian Chevallo,
  Cavallo; Polish Siwek, Konicki; Polish or Ukrainian Kolybecki
sheep: English Lamb, Shepherd (various spellings), Withers, Agnew;
  Bulgarian Beranich, German Scheaffer (various spellings); Polish
  Beran, Kozlowski (many variants)

Sometimes animal names may be particularly appropriate. A prominent professor of agriculture at the University of Illinois was named Sleeter Bull. His specialty: meats.

Birds of a Feather

Pictures of birds were used on many business signs in the namegiving period of the Middle Ages; some people were thought to resemble birds, and others hunted, captured, or trained birds. In these ways the ancestors of an estimated one to two million Americans took their names from the avian part of the world.

The following names are among the many thus derived. Each is held by at least 10,000 Americans, and some, such as Crane and Aguila, by 35,000 or more.

Adler: German 'eagle'
Aguila: Spanish 'eagle'
Ahrens: Dutch 'eagle'
Coe: English 'jackdaw'
Corbett, Corbin: English 'raven'
  (When Irish, Corbin does not
  refer to birds.)
Crain, Crane: English 'crane'
Crow(e): English 'crow'
Culver, Dove: English 'dove'
Falco(n)(ne)(ner), Faulkner:
  Falco or Falcone is Italian for
  'falcon' or 'hawk'; English
  Falconer or Faulkner trained
  falcons or hunted with them

Finch: English
Fink (several spellings): German
  'finch'
Hawk: English
Ortega: Spanish 'grouse'
Palumbo: Italian 'dove'
Partridge: English
Poe: English 'peacock' (But may
  also have other derivations.)
Schwann: German 'swan'
Sparks: English 'sparrow hawk'
Swan: English
Wren(n): English

In addition, more than a score of other birds have lent us their names, although fewer than 10,000 Americans now use any one of the forms. Note that Slavs in particular seem to like birds' names.

blackbird: Kos, Kosiek
black daw: Kafka
cuckoo: Kukulka
lark: Skowron(ek)
linnet: Konopka
magpie: Pye, Agassiz, Sroka
mallard: Mallard
nightingale: Nightingale,
  Nachtigall, Slovick, Slowick
owl: Sowa
robin: Cermak (The English
  surname Robin is usually
  derived from Robert.)
grosbeak: Ziemba

heron: Her(r)on, Caplenko
lapwing: Czej(k)a
rook: Rook
snipe: Snipe, Kulik
starling: Starling, Szpak
stork: Stork, Capek
teal: Teal(e), Teel(e)
thrush: Drozd
titmouse: Sikora
vulture: Geier, Geyer
wagtail: Pliszka (In 1641 an
  Elizabeth Wagtail was living in
  Grimsby, England.)
woodpecker: Speck, Specht

Finally, general names meaning 'bird' are not uncommon. Bird itself is the name of over 30,000 Americans, and Byrd even more—about 85,000. German-American Vogel is used by another 30,000, and the Americanized spelling Fogle or Fogel by about 15,000. Finkel 'little bird' in combination with Finkelstein 'little bird stone' may account for another 15,000. Spanish Garza, which may mean 'bird' or more specifically 'heron' or 'dove' is the name of some

75,000 Americans. Polish Pta(c)k means 'bird,' and Czechoslova-kian Ptacek is a dimunitive form 'little bird.'

Matronyms

Matronyms (surnames based on mothers' names) are more often called metronyms or metronymics, but matronym, more clearly based on *mater* 'mother,' is less confusing.

To form the surname of a daughter, in Iceland or in earlier times in the other Scandinavian countries as well, the equivalent of *daughter* was attached to the father's name. Thus, in Iceland, the president first elected in 1980 is a woman named Vignis Finnbo-gadottir. That means 'Vignis the daughter of Finnboga.' In 1925 the Iceland legislature decreed that having a patronymic was a re-quirement for citizenship. If Vignis has a brother, his patronymic is Finnbogason. If she has a husband whose first name is Thorsteinn and they have a son named Olafur, the son's full name is Olafur Thorsteinson and the daughter may be Guthrun Thorsteinndottir. The best-known work of Norwegian novelist and Nobel Prize winner Sigrid Undset is the trilogy *Kristin Lavransdatter*, which is set in medieval times when -*datter* was a common ending for girls' sur-names.

Those names are less sexist than most European names, be-cause they do not impose -*son* or the equivalent on girls and boys indiscriminately. But they are not matronyms, for they do not me-morialize mothers, as Hanson and Sorensen, for example, memo-rialize fathers. In fact, Finnbogadottir and Lavransdatter honor fa-thers named Finnboga and Lavran(s).

Not only patronyms but also descriptives and occupational names relate almost exclusively to men rather than women. De-scriptive names such as Strong or Long, for example, recall char-acteristics more often associated with men than with women; few people have the name Buxom or any other that suggests feminine appearance or traits. Few women have been smiths, carters, wheel-wrights, and the like, but it is such predominantly male occupations that are the sources of great numbers of names; in contrast, women or men named Milkmaid are few.

Some occupations, however, especially those in which many women worked, do have feminine forms beside the masculine ones.

Thus Webster is a female Web(b)er or Weaver, Baxter is a female Baker, and Brewster is the feminine equivalent of Brewer. Those and a few more names are occupational names, then, but in a sense are matronyms as well.

The true matronyms, however, are those in which a woman's name appears. They are not numerous, although someone has estimated—probably much too optimistically—that 10 percent of "patronyms" are matronyms.

The most common example of a matronym is Allison, but like the other examples, that name may refer to either a female or a male progenitor. It may be derived from Alice, which appeared in various spellings (Allis, Alys, etc.) in the Middle Ages, but it also may be based on the male Ellis or even Allen or Alexander.

Similarly, Emmett and its variants may honor a medieval Emma, but also a male Emery or Emory, or German Emmerich. The rare name Ibbot(son) may be traced to a nickname for Isabel, but the same nickname was apparently used for the masculine Ilbert. Anson is usually 'son of Ann.'

Till was a nickname for Matilda and also for several rather rare medieval men's names, such as Tilbeohrt. Modern Till(ett) or Tillotson, then, may be a matronym fairly often.

There aren't many more. If it is indeed an honor to have one's name perpetuated in the names of one's descendants, then women have been consistently shortchanged.

Jewish names are not quite so sexist as most. Some husbands in the naming period, which for most Jews was considerably later than for gentiles, took their wives' names. Thus Estermann is 'Esther's husband,' Dienesmann 'Dinah's husband,' Hodesmann 'Hadassah's husband,' and Pearlman 'Pearl's husband.' Estrin is 'descended from Esther,' and Esther might also be commemorated as the founder of the Estersons. Rabbi Benzion C. Kaganoff comments, "Often a Jewish family name is associated with the wife's name in cases where she was the breadwinner or where she came from the more distinguished family lineage (*yichus*)." In *A Dictionary of Jewish Names*, he mentions several examples, including Adelman and Edelman, Edelstein (sometimes), Dobkin, Dobrin, and Dus(h)kin.

❦ 15
Wonderful People with Strange-Sounding Names

Uncommon Surnames
from the 1790 Census

President George Washington authorized the taking of the first census of the United States in 1790. Many of the surnames recorded in that year now have vanished or become quite rare. These lists and several that follow include a small proportion of those names.

The lists are classified according to their apparent meanings, but in a few instances the names may really mean something else. They may have been misspelled by the census-takers, or the words may have had different meanings two hundred years ago. *Bloomer*, for instance, then meant a flowering plant, not an article of feminine attire. The later meaning is from Amelia Jenks Bloomer, a suffragette not yet born in 1790.

Food

Almond	Custard	Lard
Beans	Dates	Milk
Beets	Fowl	Mints
Cheese	Goodbread	Mush

Mustard   Redwine   Tongue
Olives   Squash   Vinegar
Onions   Tart

Clothing and Sewing

Beads   Jumpers   Petticoat
Bloomer   Lace   Pin
Boas   Lightcap   Redsleeves
Collar   Mendingall   Scarf
Crape   Mitts   Threadcraft
Frill   Overall   Waistcoat
Frocks   Pattern

People and Their Characteristics

Barefoot   Humble   Plump
Beeman   Kicker   Rascal
Boney   Knave   Sickman
Councilman   Madsavage   Strut
Fickle   Measley   Toogood
Goodfellow   Older   Toughman
Gump   Peacemaker   Underhand
Hero   Pettyfool   Weedingman
                   Pilgrim

The Body and Its Ills

Blister   Fits   Rickets
Boils   Gout   Salts
Bowels   Gullets   Shoulders
Corns   Lips   Shiver
Cough   Livers   Thumbs
Crampeasy   Nose   Warts
Fatyouwant   Physic

Houses and Their Furnishings

Brickhouse   Buttery   Cushion
Brickroof   China   Gambrel
Greathouse   Mug   Pump
Latch   Newbowl   Spoons
Laughinghouse   Newhouse   Spout
Lockkey   Oldhouse   Stonehouse
Longhouse   Porch

Merchandise and Commodities

Awl   Barrels   Bomb
Barley   Boiler   Buckhorn

Camphor
Coal
Coop
Coopernail
Coldiron
Combs
Cowhorn
Divans

Fender
Filters
Gouge
Harness
Hogshead
Junk
Ladder
Nipper

Nuthammer
Oven
Screws
Silkrags
Smallcorn
Sulkey
Surrey
Tenpenny

Nature

Birdwhistle
Blizzard
Caraway
Chestnutwood
Coldair
Currants
Flyberry
Hazelgrove

Hornet
Marjoram
Mayberry
Oysterbanks
Parsley
Pheasants
Quince
Rottenberry
Sealion

Slush
Tails
Tallhill
Widedale
Wilderness
Woodsides
Woodyfield
Wormwood

Unusual Combinations

Beersticker
Cathole
Cockledress
Coldflesh
Crackbone
Flybaker
Goodbit
Huntsucker

Liptrot
Livergall
Milkrack
Partneck
Reedhovel
Sharpneck
Shortday
Silvernail
Spitsnoggle

Splitstone
Stophell
Sydensticker
Tallowback
Trueluck
Wallflour
Willibother
Witchwagon

Forenames and Surnames

Unity Bachelor
Joseph Came
Comfort Clock
Boston Frog
Anguish Lemmon
Christian Shelf
Truelove Sparks
Preserved Taft

Sharp Blount
Bachelor Chance
Sermon Coffin
Snow Frost
Thomas Purity
Thomas Simmers
Barbary Staggers
Peter Wentup

Wanton Bump
Mourning Chestnut
Jemima Crysick
Thomas Gabtale
Ruth Shaves
Sarah Simpers
Booze Still
Darling Whiteman

How Many Different Surnames Are There?

No one knows for sure the number of names by which we call ourselves here in America. Computers for the Social Security

Administration in their tally of 1974 found 1,286,556 *different* surnames. But of course that number has changed—changes daily in fact. The last surviving holder of a name may die, and the possessor of a name previously unheard in this country may debark from an airplane.

Besides, the SSA count was itself not complete. The computers were asked to list only the first six letters in each name. So, for example, the names Hernan, Hernand, Hernander, Hernandes, Hernandez, Hernando, and Hernani were counted as a single name (Hernan).

The computer count may have shorted the total by a quarter of a million names—a wild guess. So the total number of different surnames in the United States may well exceed one and a half million.

Unique Surnames

"I've never known any other family with a surname just like mine," a man named Kwasimady said. "Is that possible?"

Yes, indeed. The records of the Social Security Administration show a total of 448,663 one-of-a-kind names. An SSA spokesperson hypothesizes that most of the oddities are variant spellings. Someone may have misspelled the name, intentionally or not, perhaps changing just one or two letters. So, for example, a Tomlinson may possibly gain uniqueness by writing Tomlansen or perhaps Tomlinsun.

As for Mr. Kwasimady, some of his ancestors may have spelled the name Quasimodo, like that of Victor Hugo's hunchback of Notre Dame or the late Italian poet, Salvatore Quasimodo.

The Shortest American Surnames

The X, Y, and Z who perform various actions in high school algebra problems are real people. So are A, B, and C and all the other letters of the alphabet. The files of the Social Security Administration contain the records of these people for whom a single letter serves as the surname:

A (24)	H (8)	O (16)	V (17)
B (6)	I (12)	P (7)	W (5)
C (16)	J (4)	Q (2)	X (2)
D (13)	K (4)	R (5)	Y (5)
E (10)	L (11)	S (8)	Z (4)
F (3)	M (16)	T (4)	
G (10)	N (2)	U (7)	

One man explained his single-letter name in this way: "I had a five-syllable name starting with D that most people couldn't pronounce. Some of them just called me 'Mr. D.' So I made the change legally."

Since I is the skinniest letter, the people named I may claim the smallest name.

Outside the United States, names equivalent to E and U are occasionally found as Burmese surnames, and U may also be a given name. In Korea the surname transliterated as O is rather common.

The Longest American Surnames?

It is not certain whose surname is longest, if we eliminate obviously contrived names. Somebody is probably piecing together, even as you read this, twelve hundred letters or so to gain notice in Guinness.

Names of unquestionably legitimate candidates are much shorter than that. Perhaps the most likely was recorded by the U.S. Army as Lambros A. Pappatorianofillosopoulos—25 letters.

Philadelphia had a long-term resident, born in Germany, whose letterhead read Hubert Blaine Wolfeschlegelsteinhausenbergerdorff, translated by Elsdon Smith as "a descendant of Wolfeschlegelstein (one who prepared wool for manufacture on a stone), of the house of Bergerdorf (mountain village)."

But that wasn't the half of it. The parents of the infant, born in Bergerdorf on February 29, 1904 (could Leap Year Day have had anything to do with the eccentricity?), inflicted upon him the following names: Adolph Blaine Charles David Earl Frederick Gerald Hubert Irvin John Kenneth Lloyd Martin Nero Oliver Paul Quincy Randolph Sherman Thomas Uncas Victor William Xerxes Yancy Zeus Wolfeschlegelsteinhausenbergerdorffvoralternwarengewissenhaftschaferswessenschafewarenwohlgepflegeundsorgfaltig-

keitbeschutzenvonangreifendurchihrraubgierigfeindewelche-
voralternzwolftausendjahresvorandieerscheinenvandererersteer-
demenschderraumschiffgebrauchlichtalsseinursprungvonkraft-
gestartseinlangefahrthinzwischensternartigraumaufdersuchen-
achdiesternwelchegehabtbewohnbarplanetenkreisedrehensighund-
wohinderneurassevonverstandigmenschlichkeitkonnteffort-
pflanzenundsicherfreuenanlebenslangelichfreudeundruhemit-
nichteinfurchtvorangreifenvonandererintelligentgeschopfsvonhinz-
wischensternartigraum.

The whole surname is a concatenation of words ending with what is apparently good wishes for a long and happy life. People who know German may enjoy trying to puzzle it out. The initials for the 26 given names, as you may have noticed, cover the alphabet from A to Z.

The Guinness editors comment that late in life Mr. W further shortened the surname to Wolfe + 590, Senior. Whether there is a Junior, and if so, what he calls himself, is not mentioned.

Later editions of the Guinness books refer to—but do not include—two even longer contrived names, both of which were "made in America." The Guinness folks and Paul Dickson, author of a fine book called *Names,* though disagreeing about the length of the two girls' first names, tell essentially the same story but do not print the names—perhaps because they wanted to leave space in their books for something else. In Missoula, MT, in 1980, Mr. and Mrs. Scott Roaul Sör-Lökken called their daughter S. Ellen Geogianna. The S. stands for a 598-letter name (Dickson says 611) designed "to throw a wrench into the computers of federal bureaucracy," according to the father. The girl, says Guinness, is known as "Snow Owl" for short and "Oli" for shorter.

A mere 598 or 611 letters wouldn't suffice for Mr. and Mrs. James E. Williams of Beaumont, TX. In 1984, they originally named their infant daughter Rhoshandiatellneshiaunneveshenk Koyaanesquatsiuty but then amended the first name to 1,019 letters (Dickson says 948) and the middle name to 36.

Both of those girls may encounter difficulties with the IRS, Social Security, and college registrars. And when a notary public is asked to witness the legal signature of one of them, he or she may fall asleep before signing is complete.

Some Unusual Beginnings of Surnames

Theoretically, any two letters could begin a surname, but in actuality some combinations are very rare or even nonexistent. In a recent Manhattan phone book there is only one name listed with the two letters that start each of these names:

Bpgen	Jn	Qvarnstrom
Bschorr	Kdenovic	Tfank
Dfsell	Kgositsile	Ttappalou
Dkada	Ldova	Uosikkinen
Dsouza	Mshar	Vhugen
Equinda	Mwangosi	Vjesner
Fhagen	Mzimela	Vnuk
Fteha	Nhan	Wcislo
Gdanski	Nnamdi	Wdowka
Hforoobar	Nsubaga	Wfoulkes
Hmura	Nxumalo	Wg
Htain	Pniewski	Wsiaki
Ijams	Pvar	Zjawinski
Iqbal	Pzena	Zkhiri

Some of these names come from northern or eastern Europe, others from the Middle East, Africa, or Asia.

The same directory shows only about a dozen or fewer names beginning with these letter combinations: BZ, CM, DF, DH, DK, DL, DM, DV, DZ, EJ, EO, FF, FJ, GB, GJ, GM, GN, HJ, HL, HN, HR, HV, IU, JH, KJ, KP, KS, KV, LJ, LV, MB, MJ, ML, MN, MP, MR, ND, NK, NT, NW, PT, QA, RZ, SB, SD, SF, SG, SJ, SS, TC, JJ, TK, TL, UI, UY, WL, WN, WS, XH, YZ, ZS, ZD, ZG, ZN, ZR, ZS, and ZV.

Which Name Is the Surname?

In Chinese, Korean, and Hungarian names, the surname comes first, so Chin Wu, for instance, is Mr. Chin rather than Mr. Wu, and Nagy István in England or America would be Stephen Nagy. To avoid confusion in the United States, Mr. Chin, too, is likely to sign his name Wu Chin; the listing in the phone book would be Chin, Wu.

Spaniards and Portuguese put the father's surname in the middle, with the mother's surname at the end, sometimes prefaced by *y* (Spanish) or *e* (Portuguese) to signify 'and.' So Enrico Garcia y

Lopez is Señor Garcia. Garcia, like Chin, will probably list himself under the surname (Garcia), although Pablo Picasso and others have chosen to be known by the matronym.

What's Your Last Initial?

More American surnames start with S than with any other letter, and X—not unexpectedly—begins the smallest number.

B gets second place, M is third, and K a close fourth. Z surprisingly ranks ahead of Y, and ahead also of I, J, Q, U, and X.

Here are the complete percentages:

Letter	Percentage	Letter	Percentage
A	4.8	N	2.7
B	7.0	O	2.6
C	5.5	P	5.5
D	5.9	Q	0.3
E	2.5	R	4.4
F	3.3	S	9.8
G	5.2	T	4.6
H	4.4	U	0.9
I	1.2	V	2.7
J	2.0	W	3.1
K	6.4	X	0.1
L	5.0	Y	1.3
M	6.5	Z	2.2

Some people (usually with names between Aaron and Myles) have claimed that men and women with surnames starting with A through M generally accomplish most in life. They say, for example, that almost two-thirds of our U.S. presidents—27 of 41—have had names in the A to M group.

The journal called *Names* disputed that. R. V. Dietrich and L. T. Reynolds (impartial, since their last initials are D and R) made a count based on *Who's Who in America* and similar compilations. Their conclusion should comfort people in the maligned N to Z group: "There is no good basis for any statement to the effect that a discordant relationship exists between the initial letter of a person's surname and his or her characteristics or achievement."

Another researcher, Gary S. Felton, set out to find whether *low* achievers among students tend to cluster in one-half of the alphabet. He reported in *Names* that poor test scores are spread proportionately, regardless of the alphabet. If, for instance, almost twice as many S's and L's make low grades, it is because there are almost twice as many S's in the student body.

Presidents' Nicknames

Some American presidents had as many as a dozen nicknames—both favorable and unfavorable; others had none that were widely known. Try to match each president with the nickname from the group opposite each list. (Answers are at the end.)

Before 1900

1. George Washington	A.	Era of Good Feelings
2. John Adams		President
3. Thomas Jefferson	B.	Tippecanoe
4. James Monroe	C.	Bachelor President
5. Andrew Jackson	D.	Prince Arthur
6. Martin Van Buren	E.	Emancipation President
7. William H. Harrison	F.	Kinderhook Fox
8. Zachary Taylor	G.	Duke of Braintree
9. James Buchanan	H.	Granny
10. Abraham Lincoln	I.	Old Hickory
11. Ulysses S. Grant	J.	Old Rough and Ready
12. Rutherford B. Hayes	K.	Little Ben
13. Chester A. Arthur	L.	Perpetual Candidate
14. Grover Cleveland	M.	Surveyor President
15. Benjamin Harrison	N.	Unconditional Surrender
	O.	The Sage of Monticello

Since 1900

16. Theodore Roosevelt	P.	Give 'em Hell
17. William Howard Taft	Q.	Silent _____
18. Woodrow Wilson	R.	Big Bill
19. Calvin Coolidge	S.	Big One of the Peace
20. Herbert Hoover		Conference
21. Franklin D. Roosevelt	T.	Tricky Dick
22. Harry S Truman	U.	Dutch
23. Lyndon B. Johnson	V.	The Roughrider
24. Richard M. Nixon	W.	The Squire of Hyde Park
25. Ronald Reagan	X.	Prosperity Around the
26. George Bush		Corner
	Y.	Big Daddy
	Z.	No New Taxes

Answers

1. M   2. G   3. O   4. A   5. I   6. F   7. B   8. J
9. C   10. E   11. N   12. H   13. D   14. L   15. K
16. V   17. R   18. S   19. Q (Cal)   20. X   21. W
22. P   23. Y   24. T   25. U   26. Z

Pity the Postman in Amishland

A rural mail carrier in an Amish community in southeastern Pennsylvania may have unusual problems.

According to an article by Elmer E. Smith in the journal *Names*, one such postman had on his route 437 people named Stoltzfus. Ten Stoltzfuses would be fine, even a few dozen would be bearable, but 437? No way.

Because of the Amish practice of endogamy (marriage only within the sect), for a couple of centuries there has been almost no infusion of new names. As a result, says Smith, "The great majority of Amish [in southeastern Pennsylvania] have only seven different surnames, and twenty surnames constitute 96.7 percent of the total Amish population in that region."

Moreover, "An analysis of 2,611 Amish marriages since 1890 revealed the existence of only forty-two different Amish surnames, and three of those [Stolfzfus 27.2 percent, King (from König) 12.2 percent, and Beiler 10.5 percent] constituted 49.9 percent of that total. Fourteen surnames make up 90 percent of the Amish names."

Could Johnny Carson
Have Been Wrong?

Television talk-show host Johnny Carson, in his monologues, has sometimes remarked that the flush toilet was invented in the middle of the nineteenth century by a man named Thomas Crapper.

There really was a Thomas Crapper, rather well-known in his time (1837–1910) as an inventor.

However, *A History of Technology* by Singer *et al*, says that the first such water closet was designed in 1596—three centuries before

Crapper—by Sir John Harrington, and that improved models were invented in 1775 and 1778. Singer includes a drawing depicting Harrington's invention. It had a tank several feet above the stool. At the top of the tank was a water inlet and at the bottom a chain or cord to open a valve that permitted water to flow down to the stool. Essentially the same device may be found in some old buildings today.

Obviously, despite Johnny Carson and others, the device slangily called a "crapper" should be called a "harrington" or possibly a "Sir John."

The Owl without a Vowel

From 1949 to 1951, a basketball player named William Mlkvy performed for the Temple University Owls, earning a nearly unanimous All-American rating. The press was understandably delighted by his name, calling him "the Owl without a vowel," overlooking the fact that y is sometimes a vowel. The player later became Dr. William P. Mlkvy.

During the Vietnamese war another vowelless name, Ng, was often in print, and some Americans learned to pronounce it as what was described as "a tight *unn*." Columns of Ng's may now be found in some big American city directories.

From Czechoslovakia have come a number of names that appear to have no vowels in their spelling. These ordinarily contain an r, which in Czech may serve as a vowel but still gives a vowelless look (in American eyes). Elsdon Smith gives these examples of such odd-seeming names:

Chrt	Srb	Trlt
Krc, Krch 'cramps'	Srch	Trh
Smrt 'death'	Srp 'sickle'	Vlk 'wolf'
Smrz	Trc, Trch	

When immigrants first arrived on these shores, such names were not extremely uncommon, but out of kindness to people who would be baffled by them, immigration officials or the newcomers themselves generally stuck in an obvious vowel.

A Manhattan directory still has Jn and Nj, and many Ng's, and comes close to vowellessness with Brchnel, Brlik, Brztwa, Hrnclar, Hrynklw, and Zmrzlik.

The all-time vowelless champ, however, if we again ignore a *y*, was a fictitious character named Mxyztplk, who came to Earth from the fifth dimension, in one of the first episodes of the comic book version of Superman, who was dreamed up by two teenage boys.

The Truth about the Hoggs

Nineteenth-century journalists learned with glee that Texas Governor James Hogg (1851–1906) had a daughter named Ima. They began making up stories about fictitious members of his family, and his political opponents rejoiced. According to these stories, the governor also had daughters named Ura and Bea and a son Hesa.

Not true, said R. M. Rennick, writing in the journal *Names* in 1982. Ima was the Hoggs' only daughter. Their sons had ordinary names: William, Michael, and Thomas.

Why did the Hoggs name their daughter Ima? Rennick suggests that it was because Hogg's brother Thomas had written a novel in which a heroic Civil War nurse was named Ima. The Hoggs liked the name.

They intended to play no cruel joke on their infant daughter. They rejoiced in her. Just after her birth, her father wrote to a relative, "Our cup of joy is now overflowing. We have a daughter of as fine proportions and of as angelic view as ever nature favored a man with, and her name is Ima."

Did the name affect her badly? Apparently not. She became an accomplished pianist and a respected music teacher, a leader in Houston society, a member of the school board, a sponsor of a University of Texas health foundation, and a founder of the Houston Symphony Orchestra.

Mr. Reardon Couldn't Be There

A prankster invited a number of people, strangers to each other, to dinner. He asked them to introduce themselves and said he would leave it to them to discover during the evening what all of them had in common. They finally figured it out. Two women had the given name Fanny, and the other guests had surnames such as Bottomley, Duff, Pratt, Hinds, Butts, and Botham.

Trends in American Surnames

The first United States census was taken in 1790. According to analyses made much later, 83.5 percent of the surnames in that year were English or Welsh; Scots contributed another 6.7 percent and Irish 1.6 percent, making a total of 91.8 percent British. Germans were far behind with 5.6 percent, the Dutch had 2 percent, a few people were unclassifiable, and French and all others made a total of less than 1 percent. The "all others" represented only about five thousand people.

No similar detailed analyses of later census reports have been made, but the predominance of British names was greatly reduced by successive waves of immigration. English, Welsh, and Scots kept coming, but until 1860 or so the Irish and Germans were the most numerous newcomers, bringing in hundreds of thousands of people with names such as O'Rourke and Schneider. Scandinavians joined the throngs gradually, and from 1880 to 1914 immigrants from southern, central, and eastern Europe crowded in, sometimes averaging more than a million a year and bringing with them names ending in vowels or in -*vich*, -*wich*, -*ski* or -*sky*, -*opoulos*, and the like.

After World War I, immigration restrictions soon limited the flow, although many German Jews fled here from Hitler's Europe in the 1930s. After World War II, Asian immigrants greatly increased, bringing the one-syllable Chinese and Korean names such as Lee and Kim, the two-part Japanese names such as Yamamoto, the frequently Spanish names of the Philippines, and the Vietnamese names that often had a hard-to-pronounce Ng- beginning or other sounds uncustomary in America. More Asians came in between 1960 and 1990 than had entered during all our earlier history. Especially, though, people with Hispanic names came by the hundreds of thousands from Mexico, Cuba, and Puerto Rico.

What of the future? No one can predict with certainty, but probably the Hispanic names will continue to outpace most others in growth. In some places, as has already happened in Miami and some California cities, Hispanic names will outnumber Smith and Johnson. The flow of people from Central and South America, speaking either Portuguese or Spanish, seems likely to grow, and unless immigration laws are changed from those adopted in 1965, more and more Asians may enter.

Wonderful People
with Strange-Sounding Names

Sometimes a person with a strange-sounding name does well. The late actor Humphrey Bogart achieved fame in his own lifetime, and both Bogart cultists and many in the general public are still happy to see reruns of Bogey movies. W. Atlee Burpee got rich selling seeds (it's not significant that the company now offers "burpless" cucumbers). Mrs. R. O. Backhouse is remembered in a daffodil named for her. Robin Fox and Lionel Tiger made important studies of animal behavior. C. T. Onions (he pronounced it *o-NIGH-unz*) compiled dictionaries. Bedrich Smetana composed memorable music, even though his surname means 'sour cream.'

❦ PART III

We Name Almost Every Place We Know

❦ 16
The Continents and the States

How the Seven Continents Got Their Names

Some high school graduates and probably most college graduates know how the American continents came to be called America, but it is doubtful that one person in a hundred can say much about the origins of the names of the other continents.

Until less than five hundred years ago, the sketchy world maps that existed showed only Europe, Asia, and Africa, along with other undefined areas sometimes labeled Terra Incognita 'unknown lands.' But in 1507 Martin Waldseemüller, a German geographer and cartographer, drew in, roughly, a fourth area. He knew of the voyages of Columbus and the other sea captains who followed him. These men included the Italian Amerigo Vespucci, whose name in Latin was Americus Vespucius. He had made perhaps four voyages to explore the coasts of what are now called South and Central America, and possibly Florida. Waldseemüller proposed a name for this large area:

> A fourth part [of the world] has been discovered by Americus Vespucius (as will appear in what follows). For that reason I think that nothing should prevent us from calling it Amerige or America, that is, the land of Americus, after its discoverer Americus, a man of brilliant mind, [using a feminine ending] because both Europa and Asia are also named for women.

The proposal was adopted, although there are still those who argue persuasively that Columbia or Colombia would have been a more logical choice.

The name Europe, as Waldseemüller commented, seems to be the name of a woman (especially in its Latin form), Europa. Mythology tells us that Europa was a beautiful maiden whose father may have been Agenor, the king of Phoenicia. Zeus (Jupiter), king of the gods, whose all-seeing eyes liked to concentrate on feminine pulchritude, observed her and determined to possess her. He changed himself into a handsome white bull and, as Thomas Bulfinch says in *The Age of Fable*, "mingled with the herd as Europa and her maidens were sporting on the sea-shore. Encouraged by the tameness of the animal, Europa tried to mount his back; whereupon the god rushed into the sea, and swam with her to Crete."

Alfred, Lord Tennyson, described the trip sensuously:

Sweet Europa's mantle blew unclasp'd,
From off her shoulder backward borne;
From one hand droop'd a crocus; one hand grasp'd
The mild bull's golden horn.

Once in Crete, Zeus assumed human form, and eventually Europa bore him three children. It was this Europa for whom the continent was supposedly named.

But reality is seldom so poetic. The word *europa* was once thought to mean 'sunset' and to have been applied by the Greeks to the lands to the west of them. Now, however, scholars believe that it meant 'mainland.' "It appears," says the *Encyclopaedia Britannica*, "to have suggested itself to the Greeks, in their maritime world, as an appropriate designation of the broadening, extensive northerly lands that lay beyond, lands with characteristics but vaguely known."

Asia, too, has a feminine-sounding name, but apparently it is only an indicator of a direction—east. In Greek the word meant 'region of the rising sun,' which may be related to an Assyrian word *asŭ* 'east.' It is also possible that at one time it referred only to what is now called Asia Minor, and then gradually reached out to encompass the whole continent.

The Romans were responsible for the naming of Africa. The word apparently comes from Latin *aprica* 'sunny,' which is similar to the Greek *aphrike* 'without cold.' Two other hypotheses, though, have been advanced. One is that the Romans called the relatively unexplored southern two thirds of the continent Afriga 'land of the Afrigs,' who were Berber tribes from south of Carthage. The least plausible explanation is that Africa means 'ears of corn' and was used to denote fertile land in what is now Tunisia.

Scholars of ancient history have encountered occasional references to a *terra australis incognita* 'unknown southern land,' and starting in the twelfth century A.D. there were more and more rumors of the existence of such a land. But it was not until the seventeenth century that exploration and settlement actually began. Since the Dutch were the earliest explorers, the landmass was at first named New Holland. But the Dutch did not persist in settlement, and the English did. One of their explorers, Matthew Flinders, who had demonstrated that the landmass was indeed a separate continent, argued in 1817 that because this appeared to be the most southern of the continents, the old word for 'south' should be revived and that Australia should replace the outdated New Holland. This view soon prevailed.

We now know that an even more southerly continent exists, Antarctica. The etymology of *arctic* is explained in the *American Heritage Dictionary*:

> Middle English *artik*, from Medieval Latin *articus*, alteration of Latin *arcticus*, from Greek *arktikos*, from *arktos*, bear, hence the northern constellation Ursa Major, the Great Bear, hence "north."

So *arctic*, by way of that great bear in the sky who points the way to the north star, gave the Arctic Ocean and the Arctic Islands their names. The *Ant* in *Antarctica* is short for the prefix *anti-* 'opposite.' Antarctica is opposite the Arctic—opposite the north.

State Names and Nicknames

About half of our states' names are from Native American sources, although the original meanings are often uncertain. Of the other half, several come from names of English royalty or other persons of high rank, some from places in England, one from a Greek island (Rhodes), three from French sources, five from Spanish, and one (Washington) from a president.

Some states have, or have had, more than a single nickname. The ones that appear to be most generally used are listed here.

Alabama. the Yellowhammer State: said by some to be Choctaw for 'thicket-clearers' or 'vegetation-gatherers,' but George R. Stewart says it is from the name of a Creek tribe, the Alibamu or Alabamons. AL

Alaska. the Land of the Midnight Sun or the Last Frontier: from an Aleut word 'sea-breaker' or 'mainland.' AK

Arizona. the Grand Canyon State: Indian Arizonac, for 'little spring.' AZ

Arkansas. Land of Opportunity: a Quapaw name of a tribe, the Arkansea or Arkansa, then applied to the river and the territory. AR

California. the Golden State: name in a Spanish poem, *Las Sergas de Esplandián,* by Garcia Ordoñez de Montalvo, c. 1500, California being an imaginary, rich island with Amazons as rulers. CA

Colorado. the Centennial State (admitted to the Union in 1876): Spanish for 'red' or 'ruddy.' CO

Connecticut. the Nutmeg State: Native American word early recorded as Quinnehtukqut 'beside the long tidal river.' CT

Delaware. the Diamond State or the First State (first to ratify the U.S. Constitution, 1787): Delaware river and bay, named for Sir Thomas West, Lord De la Warr, the first governor of colonial Virginia. DE

Florida. the Sunshine State: Spanish 'feast of the flowers' (Easter). FL

Georgia. the Peach State or the Empire State of the South: named to honor George II of England. GA

Hawaii. the Aloha State: uncertain origin, but the islands' discoverer is said to have been named Hawaii Loa. The traditional home of Polynesians also was called Hawaii or Hawaiki. HI

Idaho. the Gem State, the Panhandle State, or the Spud State: origin obscure, but may be from the Kiowa-Apache name for the Comanche tribe (Idahi) or may be from a word meaning 'gem of the mountains.' ID

Illinois. the Prairie State: a Native American tribe (Illini), with a French affix. Said to mean 'tribe of superior men' or simply 'the men.' IL

Indiana. the Hoosier State: *Indian* + *a*, said to mean 'land of Indians.' IN

Iowa. the Hawkeye State or the Land Where the Tall Corn Grows: Native American for 'the beautiful land' or 'this is the place'; early spelling recorded as Ouaouiaton, shortened to Ouaouia. IA

Kansas. the Sunflower State or the Jayhawk State: Siouan for 'people of the south wind'; Spanish wrote the name as Escansaque, French as Kansa, then Kansas. KS

Kentucky. the Bluegrass State: Iroquoian Ken-tah-ten 'land of tomorrow' or Ken-ta-ke 'meadow land.' KY

Louisiana. the Pelican State or the Creole State: for King Louis XIV of France; Spanish changed the French Louisiane to Louisiana. LA

Maine. the Pine Tree State: sometimes considered a compliment to Queen Henrietta Maria, wife of England's Charles I, who was associated with a French province, Mayne, but more likely means 'the main,' that is, the mainland in contrast to nearby islands. ME

Maryland. the Free State or the Old Line State: for Henrietta Maria, queen of Charles I of England. MD

Massachusetts. the Bay State or the Old Colony State: Algonquian (Natick) words meaning 'great mountain place.' MA

Michigan. the Wolverine State: Algonquian words meaning 'great lake'; early reported as Machihiganing. MI

Minnesota. the North Star State, the Gopher State, or the Land of 10,000 Lakes (actually about 22,000): Dakotah word for 'sky-blue water' or a Siouan word for 'water-cloudy.' MN

Mississippi. the Magnolia State: Algonquian for 'father of waters' or 'big river'; early form Messipi. MS

Missouri. the Show-Me State: Missouri Indian tribe, the name said to mean 'place of the large canoes,' but more likely 'big and muddy'; early recorded as Ouemessourit. MO

Montana. the Treasure State: Latinized Spanish word, chosen by Representative J. M. Ashley of Ohio; means 'mountainous.' MT

Nebraska. the Cornhusker State: Oto or Omaha for 'flat water'; early reported as Nibthaska. NE

Nevada. the Sagebrush State, the Silver State, or the Battleborn State (for the Mexican War): Spanish for 'snow-capped.' NV

New Hampshire. the Granite State: English county of Hampshire. NH

New Jersey. the Garden State: Channel Isle of Jersey. NJ

New Mexico. the Land of Enchantment or the Sunshine State: from the country of Mexico (Nehuatl Mexihco). NM

New York. the Empire State: for the English Duke of York. NY

North Carolina. the Tar Heel State: named to honor England's King Charles I (in Latin, Carolus). NC

North Dakota. the Sioux State or the Flickertail State: from the name of the Dakotah tribe, meaning 'allies.' ND

Ohio. the Buckeye State: Iroquoian for 'great river.' OH

Oklahoma. the Sooner State, for settlers who arrived sooner than officially permitted: Choctaw words for 'red people.' OK

Oregon. the Beaver State: origin unknown, but may be Native American; place-name authority George R. Stewart said it came from a misprint in a French map of 1715. OR

Pennsylvania. the Keystone State: honors its founder, William Penn; means 'Penn's woods.' PA

Rhode Island. the Ocean State: from the Greek island, Rhodes. RI

South Carolina. the Palmetto State: honors England's Charles I. SC

South Dakota. the Sunshine State or the Coyote State: from the name of the Dakotah tribe, meaning 'allies.' SD

Tennessee. the Volunteer State: Cherokee town name, meaning obscure; early recorded as Tanasqui, much later as Tinnase. TN

Texas. the Lone Star State: from Native American *teyas* 'friends,' which the Spaniards mistook for a tribal name. TX

Utah. the Beehive State: named for the Ute tribe, said to mean 'the people of the mountains.' UT

Vermont. the Green Mountain State: French *vert mont* 'green mountain.' VT

Virginia. the Old Dominion State or the Mother of Presidents: name honors Elizabeth I, called the Virgin Queen. VA

Washington. the Evergreen State or the Chinook State: for George Washington. WA

West Virginia. the Mountain State: same as Virginia. WV

Wisconsin. the Badger State: French version of an Algonquian name, meaning uncertain: early reported as Mescousing or Mesconsing, later Ouisconsin(g). WI

Wyoming. The Equality State: named for the Wyoming valley of Pennsylvania; meaning may be 'alternate mountains and valleys' or, more likely, 'big-flats-at'; early recorded as Mauwauwaming or Meche-weami-ing. WY

They Merge at the Border

These border towns or cities share parts of the names of two or more states:

Arkoma, OK (Arkansas, Oklahoma)

Calexico, CA (a state and a country: California, Mexico)

Delmar, DE (Delaware, Maryland)

Kanorado, KS (Kansas, Colorado)

Kenova, WV (Kentucky, Ohio, West Virginia)

Mardela Springs, MD (Maryland, Delaware)

Moark, AR (Missouri, Arkansas)

Tennga, GA (Tennessee, Georgia)

Texarkana, AR (Texas, Arkansas)

Texhoma, OK, TX (Texas, Oklahoma)

Texico, NM (Texas, New Mexico)

Vershire, VT (Vermont, New Hampshire—about 15 miles from the border)

Mexicali, Mexico, shakes hands across the border with Calexico, CA. Oklahoma and Texas also share a lake called Texoma.

Other combined names also exist or did exist, but do not have post offices. They include Arkana (Arkansas, Louisiana), Calzona (California, Arizona), Dahoming (Dakota and Wyoming), Nosodak (North Dakota, South Dakota), Nypenn (New York, Pennsylvania), Pen-Mar (Pennsylvania, Maryland), and Varopa (Virginia, Ohio, Pennsylvania). Cal Nev Ari (California, Nevada, Arizona, with its community post office at Searchlight, AZ) is in the triangular bottom of Nevada about halfway between California and Arizona.

Delmarva or the variant Delmarvia is a name sometimes used for the states of Delaware, Maryland, and Virginia as a group. Usually, though, Delmarva refers only to the peninsula between Chesapeake Bay and the Atlantic, consisting of most of Delaware and parts of Maryland and Virginia.

Is the United States, or Are the United States?

President John Adams used to say "The United States are ... " and so did a few lesser American dignitaries and many Britishers (who also say "the government are ..." and report cricket matches in headlines like "England Defeat Wales").

Most Americans, though, regard the nation as a unit and therefore treat the name as a singular. Carl Sandburg said what should have been the last word—but wasn't—in 1958. "The United States is, not are. The Civil War was fought over a verb."

Problems arise when someone—usually a member of Congress or some other political orator—puts these before the name. Obviously one can hardly say "*These* United States *is* . . ." with a plural at one end and a singular at the other. The solution is simple: The speaker is not talking here about the place as a nation, but rather as a group of states that are united in some way or ways. In print the construction should be spelled without capitals: "These united states are determined. . . ."

All Those Vowels in Hawaii

When people from the continental United States look at a map of the 50th state, most of the place names look strange to them. Most of the names consist of vowels and the same few consonants often repeated: Oahu, Waikiki, Waianae, Wahiawa, Kailua, Honokaa, Mauna Kea, Kaumalapau, and so on.

Almost 86 percent of Hawaiian place names are in the nearly extinct Hawaiian language, although words from English and other languages, as well as fake Hawaiian names, are reducing that percentage. The Hawaiian language has an alphabet of only twelve letters, five of which are vowels. Each syllable and, therefore, each word ends in a vowel.

Travelers in Hawaii may be interested in books that tell the meanings of the names. One of the best is *Place Names of Hawaii*, by Mary Kawena Pukui and others.

Travelers find that the same letter combinations appear in many names. *Wai*, for example, meaning 'water,' is in at least 240 names. Waikiki means 'water spouting.' Mauna means 'mountain.'

Here are a few more often-seen parts of names:

ana 'caves'
hale 'house'
kai 'sea,' 'seaweed'
kea 'white'
lani 'sky' or 'royal chief' (Okalani means 'of the royal chief.')
loa 'long' (Now you can translate Mauna Kea and Mauna Loa.)

lua 'pit, crater, hole'
Pele 'goddess of the volcano'
puaa 'pig'
puu 'hill, elevation'
uka 'inland'
ula 'red'

Mary Kawena Pukui says, "The meanings of a large proportion of the place names can be understood if one learns . . . 86 words."

The Most Consecutive Vowels

On a French map of the central part of North America, printed in 1693, was the name Ouaouiaton, spelled with seven consecutive vowels. Later, shortened to Ouaouia, the name was applied to the Native American tribe that subsequently was called Iowa. Iowa next was attached to the river, then to the territory, and now to the state.

Apparently no other American place name has been written with so many consecutive *a*'s, *e*'s, *i*'s, *o*'s, and *u*'s. Vowel-rich Hawaiians do manage five in a row fairly often, as in Ma-'ie'ie (a land section and a stream on the Big Island) or Puao-ao (a beach on Molokai). More rarely, they use the *same* vowel three times consecutively, as in Ka-'a'awa (land section and stream on Oahi), Pu'-u'uao (a Molokai peninsula), and Pu'u'ua'u (on Oahu, with a name that means 'dark-rumped petrel hills').

California's Names Show Its History

Imagine compressing California's history into four maps featuring the names in the state. That is what Erwin G. Gudde does in his *California Place Names.*

Map I is called "Names on the Land—About 1800." Its most notable feature is the lack of names away from the coast. The Sierra Nevada range was named in 1776, but other interior places remained nameless, since whatever the Native Americans called them was not recorded and so was quickly forgotten.

Along the coast, a considerable number of the names are those of "points"—toes of land testing the waters of the Pacific. Most of them are Spanish toes, recalling that this soil was once wrested by Spaniards from the natives. Pt. Concepcion 'the Immaculate Conception' 1602, Ft. Pinos 'the Pines' 1602, and Pt. Ano Nuevo 'the New Year' 1603 are among the oldest; farther north is Cape Mendocino, named for one of the exploring Mendozas in 1587. An English toe is still farther north: Pt. George, named for an English saint by an English man, George Vancouver, in 1793.

Now-familiar town or city names dot the coastline—all of them Spanish and often prefixed by San or Santa 'Saint': San Francisco (1769, but an earlier one existed a few miles north); nearby a San Francisco Draco, for the English Sir Francis Drake; Palo Alto, 1774;

Santa Clara, 1769; San Jose, 1777; Santa Cruz, 1769; San Luis Obispo, 1772; and others stretching down the coast to Los Angeles 'the Angels,' 1769, and the much older San Pedro, 1602. San Diego Bay (honoring St. James, as does Santiago) also got its name in 1602, and considerably later an on-shore settlement became San Diego.

Gudde's Map II shows the names attached to California places in the Later Spanish Period, from 1800 to the near-end of the 1840s.

By then interior California was no longer almost nameless. The rivers had been given English, Native American, or Spanish names such as Smith, Klamath, Feather, Yuba, American, Russian (mindful of the one-time Russian presence) Sacramento, Chowchilla, and on down to Amargosa and Mohave. The beautiful Cascade Range, which extends from California northward into British Columbia, got its name sometime before 1823.

For towns, which were still springing up mainly on or near the coast, Spanish names show the continuing presence of the Spaniards and the control by Mexico after 1822. Saints, both male and female, were still honored: Gregorio, Joaquin, Simeon, Miguel, Bernardino, Jacinto, Pasqual, Rosa, Maria, Ynez, Paula, and Susana.

Many of the Spanish names, however, have nothing to do with saints. There's even a Mount Diablo. We find Merced 'mercy,' 1806; Los Banos 'the baths,' because of pools suitable for bathing, named before 1841; Atascadero Miry Place, 1839; Guadalupe, for places in Spain and Mexico, 1830; Tejon 'badger,' 1806; La Jolla, either 'the hollow' or 'the jewel,' about 1828.

Cajon Pass, 1806, comes from Spanish for 'box.' But Walker Pass, Carson Pass, and Carson River are named for American frontiersmen.

In the late 1840s, as a result of the Mexican War, control of Alta (Upper) California passed to the United States, which obviously has not been the same since.

The tough forty-niners gave California tough names. There were Hell Hollow, Murderers' Bar, Jackass Hill, Humbug, and Poker Flat. Growlersburg survived as Georgetown, Hangtown as Placerville, Gouge Eye as Pleasant Grove, and Bedbug as Iona. (See also page 262).

Gudde's Map III shows more reputable names added between the late 1840s and 1880. The strip down the center of the state was filling up: Redding, Red Bluff, Chico, Oroville, Marysville, Amador, Sonora, Fresno, Visalia, Bakersfield, Palm Springs, and more.

On or near the coast, other new communities were being built: Eureka, Ukiah, Berkeley, Oakland, Redwood City, Ventura, Anaheim, and others.

Additional passes between mountains were named in eastern California: Donner (for the unfortunates who froze there in 1846–47), Luther, Ebbetts, and Tioga.

Death Valley got its name before 1861, but the tall Mt. Whitney not until 1864, Hamilton in 1861, Wilson in 1864, Humphreys in 1865.

Few names of this period, in contrast to the past, commemorated the speakers of Spanish. Chico 'small' is one exception. Speakers of Native American languages fared little better, although Tehachapi made it in 1853. A small-scale local siege made one community take the name of the besieged Russian Sebastopol. Anaheim combines a saint's name and the German word for 'home.'

But most of the names by that time were "American"—English words such as Redwood City, American men such as geologist Josiah Whitney or soldiers Robert Stockton and Thomas Baker.

A footnote to history and botany: True holly is not native to Calfornia, but the toyon is. The toyon has been called fake holly because it resembles the real thing. In 1886, when Mr. and Mrs. H. H. Wilcox named a California place Hollywood, they probably didn't know the difference. If they had, the place might have been Toyonwood.

But Hollywood is what it's called on Gudde's Map IV, for places named since 1880. Many of the new names are for physical features such as Lava Beds National Monument, 1925; Mt. Hilgard, 1896; Sequoia National Park, 1890; Lake Berryessa, 1957; or (back to the Spanish priests!) Los Padres National Forest, 1936. The towns and cities named in these years haven't become gigantic or very famous yet. Examples: Fortuna, Weed, Project City, Arbuckle, Pacific Grove, Pacifica, Burbank, Pomona (goddess of fruit trees), Blythe, El Centro (central to the Imperial Valley). Exceptions to the lack of fame: Long Beach and, of course, Hollywood.

Californians have started to name places for twentieth-century USans: Muir Woods for a naturalist; Taft for a president; Will Rogers Beach for a cowboy-entertainer-folk philosopher out of Claremore, OK.

Most of the California places named fairly recently have deservedly lovely or deservedly noncommittal names. But a few, especially in the Death Valley area, are remindful of gold rush days of almost a century and a half ago: Bad Water, Furnace Creek Inn, Dantes View, and the Devils Golf Course. (See also page 216.)

Around the World in Arkansas

With a little zigging and zagging, you can visit a large part of the world without leaving Arkansas: Athens (including Parthenon), Carthage, Damascus, Egypt, England, Formosa (not yet called Taiwan), Genoa, Hamburg, Havana, Jerusalem, London, Manila, Moscow, Oxford, Palestine, Paris, Scotland, and Ulm.

If you prefer not to leave the United States, you also can find in Arkansas Augusta, Bismarck, Charleston, Cleveland, Columbus, Concord, Danville, Decatur, Denver, Evansville, Fargo, Fulton, Helena, Houston, Monticello, Nashville, Omaha, Poughkeepsie, Tupelo, Waterloo, and about 50 other places that you probably thought were in other states.

In Arkansas you can even find Romance, and a Sweet Home, as well as Success.

Around the World in Maine

A postcard that travelers used to enjoy sending—perhaps still do—showed signboards at a crossroads pointing the way to Athens, Belfast, Belgrade, Bremen, China, Denmark, Dresden, Frankfort, Limerick, Lisbon, Madrid, Mexico, Naples, Norway, Oxford, Palermo, Paris, Peru, Poland, Rome, and Vienna.

All those places are within about 50 miles of a spot north and west of Portland, ME.

❦ 17
How Places
Get Their Names

Naming Places in the
Twentieth Century

Suppose that the United States had not sprung into being until the twentieth century, but that in other respects civilization had moved along as it has. What kinds of place names might have been chosen for the newly developing country?

There may be some clues in the names that actually have been chosen in the past 50 or 75 years.

Perhaps most famous of these was adopted from a radio show in 1950. The proprietors of that show went to a place in New Mexico and offered to hold an annual fiesta there if the townspeople would change the name from Hot Springs to the name of the program. It sounded like good publicity, and business people argued for a yes vote. Hot Springs had never before had so much excitement and such lively discussion. In the election a considerable majority approved the change, and so Truth or Consequences, NM, came into being. It was confirmed by a second vote in 1964. The radio show has long been gone, and the name is awkward. People in the area shorten it to T or C, and signs often say merely Truth or C.

Other twentieth-century entertainment has influenced names. An Oklahoma town in 1942 named itself Gene Autry, after a popular singing star in western movies. Children and sometimes adults

176

talk excitedly about going to Disneyland or Disney World, using those as place names and sometimes unaware that they will really have to buy their plane tickets to Anaheim, CA, or Orlando, FL, both of which have grown remarkably in population because of being entertainment centers. The name of the Paramount motion picture company was attached to the boulevard on which the huge movie lot was built, and later to the town of Paramount. Singer Elvis Presley's name has been given to streets and business establishments, especially in his native Memphis. Jiggs, NV, was named for the leading character in the comic strip, and Dogpatch (the habitat of Al Capp's redoubtable Yokum family and other denizens such as Marryin' Sam, Senator Phogbound, and Moonbeam McSwine) is the name applied to an amusement area in northern Arkansas and at least facetiously to many other places.

The name of Jim Thorpe, a Native American who was one of America's greatest all-round athletes, is now the name of a Pennsylvania community formerly called East Mauch Chunk and Mauch Chunk (which means 'bear mountain').

In Colorado in 1936, a place was named Uravan because uranium and vanadium were mined there. In Indiana, near a reactor testing station, is Atomic City.

TV Mountain, MT, is so called for the television transmitter built there in 1954. Somewhat older is Twenty Mule Team Canyon, CA, which became best known after a brand of borax was named Twenty Mule Team; the box showed the mules pulling a heavy wagon. Tin Mountain, CA, and Tin Mine Canyon, CA, celebrate one part of the mining industry, and Tin Can Branch, KY, memorializes a more immediate source of much of America's food supply (although, it seems, not much if any tin is now used in tin cans). The word Coal or a derivative appears in close to a hundred settlement names, some of them pre-twentieth century, and other things that are mined (silver, gold, lead, and copper, for instance) have their own namesakes. Cyanide County, MT, received the name of this deadly poison because it is a chemical used in treating ore. Several towns have Gas as a part of their names.

A California area renowned for experimentation with computers, silicon chips, and the like is publicized by journalists as Silicon Valley. Neon, Krypton, and Xena (for xenon) are near one another in Kentucky. Munition and Nitro in West Virginia got their names during World War I. Herpoco, CA, is an acronym for Hercules Powder Company.

Motorists entering Arizona may have their cars searched for illegal fruit; the official inspection station has been nicknamed Gripe.

Twentieth-century events and people are sometimes memorialized. In 1901 two Wyoming mountain climbers, reaching the top of a peak, celebrated by drinking a bottle of Pabst beer. That's how Pabst Mountain got its name. And in 1946 Phil D. Smith climbed another Wyoming mountain, which he modestly named Philsmith Peak. A well-liked Chinese consul in Seattle, named Goon Dip, died in 1936, and someone in Alaska remembered him in 1939 by naming Goon Dip Mountain for him.

One or another of the Roosevelts has frequently had places named for him, and in Colorado are some rocks called Teddys Teeth, probably because political cartoonists liked to feature TR's toothy grin. Hoover Dam, formerly Boulder Dam, was renamed in 1947 to honor the former president (and Democrats persist in calling an economic depression by his name). Other presidents have been honored in other places.

If we had, indeed, started afresh with naming in the twentieth century, names like those mentioned suggest the probable emphases—names taken from entertainment, science, war, industry, and both little-known and famous people.

Gone would be almost all our Native American names—gone Chicago, gone Massachusetts, gone Utah, gone many hundreds more. There would be no Washingtons, Franklins, Lincolns. Most French and Dutch names would probably be missing. Old names based on incidents, legends, or jokes might be replaced by names from newer happenings, imaginings, or humor.

A few of the idealistic and patriotic names might appear here and there. Assuming English as the language, maybe some Libertys, some Unions, a few Harmonys would still be here. Some places in the old world might again be remembered—perhaps London, Paris, Stockholm, Vienna, Canton.

There would still be many names describing the shape or general appearance of natural features, still names from the trees and flowers and animals found here. There could still be Great Lakes or something similar, still the Rocky Mountains. Some things last better than others.

Sources of Place Names

Unfold any state road map and you can see the names—
long and short—of once nationally prominent people and of other
people you've never heard of, pretty names and ugly names, names
of rivers and mountains, names from the Old World and from farther
east in the New, names that seem foreign, a few names that sound
funny, some that seem inexplicable. Who named all these places,
and what did they base their decisions on?

Naming practices varied somewhat from state to state, for historical reasons and especially because of differing patterns of immigration, but the 13 sources of place names described by Ronald
L. Baker and Marvin Carmony in *Indiana Place Names* are representative. The percentages attributable to each of the 13 are different
in other states, but the similarities are considerable. For instance,
in every state a high percentage of place names are derived from
people's names.

1. People's names. Eighty-five percent of Indiana's
county names, (for example, Adams, Kosciusko, Warren) are those
of people, usually "non-local people, especially military heroes."
Thirty-seven percent of the names of cities, towns, and villages are
also from people's names, although local people rather than national
figures are usually the ones thus honored—sometimes through use
of a Christian name or a nickname rather than a surname. Of Indiana streams and lakes, about 21 percent have people's names.

2. Names of other places. Eleven percent of Hoosier county names are for other places—sometimes far away (Switzerland, Orange), but more often local rivers or lakes (Ohio, Tip-
pecanoe, Lake). Twenty-eight percent of town names are from other
place names (Bunker Hill, Salem), with about half of those being
names of natural features (Lakeville).

3. Names indicating direction or position. Two
percent of settlement names (North Liberty, West Terre Haute) are
of this sort, and 4 percent of natural features (East Fork Tennessee
Creek).

4. Descriptive names. One county, La Porte 'the
door,' has a descriptive name, referring here to a natural forest open-
ing that was a good place for a trail or a road. Eight percent of

settlement names are descriptive (Badger Grove, Cloverdale, Edgewood, Quakertown, Pleasant Ridge); 20 percent of streams and lakes have descriptive names (Blue Lake, Butternut Creek, Buck Creek).

5. Inspirational names. This source includes idealistic, classical, literary, biblical or religious, and commendatory names—the last being most numerous. In all, 7 percent of Indiana settlement names fit these categories (Harmony, Mt. Olympus, Waverly, Palestine, Acme, Fairfield, Prosperity). Union is the only county and St. Joseph the only stream or lake classed as inspirational.

6. Native American and pseudo-Native American names. The eastern and southern parts of the nation have more Native American names than do the midwest and west. In Indiana only two counties owe their names to Native Americans, and fewer than 2 percent of settlements. However, 33 percent of Indiana stream and lake names are of Native American origin (Big Shawnee Creek, Iroquois River, Kickapoo Creek, Shipshewana Lake, etc.). As is true elsewhere, the Native American names are often distorted from what the Native Americans probably said: thus the village of Mongo seems once to have been Mon-go-quin-ong 'big squaw,' and Baugo Creek was Baubaugo 'devil river.'

7. Humorous names. "Hoosier namers apparently were a sober lot," the authors complain, and although they relate humorous anecdotes about places called Pinhook, Popcorn, and the like, they say that only one name, Santa Claus, "clearly reflects humorous motivations."

8. Names from languages other than English. New York has more Dutch names than Indiana has; Illinois, Louisiana, and several other states have more French names; and the southwest has far more Spanish names. Three Indiana counties (La Porte, which is also descriptive, and Fayette and La Grange) are French, and a few settlements are, too (Terre Haute, Vincennes). Only here and there can one find a trace of any other language, such as German Haubstadt, Greek Eureka, and Spanish Plano.

9. Incident names. Local happenings inspired no Indiana county names, and the names of only five settlements (including Battleground and Cyclone), and just three streams (creeks named Hurricane, Poison, and Treaty).

10. Folk etymology. People sometimes mishear or misinterpret an unfamiliar word, and then they pronounce it like a different, more familiar word—a process called folk etymology. Fewer than 1 percent of Indiana place names arose in this way. Examples include Koleen, which comes from kaolin, a kind of clay; Russiaville, which was actually named for a Miami Indian chief with the unlikely name of Richard; and Weasel Creek, from Wesaw, another Miami chief.

11. Coined names. Coinage also is responsible for fewer than 1 percent of Indiana names. Kyana and Michiana Shores blend parts of Kentucky and Michigan with parts of Indiana. Elwren uses parts of the names of four resident families: Eller, Whaley, Baker, and Breeden.

12. Mistake names. Again, fewer than 1 percent. Moores Mill was once the name of a town, but perhaps the second M looked like an H on the application for a post office. So for over a century the little town has been Moores Hill.

13. Legends and anecdotes. For about 40 Indiana names, Baker and Carmony supplied unverifiable anecdotes or legends to account for the origin—a little over 1 percent of the settlement names and a similar proportion for lakes and streams. Limberlost Creek and Limberlost Swamp, for instance, are said to owe their name to "Limber Jim" McDowell, who went bear hunting and was lost in a swamp for three days.

Ancient But Still Living

The ancient city of Troy, famed in the *Iliad* as the home of the Trojans who fought valiantly against the Greeks, has become mainly an archeological dig, but its name survives in Troy, NY, and 21 smaller towns from Maine to Texas.

There's only one Cincinnati, though; it recalls the Roman statesman and general who, after retiring to his farm in his old age, reputedly left his plow in the field and returned to his command when Roman forces were imperiled. Phoenix, best known now as Arizona's largest city, exists also in Maryland, New York, and Oregon and in Phoenixville, PA, Phenix, VA, and Phenix City, AL. The name keeps alive the Egyptian bird that burned itself each five hundred years and then magically was reincarnated from its own ashes.

Classical names, though not unknown in America's colonial days, increased in popularity after the Revolutionary War and continued to be chosen for well over a half-century more. Predictably, many of the named places never became large cities. Here is a sampling:

Arcadia (14 states; idyllically portrayed district of Greece)
Athena, OR (goddess of wisdom)
Athens (15 states; Greek city-state)
Aurora (16 states; goddess of dawn)
Calypso, NC (girlfriend of Odysseus for seven years while he allegedly rested during his travels)
Cato, NY, WI (noted Roman political family, orators)
Cicero, IN, NY, and Chicago suburb (Roman orator; in Indiana the town was named for Cicero Creek, so called because a boy named Cicero fell into it)
Delphi, IN; Delphi Falls, NY; Delphos, IA, KS, OH (oracle)
Elysian, MN; Elysian Falls, TX (heavenly fields)
Eros, LA (Cupid, symbol of romantic love)
Hesperia, CA, MI; Hesperus, CO (Venus as the evening star; also "the Western Land")
Ithaca, MI, NE, NY (Greek island home of Odysseus when he wasn't with Calypso or elsewhere)
Nestor, CA (wise old man in the *Iliad*)
Olympia, KY, WA; Olympia Fields, IL (Mount Olympus, home of the gods; in Kentucky an earlier Olympia Springs regressed to Mud Lick)
Rome (7 states and Rome City, IN; the great city of Italy)
Romulus, MI, NY (one of the legendary twins said to have founded Rome)
Scipio, IN; Scipio Center, NY (Roman statesman; the Indiana town was earlier called Philanthropy)
Seneca (11 states plus 4 combinations; Seneca Castle and Seneca Falls in New York, as well as some others, involve respelling Native American name to resemble the Roman dramatist's. In New Mexico something similar happened to the Spanish Cienaga.)

Place Names of Australia

Are most Australian places given native names or names carried over from the British Isles? John Algeo writing in *Names*, analyzed one thousand of the several thousand reported in A. W. Reed's *Place Names of Australia*. He found that words from the

Aborigine language and names of prominent Australians accounted for 57 percent of the total. His statistics, and an example of each type of name, are as follows:

1. Aboriginal (Canberra), 29%
2. Australian persons (Macquarrie River), 28%
3. British persons (Victoria), 8%
4. Other persons (Mount Kosciusko), 3%
5. Descriptive (Blue Mountain), 13%
6. British places (New South Wales), 8%
7. Other places (American River), 3%
8. Events (Attack Creek), 4%
9. Ships (Adventure Bay), 2%
10. Miscellaneous (Lochinvar), 1%

Royalty in American Place Names

In 1861, when they weren't thinking about their newly inaugurated President Lincoln or the start of the Civil War, many residents of Illinois were fascinated by a real princess who was in their midst. Her name was Princess Clotilde of Savoy. Many Illinoisans had never heard of Savoy, a French-speaking dukedom just south of Switzerland, but they learned that the father of the princess was none other than Victor Emmanuel II, who had a role in the unification of Italy and had just been crowned its king. Besides, the princess was married in 1859 to Napoleon Joseph Charles Paul Bonaparte, nephew of *the* Napoleon Bonaparte and himself known as Prince Napoleon.

To honor the princess, the good people of eastern Illinois decided to name a place for her. A village in Champaign County, adjoining what is now the University of Illinois airport, thus became Savoy.

On the surface it seems remarkable that so many places in a democratic country have names suggesting royalty, particularly when you consider that the American colonies had become independent by rebelling against a king. There are towns named King in North Carolina and Wisconsin, and one in Virginia called King and Queen Court House, named for King William and Queen Mary of England. About 60 other post office towns have King as the first word or first syllable.

But such facts are misleading, since the majority of American place names suggesting royalty are much less authentically so than is Savoy. Most of the places with kingly connotations (or queenly

or princely) are named for common people such as the Captain
King for whom Kings Peak, CA, was named or a one-time railroad
official whose name the people in Kingsley, IA, speak every day.
Kingfisher, OK, and Kingbee, AZ, are obviously not named for
throned monarchs, though the former *is* named for a person, King
Fisher.

The majority of the genuinely royal names are in the East or
Southeast and date back to Revolutionary days, when tact, loyalty,
or affection demanded some sort of obeisance to the royal family.
Seven state names come from royalty: Georgia, which did not change
its name even when the people rebelled against the son of George
II; North and South Carolina, for Charles II; Maryland for Henrietta
Maria, wife of Charles I; Virginia and its offspring West Virginia,
for the Virgin Queen, Elizabeth I; and Louisiana, for the French
King Louis XIV.

Some town names refer to specific kings, too, including King
George, VA, and King of Prussia, PA. Alfred, ME and NY, are
named for a much earlier English king, Alfred the Great. Charles-
town, MA, was so called to honor Charles I, and its namesake in
Rhode Island probably was named for his son Charles II.

Some foreign equivalents of *king* appear here and there. Del
Rey, CA, and the misspelled Delray, WV, and Delray Beach, FL,
are Spanish for 'of the king.' The French form *roi* appears as Roy
a couple of times and as Le Roy or Leroy in 11 post office names.
Most of those, however, are actually based on the surnames of com-
moners. Georgia and North Carolina have places named Rex, and
there's a Rex Lake in Wyoming.

The royal Stuart family name *appears* to be honored in some
places, but most of those are actually named for rather ordinary
American citizens, although Kings County, NY (which is Brooklyn),
does refer to the Stuart dynasty. The French Bourbon family is
probably remembered in Indiana and Missouri towns and a county
in Kentucky, as well as in Bourbonnais, IL, and a famous street in
New Orleans.

Some Oranges also have a royal heritage. Originally in southern
France, the House of Orange became the ruling family of The Neth-
erlands and provided the English with King William III. So Orange
County in New York, North Carolina, Vermont, and Virginia (but
not in California, Florida, and Texas, which celebrate the fruit) get

their name from that family, as do Orange, MA and CT, and Orangeburg, SC, and possibly the Oranges of New Jersey.

Pennsylvania has a Queen—a tiny village in Bedford County. Missouri and Texas have a Queen City, Arizona has a Queen Creek, and Maryland a Queenstown. One or another of England's Queen Annes is honored in Cape Ann, MA, and in the three Virginia rivers North Anna, Rivanna, and Southanna.

There are 18 post offices named Princeton, as well as one Prince, one Princeville, and one Princewick, but again most of those are for people who never saw a palace. There are, however, Prince Frederick, Prince Georges Facility, and Princess Anne, all in Maryland, and Prince George without a Facility in Virginia. Amelia, VA, commemorates the daughter of George II, and it is asserted that North Carolinians honor a crown prince of Russia, Alexis.

Among county names there are King, WA; Kings, CA; and Queens, NY; as well as Kings, and King and Queen, VA. Caroline, VA, honors Mrs. George II, but Caroline, MD, was the daughter of a mere lord, the fifth Lord Baltimore. Charlotte, VA, as well as Charlottesville, pay their respects to Charlotte Augusta, Princess of Wales. Another woman so honored in Virginia is Louisa, another daughter of George II. In Virginia and other states, various royal men are saluted, including Charles, William, Frederick, Edward, and George, and in Pennsylvania the Dauphin of France, son of Louis XVI.

There are a dozen places named Royal, Royalty, Royalton, Royal City, and the like. Of these the most interesting story lies behind Front Royal, VA. It used to be called Royal Oak because a kingly oak stood there and reminded folks of Bonny Prince Charlie's having once saved his life by hiding in such a tree. A colonial officer wanted his regiment to face the oak, but couldn't recall the correct command. So he ordered them to "front the royal." Townspeople were so amused that they began calling the place Front Royal. Or so the local legend has it.

It Happened Right Here: Names from Incidents

In the winter of 1873 to 1874, Alfred Packer and five companions were snowbound on a plateau of the Rocky Mountains in Colorado. Their food was soon gone, and the men were weakening. The remaining details are skimpy and not well authenticated, but according to local accounts Packer killed the other men and lived off their flesh until the winter was past. The place where that incident occurred has since been called Cannibal Plateau.

Ten years later, Packer was arrested in a canyon in Wyoming. Its name, as a result, is Man-Eater Canyon. But Packer's guilt, and therefore the accuracy of the two names, is still contested.

Several hundred American place names—certainly many more if very local names are counted—are derived from incidents, some unquestionable, others probably invented. Most of the incidents are relatively trivial: someone named Cicero fell into a creek and so the creek was named for him; a deer was seen and so a place was called Deer Lake or Buck Creek; a climber in Alaska in 1931 called the mountain Shivering Mountain because he was shivering from cold as he climbed, and similarly two other climbers of a small peak in Wyoming in 1959 called it Mount Quiver because the dangers they faced made them quiver. Some Nebraska cowboys ran out of supplies except for beans, and Bean Soup Lake remembers their temporary discomfort. Two flocks of sheep became hopelessly intermingled at Mixup Spring, OR. And so on.

However, other name-creating incidents are less hohum.

In a lake in New Mexico, a man's body was found floating, pierced by several arrows. He was identified as a man named Ambrosio, and so the lake was called in Spanish "the lake of the dead Ambrosio." But Ambrosio was soon confused with *ambrosia*, the food of the gods, alleged to impart immortality. Today the place is Lake Ambrosia, and in a way Ambrosio has immortality.

At what was afterward called Bloody Point, CA, Native Americans in 1852 killed 63 whites. But a creek in Nebraska got its name because a group of surveyors anticipated an attack that did not materialize, so they called it Bloody Creek as a joke.

Bones of prehistoric mastodons and mammoths were found at the salt deposits thereafter named Big Bone Lick, KY.

There was plenty of brandy aboard a schooner that went aground on an Oregon reef one nightfall in 1850. Making the best of their troubles, the passengers and crew spent the night carousing, but were still able to free the boat sometime later. The place was then called Brandy Bar. Jim Jam Ridge, CA, marks the location of a longer spree in 1890—one so bad that the three miners involved got the jimjams, an old slang term for *delirium tremens*. The number of pink elephants they saw was beyond counting.

Governor John Winthrop had only cheese for dinner on February 7, 1632, because his servant had been neglectful. He named the Maine spot where he had his unaccustomed light meal Cheese Rock.

A half dozen or more places are named Christmas because of big or small events that happened on that day. For example, at Christmas, FL, a military post was established on Christmas Day, 1837.

Conquest, NY, got its name because one faction defeated another in an attempt to create a new settlement. However, the names Union Ridge, NC, Union County, SC, and Union Grove, MN, all celebrate the uniting of formerly rivalrous church groups.

A creek in Wyoming was named Damfino because someone who asked a local what its name was, got the reply, "Damn if I know."

A cooperative postman in a little place in Texas reportedly liked to do favors for people, but thought he should be paid at least a token amount. He put up a box into which people could drop dimes to pay him for his trouble. The place is now known as Dime Box.

Disaster Peak in Nevada commemorates a group of prospectors attacked by Native Americans in 1856. In contrast, John Vancouver escaped an attack on an Alaskan point in 1793, and the name Escape celebrates his safety.

The gondola from a stratospheric explorer balloon landed in South Dakota in 1935. The landing place was afterward named Gondola Lake.

No one seems to know for sure who needed help in or near an Alaska creek. But the name Goshelpme suggests that someone must have been in trouble there. Helpmejack Creek in the same state also hints at some perilous occasion. But Oh-Be-Joyful Gulch, CO, proclaims a lucky strike. Nil Desperandum Gulch in Arkansas was apparently an erudite message of hope for someone who needed cheering up; it is Latin for 'Don't despair.'

In 1812 or 1813, Jack Storm's horse got mired in the mud of a little Indiana stream that flows into Beanblossom Creek. Jack had great difficulty in extricating himself and his mount. A sign, Jack's Defeat Creek, marks the spot at the edge of Ellettsville, where some natives may tell you a much-embroidered version of the story, complete with an exciting love affair and competing suitors.

In parts of South Dakota, the roads go uphill a short distance, then down, then up, and so on for miles and miles. In the 1840s a slang term for alternating ridges and depressions in a road was kiss-me-quicks—probably to suggest the need for a quick kiss before the next bump. Travelers in South Dakota at that time or perhaps later translated the term into a name, the Kiss-Me-Quick Hills.

A South Dakota cowboy who couldn't spell very well found a calf with characteristics of both sexes. He named the place Morphradite Creek, by which he meant 'hermaphrodite.'

The name Lovers Leap is attached to dozens of places, memorializing one or two lovers, oftentimes Native Americans, who in despair jumped from a high place to certain death. A touching, beautiful, romantic tale, but, says George R. Stewart, "No authentic story is recorded."

During the years of Queen Victoria's reign in England, many American women became linguistically squeamish. Tables and chairs, for instance, no longer had legs (a naughty word), but only limbs; and *bull* was a word that no lady would utter. So when in 1890 a young California woman was chased by a bull and had to take refuge on a large rock, the place was named not Bull Rock, but Man Cow Rock.

A geologist in Alaska in 1950 became greatly concerned when other members of his party did not show up when they were expected. After they came, he decided that the creek where he had awaited them should be called Panic Creek.

On June 1, 1778, James Cook displayed the British flag on a point in Alaska and "took possession for Great Britain." The point became Possession Point.

A party of explorers in Nevada in 1846 needed water badly. They finally found a spring by following rabbit trails, for rabbits know where to go when they're thirsty. They attached the name Rabbithole Spring.

We began with a gruesome incident of alleged cannibalism and will end with something no more pleasant. Once the Apache and Maricopa Indians fought a bloody battle in Arizona and left their dead behind them. Some of the skulls were found many years later by white Americans. They called the place Skull Valley. Then, in 1866, Native Americans and whites fought there, and the whites left behind the bodies of the Native Americans who had been killed. Thus the accuracy of the name Skull Valley was recertified. If you are so inclined, you can still visit the town, a few miles west of Prescott. (The skulls have been picked up.)

Bringing the Holy Land to America

John Leighly reported in 1979 an analysis of biblical place names that he found among 61,742 United States place names.

In all, there were 803 (1.3 percent) that were clearly biblical in origin—101 *different* names.

Salem, as Jerusalem was anciently called, was the top choice, with 95 namings. Salem, MA, was the first town in North America to be given a biblical name.

In colonial times, New England and Pennsylvania made more use of biblical names than did other colonies. Before the Revolutionary War, New England had already chosen 21 such namings (12 different names).

Areas that now have the greatest density of biblical place names, in addition to New England and southeastern Pennsylvania, are southeastern Ohio, northeastern South Carolina, and central and west central Georgia.

Here are the most common biblical place names in the United States, and the frequency of their occurrence, as counted in Leighly's research:

Salem (95)

Eden (61)

Bethel (47)

Lebanon (39)

Sharon (38)

Goshen (33)

Jordan (27)

Hebron (26)

Zion (24)

Antioch (18)

Paradise (18)

Shiloh (18)

Beulah (17)

Bethlehem (16)

Canaan (16)

Mount of Olives (various forms) (15)

Bethany (Bethania) (14)

Corinth (14)

Palestine (14)

Carmel (Mount Carmel) (13)

Smyrna (13)

Tabor (Mount Tabor, Taber) (12)

Leighly's figures demonstrate the relative popularity of each of these names, but the actual total for each must be much higher, since the research covered only 61,000 of the estimated several hundred thousand U.S. place names.

Biblical names often occur in combinations or somewhat altered forms. There are, for instance, three post offices named Mount Zion, in addition to Zion, AR and IL, Zion City, LA, Zionsville, IN and PA, Zionville, NC, Zion Grove, PA, Zion Hill, PA, and Zion National Park (CPO Springdale, UT). One of the oldest towns in Washington, settled in 1854 and close to what is now Sylvan Lake State Park, is Montesano. Some early settlers wanted to call it Mount Zion, but the majority wanted the different emphasis of the name that is similar in sound. Montesano means 'mount healthy.'

Bethalto, IL, combines *Bethel* with *alto* to give the meaning 'a higher Bethel,' so named because Illinois already had one Bethel.

Onomatists disagree about whether Manassa, CO, and Manassas, GA and VA (where a bloody Civil War battle was fought), are based on a Native American word or the biblical Manasseh, referring to individuals and a tribe. The place in Virginia was first spelled Manasseh's.

The Muslim holy city, Mecca, has two post office namesakes. The one in California is located in a desert. An Indiana church on a sandy hill in Parke County was nicknamed the Arabian Church, and its members were said to go to their Mecca each Sunday.

On Peculiar, Humptulips, and Other Oddities

Many apparently odd place names have more or less logical explanations. But now and then, the reason for a name has fallen through a crack in history.

Anaconda, MT An anaconda is a large, nonvenomous snake that wraps itself around its prey and squeezes it to death. Late in the Civil War, word reached Copperopolis, MT, that General Grant's forces were encircling General Lee's troops "like an anaconda." The news pleased the owners of the local copper mine so much that they changed its name to Anaconda, and the town later agreed that it should adopt the name of its largest industry.

Auto, WV Janssen and Fernbach say, "Name may have originated in the early days of the automobile when the level roads here were used to test the speed of those new-fangled cars."

Bicknell and Blanding, UT In 1914 a Utahan named T. C. Bicknell offered to start a library in any town in his state that would become Bicknell. Because two places agreed, he named one Bicknell and the other Blanding, his wife's maiden name.

Bushong and Latham, KS Even the most historically minded baseball fan is unlikely to have heard of St. Louis Browns players named Arlie Latham (shortstop) and Doc Bushong (pitcher). But on the map of Kansas these men are remembered. Why Kansas? Because in the 1880s workers for the Missouri Pacific railroad were building a line across Kansas and, to celebrate the then-often-victorious Browns, they named 14 Kansas stations for players. Apparently only Latham and Bushong haven't struck out. In a sense, they're in the Hall of Fame.

Cando, ND In a legal battle of 1884, one of the participants said, "We're not powerless. To show what we can do, we'll name the county seat Cando."

Cheapside, TX In southeastern Texas. The name is for the principal marketplace of old London, England. In Old English, *ceap*, the ancestor of *cheap*, meant 'barter, buying and selling, price, merchandise, stock, or cattle,' not necessarily 'low cost.' In Cheapside, *side* referred to the south part of the district. So a place called *Cheapside* is the south part of an area devoted mainly to buying and selling—both low-priced and expensive items. Cheapside, TX, which has ten post office box customers, has apparently not become a thriving marketplace.

Crackertown, FL Hoosiers who in 1920 moved to Florida and built houses and a fishing camp on the Gulf coast wanted to call the place Knotts—the name of some of them—but earlier settlers derisively called it Yankeetown. In 1925 the Hoosiers chose that as the official name. They also laid out a subdivision in honor (?) of the earlier residents. They called it Crackertown.

Dixie, WA In a village in Washington the Kershaw brothers, a musical trio, gained a measure of fame by their enthusiastic rendition of their favorite tune, "Dixie." They often played for visitors and were invited to perform in other communities. People called them the Dixie Boys, and their home became known as Dixie Crossing, shortened to Dixie.

Eighty Eight, KY Postmaster Dabney Nunnally's handwriting was poor. His village was 8.8 miles from Glasgow. "Let's call our place Eighty Eight," he proposed, "but spell it 88. I can write that so anybody can read it." But the Post Office Department ruled that figures can't be names and insisted on Eighty Eight (which didn't help poor Mr. Nunnally).

Eltopia, WA Railroad workers in southern Washington, after heavy rains caused washouts and long construction delays, said that the place should be called Hell-to-Pay. The residents disliked that idea, but modified the name to the pleasant sounding Eltopia—the only one in the United States.

Farwell, NE Farwell was earlier called Posen for the Polish city from which many of the first settlers came. After Danes moved in, they put through a petition to change the name to Farwell, a variant of the English *farewell* and its Danish equivalent. The implication was "Goodbye, Posen!" (Later the population again became mainly Polish, but the name was never changed back.)

Felicity, OH Named for founder William Fee. Felicity, first spelled Feelicity, sounded much less forbidding than Fee City would have.

Humptulips, WA No connection with humps or tulips. It's an adaptation of a Native American word alternatively defined as 'hard to pole' (referring to the river) and 'chilly place.'

Itasca, MN Scholarly H. R. Schoolcraft discovered the lake and declared it the "true head" of the Mississippi river. He borrowed *Itas* from Latin *veritas* 'truth' and *ca* from *caput* 'head.'

Joliet, IL A township and village in northeastern Illinois were named Juliet for Juliet Campbell, pretty daughter of the founder. But another woman, Harriet Martineau, an English writer who traveled in America, cheated Juliet out of her heritage. She recommended that the place be renamed to honor French explorer Louis Jolliet, who had visited the area in 1673. The residents agreed with the popular and influential writer, but chopped out an *l* from

Jolliet's name, and Juliet thus became Joliet, now an industrial city of about 100,000.

Lejunior, KY For Lee Bowling, Jr., son of a coal mine owner.

Liberal, KS During a drouth in 1886, water was so scarce that many people charged for it, but the postmaster here was "liberal" with water, giving it to all comers.

Loop, TX The postmaster-designate was playing with the loop of his lasso while trying to think of a good name.

Lufkin, TX When E. P. Lufkin, a surveyor, was planning a railroad route, some railroad workers were jailed in Homer for drunkenness. In retaliation, Lufkin changed the route to miss Homer. The newly located station was named for him. (Kelsie Harder says that Lufkin flourished, "while Homer died.")

Mad River, CA The river isn't mad, but an early explorer, Josiah Gregg, became extremely angry about some occurrence on its banks.

Maytown, PA On May Day, 1762, settlers danced in the "streets" that had just been staked out.

Mystic and Old Mystic, CT These places took their names, not from anything mysterious or mystical, but from the tidal river there. The name comes from Algonquian, not Latin or Greek. Georgia and Iowa borrowed the name from Connecticut.

Owyhee, NV Named for Hawaii. Isn't that obvious? (The same spelling is used for a county in Idaho and a river in Oregon.)

Pe Ell, WA Pierre Charles, a Hudson Bay Company employee, was well known to the Native Americans. They could not say Pierre, but called him Pe ell.

Peculiar and Protem, MO Robert Ramsey explains (tongue in cheek) these and two other names: "One harried postmaster was instructed [by the Post Office Department] that he must find a name that was peculiar; another that he must select a name that would avert confusion; another that he could use any name protem until he had made up his mind; and still another that the number of names he had already sent in was enough. In humble obedience to these instructions, the names of these four towns have become **Peculiar, Avert, Protem,** and **Enough.**" (Avert and Enough no longer have post offices.)

Penn Yan, NY Pennsylvania and New England settlers both wanted a name representing their old homes. They compromised on Penn for Pennsylvania and Yan for Yankee.

Pillager, MN Ojibway Indians here in 1767 or 1768 stole the goods of a trader named Berti, and he denounced them as "pillagers." The word was unfamiliar to many other whites, but they began using it and applying it to this village, a creek, and the Ojibway.

Qulin, MO The only post office name in the United States in which *Qu* is not followed immediately by a vowel. Ramsey says, "we have no solution at all." (Only one name starts with *Quo*: Quogue, NY. That's an improvement over its earlier name, Quaquanantuck.)

Ravenna, OH An Ohio landowner admired the Italian Ravenna so much that he took the name for the town where he lived. But people in Nebraska went further in Italolatry: their Ravenna (earlier Beaver Creek) has streets with such names as Genoa, Verona, Seneca, Padua, Pavia, Alba, Sicily, and Milan. It had an Appian Way, but for some unknown reason that was changed to Grand Avenue. Michigan also has a Ravenna, as does Texas, but the latter is a poor pun based on the fact that the town lies between two ravines. New York modifies the spelling to Ravena.

Show Low, AZ Two partners, unable to get along, played seven-up to determine who should stay and who should go away. In the deciding hand, one of them won because he could "show low" (win without playing, by showing the lowest card).

Titusville, FL Residents of Titusville say that Henry Titus and Charles Rice in 1873 played a friendly game of dominoes to determine whose name should be chosen for the town. Obviously Titus won.

True, WV The local explanation of the name is that when the village applied for a post office the application ended, "All these facts are true." Someone in the Post Office Department may have been sleepy or perhaps had a sense of humor, choosing the final word as the name.

Vandalia, IL Vandalia, the one-time capital of Illinois, where both Abraham Lincoln and his rival Stephen A. Douglas practiced law, took its name from the savage ancient Germanic tribe called Vandals (from which *vandalism* and *vandalize* also come). Some onomatists believe that uneducated early settlers thought the Vandals were a famous Native American tribe. The pretty *ia* ending they added may have softened the blow when they realized that the Vandals, among other depredations, sacked the city of Rome. Vandalia, Mississippi, Missouri, Montana, and Ohio shared the belief that the name is attractive, regardless of who the Vandals were.

Watersmeet, MI In northwestern Michigan, rain that falls in different spots close to Watersmeet may flow into Lake Michigan, Lake Superior, or the Mississippi River. Perhaps a more accurate name for the place would be Watersdivide or Watersplit.

The Only *Virgin*

Virgin, UT, is the only Virgin in the United States that has a post office.

There is, however, a Virginville in Pennsylvania. Also, a western river, originally called Virgen by Spaniards, is now spelled Virgin.

Las Virgenes Creek, CA, is probably a religious name derived from a story about Saint Ursula and her 11,000 virgins who reportedly made a pilgrimage to Rome in the fourth century, but were slaughtered by Huns as they were returning to England. The Virgin Islands take their name from the same story; they were earlier called Santa Ursula y las Once Mil Virgenes. The Ursuline nuns, who devote themselves to the education of girls, are named for this Saint Ursula, whose feast day is October 21. Unfortunately, the details of the story about the pilgrimage have not been proved true, and Ursula is no longer sanctified.

Most geographical features called Virgin are named after families, but a few others may refer to unspoiled nature or to the Virgin Mary. Virginville, PA, is said to be a translation of Native American words.

Those Charming Kentucky Names

No one can say which state has the most interestingly named towns and villages, but Kentucky is certainly in the running.

Just in the small area south of Paducah are Moscow, Dublin, and Cuba; Bandana, Ragland, and Lovelaceville; Water Valley, Cold Water, and Spring Hill; Oak Level and Pilotoak; Camelia; Crossland, Sharp, and Wolf; Fairdealing; and State Line, where Kentucky and Tennessee come together.

The rest of the state does equally well. If you're patriotic, Kentucky has a Banner for you. If you enjoy old-fashioned songs, there's Bardstown.

Kentucky is a state of trees: Magnolia, Elmrock, Locust Hill, Maple Mount, Poplarville, PawPaw, and Willow Shade, among others. And of course since it's the Blue Grass State, it has Blue Grass.

Animal lovers find not only Wolf but also Beaver and Beaver Dam, Bruin and Cub Run, Buffalo, four places with Elk in their names, Fox Town and Red Fox, Horse Cave and Horse Branch, Raccoon, and Wild Cat.

Map enthusiasts and tourists can feast on many other Kentucky names, including Goose Rock and Fancy Fare, Quality and Beauty.

More Than One Bard in Bardstown

Visitors sometimes mistakenly suppose that Bardstown, KY, was named for that great American bard, Stephen Collins Foster, who is now one of the town's important industries. That supposition attracts thousands of tourists annually.

Actually, a family named Bard (some of whom spelled it Baird or Beard) are the eponyms. When Kentucky was still part of Virginia, Governor Patrick Henry of Virginia gave one of the Bards a thousand-acre tract in what later became the Bardstown, KY, area.

Many *Bottoms*

Ramsbottom, once a not uncommon name, is now seldom heard or seen—not at all in Chicago, for example, and in only one instance in Manhattan. No doubt both the personal and the place name were almost laughed out of existence through ignorance.

The *rams* in the name are not sheep, but wild garlic plants that grow in some moist places. They used to be called *ramps,* and still are in parts of England and the American South. As for *bottom* (sometimes spelled *botham*), it is a word for low-lying land, often close to a stream, and is still called "bottomland" or "the bottoms" in many places.

Ramsbottom, then, means simply 'low land where wild garlic grows.'

Similarly, Bottom(s) is 'low land,' Sydebotham 'wide valley,' Longbottom 'long valley,' Higginbotham 'Richard's valley' (Higgins being a nickname for Richard), and Winterbottom 'valley into which sheep were driven for protection against wintry weather.' The ancestors of Jim Bottomley (once a superb first baseman for the St. Louis Cardinals) lived in a valley grove or valley meadow.

American telephone directories show many other names that refer to valleys or other low land. Here are a few of them, some of which may have unrelated secondary meanings:

English: Clough, Combs, Dale, Dean, Dell, Hellman(n), Hope (may
   also refer to high ground), Pittman, Pitts, Slade, Vail, Vale, Valley
Irish: Corey, Cor(r)y
Irish or Scottish: Cowan or Cowen (may also be a smith, or a
   descendant of Colquhoun, or if Jewish a respelling of Cohen)
Welsh: Glenn, Glynn
French: Deveaux, Duval, Valle, Lavalle, Laval
German: Dobler, Grund(mann), words ending in *-tal*
Italian: Serra, Serritella
Portuguese: Vale
Spanish: Valle

Many *Minne's*

Minne is the way we spell a Sioux word for 'water.' Blended with Greek *-polis* for 'city,' it gave us Minneapolis, although that name was suggested in part by Minnehaha, which means 'water falls' and not 'laughing waters,' as Longfellow asserted in *Hiawatha.* (Minnehaha Falls, by the way, is redundant, because it means 'water falls falls.')

Minnesota is 'water cloudy' rather than the wishfully invented 'land of the sky-blue waters.' The state has other *Minne's,* too, including Minneota 'much water,' Minneola (with the same meaning), Minnesota City, Minnesota Lake, Minnetonka Beach and Lake Minnetonka 'water big,' Minneopa 'water falling twice,' Minneiska 'water white,' Minnetrista (in which *trista* may come from English *twist,* so that the name means 'crooked water'), and Minne-washka(t)a 'water good,' which is simplified in New York to Min-newaska.

Other states share *Minne,* although Minneola, KS, and Mine-ola, TX, commemorate girls named Minnie and Ola. North Dakota has Minnewaukan 'water spirit bad,' and its sister state to the south has the Minnechadusa 'water swift' River and Minnesela 'water red' Creek, now translated to Redwater Creek; the spelling of Minnie-sechi 'water bad' Creek adds an *i.* In New Hampshire is the Min-newawa River, an Algonquian name that perhaps means 'many waters.' Minnequa, PA, may mean 'to drink.' Minnehaha Springs, WV, was named for the Native American girl in *Hiawatha.*

The Coldest-Sounding Names

The most amusing frigid name didn't start out to be funny. It's for a New Jersey creek called Shiver-de-Freeze. During the Revolutionary War, poles were driven at angles in the Delaware River to obstruct boats, in a crisscross form known by the French name *cheval-de-frise.* By folk etymology, this later became Shiver-de-Freeze and was applied to the creek.

A more legitimate use of *shiver* is Shivering Mountain, AK. Alaska also has, unsurprisingly, a Snowcap Mountain and an Icy Cape. Ice appears as three Ice Mountains in West Virginia, although one of those was named for a man rather than for congealed water. Colorado has an Ice Lake, Washington an Iceberg Point, and both Montana and California boast an unlikely Iceberg Lake.

There's a Snow Hill as far south as North Carolina, and a slightly misplaced Polar in Wisconsin. Idaho understates its winter temperatures with Chilly and Chilly Buttes (which some locals in-tentionally mispronounce as Chilly Butts), but also has a more realistic Blizzard Mountain. Michigan has Coldwater; Virginia, a Cold Harbor; and California both a Cold Mountain and a nearby Cold Canyon. Frio County, TX, uses the Spanish word for 'cold.'

Freezeout, AZ, and Freezeout Creek, CO, both recall incidents when the temperature was far below comfort. Two South Dakota creeks are called Frozen Man because someone froze to death beside each, and at Frozen Run, WV, a man saved his life by wrapping himself in the skin of a recently killed buffalo; even so, his friends had to thaw it to get him out.

Most places called Winter(s) are named for people, and a few, such as Winterhaven, FL, suggest refuge from the cold. However, explorer John Frémont gave Winter Ridge, OR, its name because it seemed so much colder than nearby Summer Lake.

California is usually thought of as a warm state, but it once held and perhaps still holds the championship for a cold-sounding name. Siberian Outpost, in Sequoia National Park, was given that name in the winter of 1895 because to the park developers the area seemed excessively cold and unpleasant. Now it's just called Siberia.

Local Legends about Hoosier Names

Probably Noblesville, IN, is named for the first U.S. senator from the state. But locals prefer a more romantic origin. A village founder, James Polk (*not* the future president), was engaged to Kathleen Noble, a city woman from nearby Indianapolis, and he loved her so much that he spelled out her name with long rows of vegetables in his garden. But she was insulted and broke off their engagement. "Flowers yes, but not radishes and cabbage!" she may have said. However, so many village folk saw the display that they chose Noble (with *sville* added) as the name for their little community.

A town in eastern Indiana is now called Redkey for a former resident. It started out as Half Way and then was platted as Mt. Vernon. A boarding house made some nicknames popular for years, even though they never became official. The meals served there to the sawmill workers were said to be both skimpy and much less than tasty. The boarders referred to the little town as Lick Skillet and Grab All because there was never enough food for hungry workmen, and Buzzards' Roost because allegedly the food was fit only for buzzards.

It's not easy to come up with a pronounceable town name that sounds unlike any other in the country, but it is said that the residents of Poneto, IN, chose the name for that reason. Now, though, we find similar sounding names in Bonita, CA and LA, as well as Bonita Springs, FL, and Pantego, NC.

Backward Places

Only a few post office names that are backward spellings now exist. Remlap, AL, and Reklaw, TX, are examples. In general, whatever the reason, most "backward" places never amount to much. Mapmakers are unlikely to find it necessary to include Yewed, OK (for Spanish-American War Admiral George Dewey), Yesmar, AL, or a trio of places in Florida: Nolem, Ekal, and Senyah.

One of the most interesting reversals isn't precisely a reversal. Father Pierre DeSmet, a Jesuit missionary, is more or less remembered in the name Tensed, ID. Residents wanted to name their village Desmet in his memory, but another place in the northwest corner of the state had beaten them to it. So they reversed the name to Temsed. Somebody in the Post Office Department may have let his pen slip or may have thought Temsed too hard to pronounce, and put the name down as Tensed. The other Desmet still exists, so Idaho honors the missionary with two post office names.

For a Beloved Poet

Although now unfashionable, in much of the nineteenth century and the first part of the twentieth, Henry Wadsworth Longfellow was America's most loved poet. Children learned, willingly or not, some of his shorter poems; McGuffey included much of the poet's work in the readers from which America learned not only reading but also morality; and a dramatized form of *Hiawatha* was performed in countless schools. Givers of names borrowed liberally from him, especially from *The Song of Hiawatha*, often referred to as a "noble epic" and compared to the Finnish *Kalevala*.

Many of these names belonged to villages no longer on maps, but some still endure as post office towns: Hiawatha, IA, KS, UT, WV; Nokomis (Hiawatha's grandmother), FL, IL; Minnehaha Springs, WV; Onawa, IA; Onaway, MI (Longfellow said that in Ojibway (Chippewa) it meant 'Awaken!').

In Minnesota the names are most abundant, with Hiawathan names of lakes, parks, streets, avenues (even a Bowdoin Avenue in Hiawatha Park because the poet graduated from that college), as well as post office towns based on Longfellow's versions of Ojibway words: Bena 'partridge or pheasant' ("Heard the pheasant, Bena, drumming"); Keewatin 'north wind'; Mahnomen 'wild rice'; Osseo (called "Son of the Evening Star"; also in Michigan and Wisconsin); Ponemah 'Land of the Hereafter'; Wabasso 'rabbit'; Waubun 'east, dawn, morning.'

Longfellow's "Excelsior" 'higher' inspired many Americans to aspire to higher things; Minnesotans and Pennsylvanians borrowed the title as a town name, and Missourians called a place Excelsior Springs. Minnesota, Missouri, and Pennsylvania also chose Revere for towns, but the name might not have been familiar had not Longfellow written about Paul's ride. Evangeline is memorialized in Louisiana, but not elsewhere.

Minneapolis, of course, has a Longfellow Street and a Longfellow Avenue. The latter, appropriately, is 50 blocks long.

Tributes to Sir Walter and His Ilk

The poems and novels of Sir Walter Scott were more popular in the Unites States in the nineteenth century than those of any other foreign author. The following post office towns bear Scott-influenced names, although sometimes the naming reflects additional influences. Montrose, for instance, carries a connotation of mountains and roses, and in Pennsylvania the founder of the town was Robert Rose.

Ivanhoe, CA, MN, NC, TX, VA (Novel)
Kenilworth, IL, NJ (Novel; also a castle and an English town)
Melrose (in 10 states) (Town and abbey; a name used in *The Lay of the Last Minstrel*)
Montrose (in 15 states) (In the title *The Legend of Montrose*)
Midlothian, IL, MO, TX, VA (County in Scotland; in the title *The Heart of Midlothian*)
Waverly (in 18 states) (Scott's novel is *Waverley*, but the Post Office Department discourages unneeded letters. In Waverly, NE, streets also have names from Scott.)

Other town names with literary origins (and sometimes collateral influences) include these:

Afton (in 10 states) (The Scottish river immortalized in Robert Burns's song "Flow Gently, Sweet Afton")
Arden, NY, NC (Shakespeare's Forest of Arden, in *As You Like It*)
Ben Hur, VA (Lew Wallace's novel; the town was named by a friend of the author)
Bronte, TX (For novelist Charlotte Bronte, author of *Jane Eyre*)

Dante, SD, VA (Italian poet; people who don't like South Dakota say
   the association is with Hell)
Freeport (in 10 states) (Usually for a port that welcomes everyone, but
   in Florida probably for Sir Andrew Freeport, a character in a Joseph
   Addison play. Kelsie Harder says that Freeport, IL, was named by the
   first settler's wife, disgusted because her husband was so hospitable
   that he kept a "free port," inviting all comers to be their guests.)
Hawthorne, CA, FL, NV, NY, WI (Sometimes, as in California, for
   Nathaniel Hawthorne)
Kipling, NC, OH (Rudyard Kipling was popular in America from the
   1890s on.)
Medora, IL, IN, KS, ND (Sometimes for the tragic heroine in Lord
   Byron's long poem "The Corsair")
Orinda, CA (Seventeenth-century English poet Katherine Phillips was
   called "the matchless Orinda.")
Orlando, FL (Sometimes said to be for a character in Shakespeare's *As
   You Like It*, it also has a Rosalind Street. Others claim it is for
   Orlando Reeves, killed by Native Americans in 1835.)
Othello, WA (Shakespeare)
Pippa Passes, KY (Delightful poem by Robert Browning about a little
   girl who does good without being aware of it. "God's in His Heaven.
   All's right with the world.")
Poe, WV (The postmaster (c. 1900) was devoted to Poe's works.)
Ruskin, FL (For John Ruskin; said by Bloodworth and Morris to be
   "the only literary man after whom a Florida place was named")
Tennyson, IN, TX (For the poet Alfred, Lord Tennyson)

Too Little Music

A superficial glance through lists of place names suggests
that a fair number of them are related to music:

Alto (towns in five states)
Bass, AR
Bow, KY, WA; Bow Creek, AK, NE
Drum, KY; Drums, PA; Drum Bridge, CA; Mt. Drum, AK
Fiddletown, CA; Fiddle Creek, OR; Fiddlers Creek, NE
Fife (towns in three states)
Fluteville, CT; Fluted Rock, AZ
Horner, WV; Hornersville, MO
Organ, NM; Organ Cave, WV; Organ Mountains, NM; Organ Pipe
   Cactus National Monument, AZ
Singer, LA; Singers Glen, VA; Singing Mountain, NV
Solo, MO
Triangle (towns in three states)
Trio, SC

Tuba City, AZ
Viola (towns in nine states)

But not all is as it seems. Tuba City, it turns out, was named for a Native American chief; Viola is from the girl's name; Alto is a Spanish word for 'high.' Bow and Solo and Trio and Fluted are not applied here with reference to music; Triangle is a mathematical figure rather than a percussion instrument; Bass can be either a fish or a person; and Drum, Horner, and Singer are from surnames of early settlers. Fife is for a county in Scotland.

Fiddle does a little better. Fiddletown and probably Fiddlers Creek got their names from the numbers of fiddlers who once lived there, and Fiddle Creek is said to commemorate an injured man who played while recuperating. Drum Bridge has pillars with ends resembling drums. Fluteville was once a center for flutemaking. The names with Organ all apparently relate to rock formations that look like organ pipes. Singing Mountain is a dune where wind-driven sand sometimes makes the sound of weird singing.

Those are slim pickings, however, and hardly impressive to the musically minded. Where are the Pianos, the Violins, the Cellos? (Monticello doesn't count; the word is Italian for 'little mountain.') Where are the Piccolos, the Oboes, the Bassoons, the Timpani? There's not a Cornet or a Trumpet, and of course not a Clarinet, a Saxophone, or a Sousaphone. Nor a Guitar and, surprisingly, not a Banjo. Where can one find a Symphony, a Concerto, a Fugue? There's not even a Waltz or a Polka among our thousands of towns and cities.

More important, what places are named for musical performers or composers? Here and there a street perhaps, such as Presley Boulevard in Memphis or Mozart Street in Chicago. Why in our town names do we almost exclusively honor military men, early settlers, and politicians? Have they contributed more to civilization than Beethoven, Brahms, and Chopin, or even than Gershwin or Charles Ives?

A small consolation: The name of Ladora, IA, is a music teacher's coinage based on the scale notes *la, do,* and *re.*

Musicians join other prominent people in being neglected by those who choose names. True, some literary figures and their works are remembered: John Greenleaf Whittier in California, and Walt Whitman has a bridge. But what painters are memorialized? What architects except in their own buildings? Outside the arts, what scientists are found on maps? What great teachers? What doctors and medical researchers? People who save thousands of lives—Jonas Salk, for instance—deserve to have their names on a few maps, right next to the now-missing Beethoven and Orchestra and the omnipresent business people and politicians.

❦ 18
Whimsy and Humor

We Laughed All the Way to Cucamonga

"Mention chickens and people laugh. Substitute hens in the same joke and die. Kokomo is funny; Muncie, 55 miles away, isn't. Brooklyn and the Bronx get laughs; Manhattan draws a respectful silence. Pickles are funnier than relish, and a porcupine is funny but a wolverine, with the same rhythm, isn't."

So says Jack C. Horn in a brief filler in *Psychology Today*. Comedians Mel Brooks and Buddy Hackett (each of whom coincidentally has a *k* in his name) once told talk-show host David Susskind that the *k* sound is the greatest laugh-getter. Podunk (the name of small but real places in New York, Connecticut, and Maine) is a favorite among comics. Hackett and Brooks also might have mentioned Keokuk and Kankakee, which get their share of yucks. If the little old lady from Dubuque had been from Davenport or Dyersburg, we probably would never have heard of her. Kalamazoo also stretches the risible muscles. Comedians haven't yet done much with Kaskaskia, IL, and too few people have ever heard of Keosauqua, IA.

Other comedians say *p* also can cause laughter. Podunk starts with it, and Peoria sounds much funnier than nearby Springfield. Poughkeepsie, like Podunk, has the hilarious good fortune to have both *k* and *p*—two *p*'s, in fact. Pago Pago (pronounced like pong-go pongo-go) often is taken lightly. Pippa Passes, KY, named by a teacher familiar with Robert Browning's poem of that name, seems

205

funniest to people who have never read Browning. Punxutawney, PA, is famous for its watchful groundhog, but is blessed by the *p* and *k* sounds in its name. Has any Johnstown groundhog ever become so widely known? All the publicity that Johnstown ever got was for a flood.

Little or nothing has ever been written about the funniest vowel. The "long *u*" or "oo" sound is hereby nominated. It helps to make poodle jokes funnier than German shepherd jokes (if there are any), and it assists the *k*'s in Dubuque and Kalamazoo.

On the old Jack Benny shows, a train announcer proclaimed a departure for "Anaheim, Azusa, and Cucamonga," a combination put together by a comic genius. It starts with the bland Anaheim, builds to a drawn-out "oo" in Azusa, and climaxes with the two *k* sounds surrounding the even more elongated "oo" in Cucamonga. The unimportant last syllables give the audience time to laugh.

How Do You Pronounce *Hawaii?*

On their flight to Honolulu, a man and wife argued about how to pronounce *Hawaii*. She opted for a *w* sound, he for a *v*. They agreed to ask the first person they met after they left the plane.

They approached a man wearing a lei over his flowery shirt. "Excuse me, sir. How do you pronounce the name of this state?" "It's Ha va ee. But I vasn't avare of that till Vensday, ven vee arrifed." (The standard pronunciation is with a "w.")

Whimsy in Place Names

Although most places are solemnly named by serious-minded people, some seem to have arisen because the namer had tongue firmly planted in cheek.

Surveyors in Maryland in 1774 made a mistake, marking off some land "by accident." So, someone must have said, why not immortalize the error? The town named Accident is still on the map. Mistake Peak, AZ, and Mistaken Creek, KY, commemorate other goofs. They were confused with a different peak and a different stream.

Once there was an Elk Cove Canyon, CA, but no elk have been seen there for years. In the oral language, Elk Cove sounds like Alcove, although the canyon has not many more alcoves than it has elk. So Alcove it became.

Where should Aloha be? In Hawaii, of course. But when the song "Aloha Oe" (farewell to thee) swept into national popularity after Queen Liliuokalani composed it in 1898, at least three places—in Louisiana, Oregon, and Washington—decided that Aloha should be their name.

Was Bayou des Amoureaux (the amorous ones) named for a pair of lovers, star-crossed or otherwise, or as George R. Stewart says, "Probably for des muriers 'of the mulberry trees' "? We can't be sure, but maybe it was the latter and then—maybe—someone noted the similarity of pronunciation and changed the name to the more romantic term.

Whimsy crosses the centuries. A Spanish explorer, Viscamo, discovered a previously unknown point on the California coast. The time was the start of a new year, January 1603. So he called the point Ano Nuevo (new year).

Another explorer, the British Sir John Franklin, was afraid that he and his men would be prevented by bad weather from reaching a point on the Alaskan coast. They did reach it (in 1826), and he commemorated his worry by calling the place Anxiety Point.

"This soil is so sandy it looks like the Sahara," an early Nebraska settler complained. "At least somewhere in Arabia," his neighbor agreed. So they called the place Arabia.

Aromatic Creek in Texas may once have been called Stinking Creek, but who would want to live near such a place? A creek by any other name would smell more sweet.

There's a little place in central Texas called Art (not far from Grit). Ask a resident how the town got its name and you may be told, "Well, it's not for Arthur or Artesian, and far as I know people here weren't ever especially arty. We've heard they picked it just because they wanted a real short name."

There's a Babel River in Alaska, named in 1956 by the author of *Dictionary of Alaska Place Names*, D. J. Orth. He chose that name "because of the 'confusion of tongues' (see Genesis 11:7) among authorities with respect to the name of this stream."

That's a good place to stop these examples of whimsy, even though we're only at the beginning of the B's. Readers of Stewart's *American Place-Names*, on which these explanations are loosely based, can find and label dozens more in that fascinating book.

"Very Like a Whale"

Hamlet: Do you see that cloud that's almost in shape like a camel?
Polonius: By the mass, and it's like a camel, indeed.
Hamlet: Methinks it is like a weasel.
Polonius: It is back'd like a weasel.
Hamlet: Or like a whale?
Polonius: Very like a whale.

Rock formations, particularly in the American West, are often named for real or fancied resemblance to something else. Guides in hilly or mountainous areas may cause tourists to ooh and ahh by pointing out faces or perching eagles or grieving Native American maidens or unicorns, all in stone. Nathaniel Hawthorne entitled one of his best short stories "The Great Stone Face," after an actual formation in the White Mountains of New Hampshire. "There was the broad arch of the forehead, a hundred feet in height, the nose with its long bridge, and the vast lips, which, if they could have spoken, would have rolled their thunder accents from one end of the valley to the other."

Here are some of America's place names for which geological quirks, slow erosion by wind and water, or the relentless movements of glaciers have been responsible.

AB Mountains, AK: when the snow melts you can read the two letters
The Alligator, AZ: a long, low ridge
Angel Terrace, WY: a white peak, especially beautiful in sunlight
Angleworm Lake, MI: long, narrow, and crooked
Anvil Rock, WA, WV
Bell Rock, AZ
Belt Mountains, MT: beltlike white rock goes around a butte
Bird Rock, CA
Biscuit Mountain, AZ
Book Cliffs, UT: resembling a set of books on a shelf
Boot Pack, AZ, several Boot Lakes, and other bootlike shapes
Bosom, WY: two peaks
Bottle Pinnacle, WY
Box Butte, NE
Bread Loaf Mountain, VT
Breast Mountain, AK
The Brothers and the Sisters, CA: two rocks on each side of a channel
Buddha Temple, AZ: one of many "Temples," "Pyramids," "Towers,"
     etc., in the Grand Canyon
Camelback Mountain, AZ
Charlies Bunion, NC: a comparatively small hill or mountain. Also
     Ropers Bunion, OR

Chetlo, OR: Chinook for 'oyster,' from the shape of this lake
Chickenbone Lake, MI: wishbone shape
Chimney Rock, NE: one of many chimney-shaped formations in various
    states
Chinese Wall, WY: long, wall-like formation
Churn Creek, CA: long, churn-shaped pothole in a rock
Cockscomb Crest, Cockscomb Peak, CA: sawtooth ridge on top
Corkscrew Peak, CA: curving layers of rock
Courthouse Rock, NE: a landmark for covered-wagon travelers
Cowhorn Mountain, OR: two pinnacles
Cross Mountain, AZ
Demijohn Mountain, CO
Mount Derby, CO: hat shape
Dumpling, MA
Eagletail Mountains, AZ: oddly shaped, like tailfeathers
Einanuhto Hills, AK: an Aleut word for 'three breasts'
Elephants Playground, CA: large boulders lying in a meadow
Face Rock, OR
Fishtail Canyon, AZ: upper end veed like a fishtail
Fluted Rock, AZ: looks like organ pipes
Fryingpan Lake, OR
Gooseneck Harbor, AK
Haystack: used often for buttes, hills, and rocks
Heckletooth Mountain, OR: rocks at the top look like a heckle, used to
    comb flax
Hole-in-the-Wall Falls, MT
Hook Arm, AK: shaped like a hook or a bended arm
Hump Mountain, WV
Lake Italy, CA: boot shape
Kidney Lake, UT
The Knobs, IN, NY: small hills
Longboat Key, FL: long, narrow island
Lumpy Ridge, CO
The Maiden's Breast, AZ
Mesa, AZ; Mesa Peak, CA: Spanish for 'table'
Mitten Butte, AZ: a pair of mittenlike formations
Moose Lake, CA: shaped like the head of a moose
Music Mountain, AZ: rock strata look like a musical staff
Natural Bridge: the most famous one is in Virginia, but Natural Bridges
    and Natural Arches are numerous in the west
Night Cap, CA: a mountain
Nipple Mountain, CO: the father of one girl named a particular
    formation Clara Bird's Nipple
Owlhead, AZ: Owl's Head, ME; Owlshead Mountain, CA
Packsaddle, TX
The Palisades of the Hudson, NJ, NY; The Palisades, CA; Palisade
    Canyon, NV: palisades were originally pales (poles) used in fencelike
    fortifications

Peapod Rocks, WA
Petticoat Mountain, CA
Preacher's Head, NM: the head of a serious-looking man
Ribbon: used for several narrow waterfalls
Rockcastle, KY
Saddle Mountain: widely used in the West
Sail Rock, NM, WA
Saw Buck Mountain, AZ: shaped somewhat like the X of a sawhorse
Table: often used to indicate a flat top; see also Mesa
Valley of Fire, NV: bright red rocks
Tepee Mountain, MI, OK; Tepee Buttes, SD
Tit Butte: common in the West
Tooth Back Mountain, AZ
Turtle Lake, MI
Wetauwanchu Mountain, CT; Algonquian for 'wigwam'
Whaleback Mountain, CA; Whale Tail Lake, MN

Heaven and Hell

Some half a hundred hills, streams, canyons, or other natural features in California are named Paradise. Near Paradise in Butte County is a supposedly contrasting place named Hell Town. But maybe Paradise itself wasn't always so heavenly. An early spelling was Paradice, which *may* have meant 'pair of dice' but was possibly only the result of limited literacy.

In South Dakota one early settler was named Adam and another, nearby, was Eve. There was no intermarrying between the two families, but even so, with such residents, the place had to be called Paradise.

Eight Paradises are listed by the U.S. Postal Service, as well as a Paradise Valley, NV, and a Paradis, LA. That Pelican State town, however, was named for a man rather than for the Garden of Eden.

Eden itself is an even more popular name than Paradise, with post offices in 14 states, although at least the one in Texas, and possibly others, are named for a man; Fred Eden owned the first store in the Texas town. There's an Eden Mills in Vermont, and there are Edentons in Ohio and North Carolina, the latter named for a onetime royal governor.

Heaven fares badly in the United States, although there's a Heavener, OK, probably named for a person. A few Horse Heavens, the Turkey Heaven Mountains of Alabama, and a Hog Heaven Branch in Georgia are obviously only facetiously descriptive.

Hades has no post office, nor does Hell, although there's a Hell station in Michigan. (Hell does freeze over every winter, the natives say.) New York has a Hell Gate station, and Wyoming a Hells Half Acre. The name Hell Gate, from Dutch Helle-Gat, was objectionable to some nineteenth-century New Yorkers, who re-named it Hurlgate, but author Washington Irving raised so much uh—fuss that Hell Gate was revived. The Hell Gate railway bridge, from Long Island to the Bronx, was opened in 1917.

Hell has been in North America much longer than that. The Hell Creek formation is what geologists call a division of Upper Cretaceous rocks that date back over 100 million years. The for-mation got its name from Hell Creek, not far from Jordan, MT, where there is an outcropping, but it shows up also in Wyoming and North and South Dakota. Remains of the Tyrannosaurus and the Triceratops have been found in the Hell Creek formation, as well as some of the most ancient primate bones known to man.

There'a a Devil's Lake, ND, a Devils Slide, UT, a Devils Tower, WY, and somehow the Devils Elbow got away from him in Missouri. Angels Camp, in California, does what it can to cope with those of the other persuasion, but obviously the largest collection of earthly angelic beings is in Los Angeles, over four hundred miles away.

USana

What is the most attractive ending for a place name?

Three of our states have names ending in -ana (Indiana, Lou-isiana, Montana). Some people believe that -ana or -anna is the best way to end a town name, too, although others prefer -ona or -ora or something quite different.

Here are some of the -ana and -anna names. Read aloud, they sound a bit like a poem. The footnotes give their states.

Anna[1], Havana[2],
Don't forget Oreana[3],
Oceana[4], Fontana[5],
In Hawaii there's Hana,

[1]Illinois, Ohio, Texas
[2]Arkansas, Florida, Illinois, Kansas, North Dakota
[3]Illinois
[4]West Virginia
[5]California, Kansas, Wisconsin

     Okeana[6], Joanna[7],
     And warm Dona Ana[8],
     Christiana[9], Urbana[10],
     And famous Amana[11],
     (Farther north is Luana[12],)
     Marianna[13], Roxana[14],
     Savanna[15], Savannah[16],
     And Vanna[17], Sultana[18].

Book Review: *The Dictionary of Imaginary Places*

If you have read Jonathan Swift's *Gulliver's Travels*, you know about the imaginary kingdom of Lilliput, whose inhabitants are all less than six inches high. If you haven't, or if you choose to reread it, consult first *The Dictionary of Imaginary Places*, by Alberto Manguel and Gianni Guadalupi. There you'll find a map showing the island and its neighbor, Blefescu; residents of the two islands fought a war over which end of an egg should be broken. You'll also find a condensed account of Lilliputian customs and beliefs, as well as of that place called Brobdingnag and other spots visited by Gulliver.

Lilliput occupies only one of the book's 454 pages, which tells you also about the physical and other features of Shangri-La, More's (and others') Utopia, Atlantis, Tolkien's Middle-earth, the town of Stepford and its roboticized women, and even the Pepperland of the Beatles.

You'll find out specifically what things looked like behind the looking-glass, whatever is interesting about OZ, locations of Robinson Crusoe's three homesites, the people of Spoon River. Did you

---

[6]Ohio
[7]South Carolina
[8]New Mexico
[9]Pennsylvania, Tennessee
[10]Illinois, Indiana, Iowa, Missouri, Ohio (and Urbanna, VA)
[11]Iowa
[12]Iowa
[13]Arkansas, Florida, Pennsylvanis
[14]Illinois, Kentucky
[15]Illinois, Oklahoma
[16]Georgia, Missouri, New York, Ohio, Tennessee
[17]Georgia
[18]California

know that Stevenson's Treasure Island was located off the coast of Mexico? that Stevenson wrote also about Suicide City, inhabited only by would-be suicides? that Toad Hall has French windows and a golf course? that each resident of Scoodlerland has a face on each side of his or her head (a removable head so that it can be thrown at an enemy)? that when Homer's monster, Charybdis, swallows enough sea water, he regurgitates it, forming tremendous whirlpools?

Your education is incomplete if you've never heard of Sas Doopt Swangranti (formerly called Normbdsgrvstt), Ruffal (where "What I tell you three times is true"), Polyglot (whose inhabitants speak all languages and have cars big enough to use as blankets on cold nights), Neverreachhereland (which can be seen but never visited) and approximately 1200 other marvelous islands, countries, continents, and cities, all created by the imaginative, questing, venturesome, far-reaching, multifaceted, multifarious human mind. (Over 200 maps and illustrations to help make the imaginary seem real.)

Don't Tell His Wife

William Safire recalled an old bilingual place-name pun in this way:

> A peccadillo is a minor fault or petty sin, from the Latin *peccare*, to sin. Its use recalls one of the great diplomatic code messages based on a pun, from Sir Charles Napier, who had been sent to gain control of the Indian province of Sind in the 1840s. After the battle of Hyderabad, the British general sent back his report in a single word: *Peccavi*. At the Foreign Office, his Latin-speaking colleagues immediately knew its import: "I have Sind."

❦ 19
Naming in the Wilds

I Think the Izaak Walton League Should Outlaw Names Like *Mattawamkeag*

Although I've fished in sun and rain,
I've never gone to fish in Maine.
The water's fine, the fish will pounce,
But the names of their lakes I can't pronounce.

The simple ones like Allagash
And Umbagog I say with dash,
But I need to take a second look
At any word like Chiputneticook.

Another one that always stops us
Is Upper or Lower Sysladobsis.
The thought of a trout in the Magagnavic River
Creates in my heartbeat nary a quiver.

(Nor does Lake Pattagumpus raise much of a rumpus.)

Medunkeunk is sunk by Nesowadnehunk.
When I see Pennamaguan I keep right agoin.
Even Walloquoik is too much like woik.
And I never give more than a crass empty look
At such a place as Chimquassabamticook.
But on the map of old Conn. I get really agog
At Chargoggagaugmanchaugagoggchaubunagungamaugg.

214

> Since New England's place names get my goata,
> I'll confine my fishing to Minnesota,
> For how can I brag how I hooked 'em and fought 'em
> If I can't say the name of the place where I caught 'em?

Actually, Minnesota may cause problems of a different sort. According to one count, it has 99 lakes named Long, 91 named Mud, and a dozen or a few dozen named Round, Rice, Sandy, or Gull.

Incidentally, people who live near Lake Chargogg . . . and the rest of those 44 letters have solved the problem of pronunciation, according to the late Odell Shepard. They call it Webster.

The Nameless Ones

Pioneers here and there, either trying to be funny, unable to agree on a name, or only unimaginative and honest, have called a number of places Nameless.

William Trogdon, writing in the *Atlantic Monthly* under the name William Least Heat Moon (and there's a tale behind that, too), tells about his search for Nameless, TN, which when he found it turned out to be "a dozen houses along the road, a couple of barns, same number of churches. . . ." He gets the story of the naming of Nameless from a couple of elderly residents who say that after going for years without a name, the community was told by the Post Office Department that it could have mail deliveries if it would just choose a name.

"The community met; there were only a handful, but they commenced debating. Some wanted patriotic names, some names from nature; one man recommended, in all seriousness, his own name. They couldn't agree, and they ran out of names to argue about. Finally, a fellow tired of the talk; he didn't like the mail he received anyway. 'Forget the durn post office,' he said. 'This here's a nameless place if I ever seen one, so leave it be.' And that's just what they did."

The woman told Trogdon, "You think Nameless is a funny name. . . . Well, you take yourself up north a piece to Difficult or Defeated or Shake Rag. Now them are silly names."

At a South Dakota cave, people who visited were invited to write down their suggestions for a name. The final tally showed Nameless Cave as the first choice, and so it was called that.

A creek and an island in Alaska bear the name, but usually Nameless gets a different name eventually. No post office town is Nameless. George R. Stewart says that there was once a Nameless in Texas and that some North Dakota visitors liked the Nameless name so well that they used it back home—but both places, apparently, are now called something else or have reverted to the post officeless state of the community in Tennessee.

There's also a Nonames Hill, NY, but that's misleading, for the name is based on that of a Native American chief who probably pronounced it very differently and to whom it had a different meaning.

When the crew of a British ship, the *Herald*, was surveying the coast of northern Alaska, a draftsman wrote *?Name* opposite one cape. A second man thought the *Name* was the name and wrote it as Cape Name. His *a* was not clearly formed, however, and Name was read by others as Nome. And so Nome, AK, once nameless and then Name, became what it is called today.

Life in Death Valley

A party of emigrants named it in 1849, when they suffered dehydration and even death in heat that has been known to reach 134° F (57° C) in the shade, and 190° F (88° C) where the sun mercilessly burns the already scorched earth.

Death Valley, CA, is now a national monument. It is close to the Amargosa 'bitter' range of mountains, which include the Black and Funeral Mountains, named for their funereal black volcanic rocks. Volcanic ash covers much of the almost waterless earth. In some years no measurable rainfall has been recorded in the valley, and the average for a year is less than two inches. Near Bad Water is the lowest point in the United States, 282 feet below the level of the sea. Modern travelers who disregard thermometers may visit Furnace Creek Inn, Dantes View, and the Devils Golf Course.

The travelers seldom see any desert life except for noisy ravens, which may croak to them "Nevermore," or they may see a lizard skittering toward a crevice. But the few residents and the more numerous geologists, pathologists, botanists, zoologists, and other scientists whose professional zeal drives them to such an apparently godforsaken place, tell us that living things are in truth not rare. There is much life in Death Valley.

A survey in the 1890s reported 78 species of birds, and later ornithologists, counting passers-through or passers-over as well as inhabitants, tripled that number. Tiny pupfish (*Cyprinidon*) live in Salt Creek and elsewhere; some of them belong to the species *diabolis* 'devil,' so named because they thrive best in hot climates. Now and then a snake may be seen searching for small prey or perhaps the egg of a bird.

Many of the animals avoid exertion in the searing daylight hours, but after dark a few rabbits venture out, as do desert wood rats or kangaroo rats with their long hind legs. Occasionally an antelope squirrel appears, a ground squirrel whose tail is white underneath; when the tail is lifted the white rear resembles the white rump of a retreating antelope.

And there are larger mammals, too: wild burros whose ancestors strayed from the campsites of prospectors or miners; cute little kit foxes; coyotes, which can survive almost anywhere; bobcats, sometimes crying shrilly from a distant ledge. Bighorn sheep from the nearby mountains infrequently descend into the valley.

Some people have brought in tamarisks, whose roots drill deep for the scanty moisture; the bushlike trees provide meager shade and pink-blossomed beauty near a few springs. Saltgrass and other salt-enduring plants grow in or near some of the hot, brackish water. Desert holly lies low in the valley. Creosote bushes, from which an acidulous gum resin called Sonora gum may be obtained, grow in many gravel fans; in season they produce bright little yellow flowers.

Spring rains, when they come, may make much of the valley bloom—less luxuriantly, though, than in the desert scenes from nearby Arizona made familiar to Easterners in the vivid pictures in *Arizona Highways*, but enough blossoms to completely dispel the notion that Death Valley is really dead.

The Longest and Shortest U.S. Place Names

In Wales a few place names may total 30 or 40 or more letters. In the late 1950s, a 20-foot sign bearing the name of a railroad station was stolen. The reason for such a large sign? The name on it was

Llanfairpwllgwyngyllgogerychwyrndrobwllllandyssilogagoch
(56 letters)

Americans seem to be shorter of breath than the Welsh. George R. Stewart says that probably the longest word among our place names is the name of some dunes in Alaska—a word of uncertain meaning that was taken over from the Inuit. It is

Nunathloogagamiutbingoi
(23 letters)

Stewart says nothing about the name of a New England lake reported several decades ago by Odell Shepard and included in this book in the verse on page 214. The name is so ungainly that almost certainly no one now uses it. It is

Chargoggagaugmanchaugagoggchaubunagungamaugg
(44 letters)

Candidates for the shortest place name include L, a lake in Nebraska, and T, a gulch in Colorado, each named for its shape. A few two-letter names exist, including Ed, Or, Oz, and Uz in Kentucky.

Some towns are or have been called unofficially by the numbers assigned to local mines. For instance, Mt. Clare and nearby Wilsonville, IL, are familiarly known simply as 3 and 4: "Go into 4 and get some salami." A West Virginia place was once 6.

The *Guinness Book of World Records* (1990) includes several one-letter names from outside the United States: Y in France, A in Denmark and Sweden, U in the Caroline Islands, and O (also called Aioi) in Japan.

No Submachine Guns?

Many creeks are near Little Soldier Mountain, ID. They include Pistol, Automatic, Winchester, Colt, Luger, Thirty-Eight, Forty-Five, and—of small value to the soldier—Popgun.

Pancakes Hard as Rocks

Villages called Pancake, in Pennsylvania and Texas, are named for George Pancake and J. R. Pancake, early settlers.

But Pancake Rock, AK, is shaped like a stack of pancakes, and George R. Stewart says that the name Pancake Summit, NV, "is probably of similar origin."

When the Names Well Ran Dry

In 1927 two geologists, responsible for naming some of the numerous small streams in Alaska, found themselves without inspiration. Their well of names had run dry, yet there was still another river to name. So that's what they called it: Another River.

❦ 20
Improper (?) Names

"Not All Names Are Considered to Be Proper"

"While names are classified as proper nouns, not all names are considered to be proper." So said Lester F. Dingman, Executive Secretary, Domestic Geographic Names, U.S. Board of Geographic Names.

One of the responsibilities of the Board is to determine which names are "proper" enough to be considered official and to appear in print on maps. For example, although Whorehouse wasn't taboo as part of the title of a long-running Broadway play (the Board has no jurisdiction over such things), it was disallowed in the geographic name Whorehouse Meadow, AZ, which on maps appears with the approved name Naughty Girl Meadow.

Just how such decisions are arrived at is not entirely clear. The same Board approved Cat House Creek, MT, and Pleasure House Creek, VA. Maybe the rules for creeks are different than for meadows.

Compromises, the Board has found, are often necessary. For S.O.B. Rapids, UT, it disallowed both the complete expression and the version with periods, changing he-man profanity to the tearful Sob Rapids.

Sometimes a name originates with no salacious intent at all, the pure-minded namer being unaware of or at least not recalling a second meaning that will offend some people. For example, a mountain in Virginia with a treeless summit was called, in all innocence, Nakedtop; a locally well-known Oregonian named Peter was bald, but the Board obviously couldn't accept Bald Peter as an official name. Wee Wee Hill, IN, makes the prurient think of something other than small size; and The Broads of New Hampshire, named for The Broads of England (a low-lying, marshy area) might sound to some folks like the title of a ribald musical comedy. Rocky John Canyon was changed to Rocky Canyon after the Board found that John in the name didn't refer to a person.

One type of name that the Board consistently frowns on is that which suggests an ethnic or racial slur. So Chink Gulch became Chinese Gulch, and other place names containing words like Jap, Gook, Dago, Nigger, and even Yankee are banned, although somehow the post office address Yankeetown, FL, was approved.

One Run, One Miss, One Error

In Virginia, at a place where staves for whiskey barrels were once made, a stream was called Whiskey Barrel Run. It was changed to Stave Run by the U.S. Board on Geographic Names, but somebody misread or miswrote one letter. It began appearing on maps as Stare Run.

The French Broad

Crossing the French Broad River in North Carolina, sexist male travelers are likely to attempt a witticism: "French Broad? Let's stop and visit her," or "Is it true what they say about French broads?"

The stream flows westward 205 miles from the Blue Ridge Mountains, joining the Holston near Knoxville, TN, to form the Tennessee River. It was originally called the Broad River, but since North Carolina already had a stream with that name, the word *French* was added to differentiate the two. At the time, a number of French settlers lived in the western part of the area through which the river flows.

A Letter to the Governor About Miss Nellie's Anatomy

When Ronald Reagan was the governor of California, he received the following letter from a woman in Omaha:

Your Excellency:

I was looking at the map of California, looking for "Bell-flower" where an old school mate of mine lives. I never did find Bellflower, but saw a mountain that I do not like, and wondered if you could change the name? It's called "Nellie's Nipple." Since I have an Aunt Nellie, I don't think this is very nice, or fit for children to study about except in Medical School! I hope to visit your beautiful State some day, if I'm lucky. But in the meantime will you please change the mountain's name at once: it seems rather scandalous.

Sexism in the Names of Towns?

Scoreboard:

Boy[1] 6, Girl 0
Guy[2] 6, Gal 0, Doll 0
Lady[3] 4, Gentleman 0
Dame[4] 1, Sir 0
Man[5] 1, Woman 0

(Males win, 13 to 5.)

Indelicate Names?

Most of the town names mentioned here are derived from people's names, and all had perfectly innocent beginnings. But the ignorant, the crude, or the prurient have found double entendres in each.

For example, after the word *gay* came to refer to homosexuality, some people made remarks that they considered funny about Gay, GA, MI, WV; Gays, IL; Gay Hill, TX; Gays Creek, KY; Gays Mills, WI; Gayville, SD; and Gaysville, VT. Each of these towns actually

---

[1]Post offices are at Boys Town, NE (for a charitable institution); at Boy River, MN (near Boy Lake, named for three small boys killed in 1768); and at Boys Ranch, AL, AZ, FL, NM.
[2]Guy, AZ, TX; Guys, TN; Guys Mills, PA; Guysville, OH; Guyton, GA (Almost always for local families)
[3]Ladiesburg, MD; Lady Lake, FL; Ladysmith, VA, WI (Marylanders say that in early years the settlement had an excess of women, but onomatists say there were residents named Lady. The Wisconsin Ladysmith is for a Lady Smith, identified by Kelsie Harder as "bride of a business official"; she did not visit her namesake.)
[4]Dames Quarter, MD (Probably for a family named Dame; *quarter* means 'tract of land' or 'area')
[5]Man, WV (An oddity. The name is the last syllable of Ulysses Hinchman, a local politician.)

bears the name of a person or persons. Gay Hill, for example, is called that because of two pioneer settlers, G. H. Gay and W. C. Hill.

Equally innocuous explanations can be found (by the pure in heart) for these:

Bloomer, WI
Bullsgap, TN
Cherry Grove, NY, WV; Cherry Hill, AR; Cherry Valley, AR, IL, NY; Cherryville, MO, NC, PA
Doctors Inlet, FL
Eros, LA
French Lick, IN
Hooker, KY, OK; Hookerton, NC
Idamay, WV

Letcher, KY, SD
Lolita, TX
Lovejoy, GA, IL
Lovelady, TX
Maiden, NC; Maidens, VA; Maidsville, WV
Mangohick, VA ("Man drink too much, man go hick")
Ova, KY
Pansey, AL

From Head to Foot

Let's check on anatomy as revealed in U.S. town names.

There's Indian Head, MD, as well as Headland, AL, Bullhead, SD, Horseheads, NY, and Head of Grassy, KY (where, however, it means 'source of a stream'). Louisiana's Grosse Tete means 'large head.' Arkansas gives us Birdeye. There are no Ears except two little Earlings (IA and WV).

The various heads are supported by Indian Neck, VA, Dutch Neck, NJ, Colts Neck, NJ, and Great Neck, NY, besides an entire Neck City, MO.

There's a Chest Springs, PA, but obviously one finds only a spelling coincidence in the various Chesters, Chesterfields, Chestnuts, and similar names. The word *breast* is apparently taboo in town names, although it or less delicate equivalents may be found in mountainous regions as names of mountains or hills.

Several hearts exist, as in Crowheart, WV, Heart Butte, MT, and Heartwell, NE. A heart is disguised in the spelling of Elkhart, IN, said to have been named for a heart-shaped island in the nearby river.

We have Big Arm, MT, Devil's Elbow, MO, and Elbow Lake, MN. Handshoe, KY, reminds us of the German word for glove, *Handschuh*. There's only a Left Hand in West Virginia. Tennessee has a single Finger, which is apparently outnumbered in South Carolina's Fingerville.

Kiester, MN, has nothing to do with *keister*, a slang term for 'buttocks.'

Kneeland is in California, but Footville is in Wisconsin. Between them (anatomically but not geographically) are Shinrock, OH, and a fascinatingly named place, Shinhopple, NY. ("Probably Algonquian, meaning uncertain," says Stewart's *American Place-Names*.) Kentucky appears to suffer from a Cutshin.

The anatomy of our four-legged friends is recalled specifically in Paw Creek, NC.

Muscle Shoals, AL, gives strength to the whole body, and the osteal system is suggested by Bonecave, TN, Boneville, GA, and Bonetraill, ND, although there is a Bone Gap in Illinois. No post office town is named Skeleton, but the West commemorates in other names some locations where human skeletons were found: Skeleton Canyon, AZ, Skeleton Creek, OK, Skeleton Gulch, CO, Skeleton Ridge, AZ, and Skeleton Springs, SD.

Blood is likewise avoided in town names. Stewart, however, mentions a Blood Gulch, CA, in which early gold miners saw blood flowing and traced it upstream to the corpse of a murdered man. And between Blood Mountain and Slaughter Mountain in Georgia, which commemorate a Native American battle, we find Blood and Slaughter Gap.

Small Town Names in Headlines

Some of the following headlines are genuine, others contrived. Each contains two or more actual names of small towns.

Sports headlines
Chestnut Upsets Canoe (Alabama)
Bumble Bee Overcomes Mammoth (Arizona)
Bigflat Travels to Pea Ridge (Arkansas)
Crows Landing at Blue Lake Tonight: Feather Falls Falls (California)
Big Indian Succumbs to Stella Niagra (New York)
Imogene Draws Stanley; Amelia Gets Tingley; Nora Springs Meets
    Waterloo; Rose Hill Travels to Loveland (Iowa)

Society news
Oblong Man Marries Normal Girl (Illinois)
Fertile Girl Weds Manly Man (Iowa)
Visitors Enjoy Intercourse; Paradise Next Stop (Pennsylvania)

❦ 21
On the Big Apple and Smaller Apples

How "The Big Apple" Got That Name

Some people say that baseball players, who are great coiners of nicknames and slang, are responsible for the nickname "The Big Apple." But it appears more likely that jazz musicians deserve the credit.

Musicians of the 1930s, playing one-night stands, coined their own terms not only for their music and its components but also for their travels, the people they met, the towns they stayed in. A town or city was an "apple."

At that time a man named Charles Gillett was president of the New York City Convention and Visitors Bureau. Learning of the jazz term, he bragged, "There are lots of 'apples' in the U.S.A., but we're the best and the biggest. We're The Big Apple."

The name did not catch on widely for some time, but in the 1970s, perhaps earlier, it became used as a tourist-attracting slogan, referring not only to New York's musical attractions but also its plays, ballets, athletic events, and convention facilities.

One More Apple

Not to be outdone by the better-known Manhattan, residents of Manhattan, KS, painted on a water tower the words "THE LITTLE APPLE."

Of Course There's Only One New York

"What town and city name do you think is most frequently used in the United States?"

"I don't know. Is it Washington?"

"Good guess. Washington is tied for second. It's used in
twenty-six of the states."

"Springfield?"

"No, but it's near the top."

"I give up."

"Try another president."

"Lincoln?"

"No. Only sixteen Lincolns. The winner is Madison."

Here are the winning numbers, along with the usual source(s)
of each name.

Madison (27)—President

Clinton (26)—Personal name

Washington (26)—President

Franklin (25)—Statesman

Greenville (24)—Personal name;
description

Marion(24)—Revolutionary War
General, nicknamed "the
Swamp Fox"

Salem (24)—Biblical place

Manchester (23)—English city;
personal name

Monroe (22)—President

Springfield (22)—Description

Troy (22)—Literature; history

Ashland (21)—Tree; home of
Henry Clay

Milford (21)—English town; ford
near a mill

Clayton (20)—Description;
personal name

Fairfield (20)—Description

Jackson (20)—President

Jamestown (20)—English king;
personal name

Jefferson (20)—President

Newport (20)—Description

Oxford (20)—English city or shire

Cleveland (19)—President; other
personal name

Lebanon (19)—Biblical place

Plymouth (19)—English city

Canton (18)—Chinese city;
French or Swiss district

Dover (18)—English cliffs and
port; a religious report of 1832

Farmington (18)—Description

Glenwood (18)—Description

Hillsboro (18)—Description;
personal name

Milton (18)—English place; poet;
other personal name

Windsor (18)—English place;
English nobleman

Most large American cities have to share their names with
much smaller places. The previous list shows that Washington, DC,
has 25 name-alikes. Here are the numbers of name-alikes for some
other cities:

Dayton, OH (17)
Buffalo, NY (16)
Columbus, OH (16)
Oakland, CA (16)
Rochester, NY (13)
Portland, OR (12)
Atlanta, Ga (11)
Denver, CO (10)
Newark, NJ (9)

Louisville, KY (9)
Boston, MA (8)
Dallas, TX (8)
Houston, TX (8)
Akron, OH (7)
Miami, FL (7)
St. Paul, MN (7)
Memphis, TN (6)
Omaha, NE (6)

There's only one New York, of course. Also standing in lonely grandeur are Chicago, San Francisco, New Orleans, Pittsburgh (with an *h*), Seattle, Cincinnati, Indianapolis, Fort Worth, Oklahoma City, Honolulu, Jersey City, and Tulsa.

For what it's worth,

Oxford beats Cambridge, 20 to 12.

Columbia wins the Ivy League, 17 to Princeton's 16. Also ran: Yale 6, Cornell 5, Harvard 4, Brown 1, Dartmouth 1, Pennsylvania 0 (although Pennsylvania Furnace scores 1).

Athens defeats Rome, 15 to 7, but loses to Troy, 22 to 15. Sparta scores 11, Carthage *delenda est* with 10.

Antelope play in five states, but Deer only in Arkansas.

The only Arctic village, not unexpectedly, is in Alaska.

The British Don't Pronounce *Gotham* Correctly

Gotham, a village in Nottinghamshire, is pronounced GOT*um*. In medieval times, to keep King John from taking up residence there, the inhabitants are said to have pretended to be stupid. For instance, they tried to drown eels.

In the United States, Gotham is a nickname for New York City that Washington Irving and some of his contemporaries made famous. On this side of the water, it is pronounced GŎTH*um*, and the residents do not need to pretend to be stupid.

British place-name pronunciation often differs from American by being more economical. Similarly, the British chop sounds or syllables out of some words, such as *secretary*, which they call SEK-*ruh-tree*. It's well-known that in England, Gloucester sounds like

GLOS-*ter*, Leicester like *LES-ter*, Worcester like *WOOS-ter*, Greenwich like *GREN-ij*, Thames like *TEMZ*, Derby like *DAR-be*, and Cholmondeley like *CHUM-lee*.

Here are some other place names and a few personal names that many British people pronounce in ways that seem odd to Americans, although some modern Britishers come closer to sounds suggested by the spellings.

Spelling	Pronunciation
Ayscough	*ASK-you* or *ASK-o*
Banbury	*BAN-bree*
Berkeley	*BARK-lee*
Berkshire	*BARK-sher*
Bicester	*BIS-ter*
Boleyn	*BULL-un*
Bottomley	*BUM-lee*
Burghley	*BUR-lee*
Cirencester	*SIS-uh-ter*
Claverhouse	*CLAV-ers*
Colquhoun	*CO-hoon*
Daventry	*DAIN-tree*
Falconer	*FAWK-ner*
Hawarden	*HAR-dun*
Heathcote	*HETH-kut*
Kirkcudbright	*ker-KOO-bree*
Leominster	*LEM-ster*
Mainwaring	*MAN-uh-ring*
Marjoribanks	*MARSH-banks*
Marlborough	*MAWL-bruh*
Ponsonby	*PUN-sun-bee*
Pontefract	*PUM-fret*
Pulteney	*POLT-nee*
Raleigh	*RAW-lee* or *RAL-lee*
Scone	*SKOON*
Seymour	*SEE-mer*
Shrewsbury	*SHROZ-bree*
Slithwaite	*SLO-it*
Sotheby	*SUTH-uh-bee*
Stanhope	*STAN-up*
St. Clair	*SIN-clair*
St. John	*SIN-jun*
Strachan	*STRAWN*
Teignmouth	*TIN-muth*
Trotterscliff	*TROS-lee*
Warwick	*WOR-ik*

| Whitefield | *WHIT-field* |
| Wriothesley | *ROTS-lee, ROX-lee,* or *RIS-lee* |

The Nowhere Cities

In an editorial the *New York Times* objected to an ad prepared for the Diors, designers and makers of French clothing. The ad asked, "What would New York be without the Diors?" It answered its own question: "Newark."

Other cities besides Newark have been the target of jokesters who like to ridicule what they consider an out-of-it, nowhere place. One old joke says that the first prize in a contest is "a week in Philadelphia." Second prize: "two weeks in Philadelphia."

The president of the AFL-CIO, Lane Kirkland, made the mayor of Hoboken unhappy when he said, "Everything outside the AFL-CIO is Hoboken."

Decades ago Gertrude Stein expressed her opinion of Oakland: "When you get there, there isn't any there there."

"The little old lady from Dubuque" has become a stock phrase to caricature not only naive, prissy, or puritanical old ladies, but also Dubuque and other communities like it as supposedly being out of date, not with it.

The *Times* answered the jokesters in this way:

> What all the jokes overlook . . . is that most of the cities on the list have in recent years proven through redevelopment of business and neighborhoods that they no longer deserve to be ridiculed [if they ever did]. That's what Newark is doing, and it doesn't need any help from the Diors.

You Know Names from Maxwell Street

The pushcarts now appear only on weekends on Maxwell Street, just southwest of Chicago's Loop, and they are much fewer in number. The street itself has been shortened, changed. Many of the shops have closed or been torn down. The street doesn't smell much, either—not as it once did. It smelled of sweat and urine, herring and lox, hot dogs and Polish sausage, nickel cigars, spoiled vegetables and too-ripe fruit, carelessly washed used clothing.

In its more than 160 years, it has known thousands of small shops, many of them short lived, and more thousands of pushcarts.

It escaped—was barely south of—the 1871 fire that consumed most of Chicago; many homeless victims found cheap lodging near or along Maxwell Street.

Ira Berkow in *Maxwell Street* says:

> Irish and German immigrants who fled famine and depression in Europe were the earliest inhabitants of the area. With the Jewish influx [which occurred especially as a result of the Russian pogroms] the Germans and Irish moved out, just as several decades later the Jews would move when blacks and Mexicans moved in. Gypsies have long lived there. Italians and Poles and Lithuanians and Greeks and Scandinavians lived on the outskirts.

In old days men called "pullers" stood close to the pushcarts or the small shops that lined the street.

They tried, with shouts or intimate whispers, sometimes even with their hands, to induce passersby to examine this or that "mahvelous bahgin." In one favorite game the puller would see a prospect examining, say, an overcoat. The puller pretended interest in the same coat. He shouted to the proprietor in the back of the shop, "How much for this overcoat?" "Thirty dollars." The puller yelled back, "Did you say twenty dollars?" The shopkeeper pretended to be hard of hearing. "Yes," he would yell. The prospect then was expected to try to persuade the puller that he himself had seen the coat first and deserved to get the coat for the bargain price, and the puller would reluctantly agree. The customer never learned that with a few minutes of bargaining he might have made the purchase for fifteen dollars or even ten.

The street smelled. But many of its people worked or fought or bargained or studied and thought, and worked more and left Maxwell Street and its smells, its noise.

It is possible that no other mile-long street in America has produced a greater number of famous names. Boss of a leading television network. Champion boxers. Show biz folk. Gangsters. An internationally known ambassador.

A Russian-born boy named Hyman Rickover grew up in the Maxwell Street area. He was always bright, ambitious, energetic, outspoken, often profane, and he never changed much. In 1922 he graduated from Annapolis, and later he commanded a minesweeper, then became an expert on nuclear propulsion. He designed and oversaw construction of the *Nautilus*, the first nuclear-propelled submarine, which was launched in 1954, and in 1956 to 1957 he helped to develop an experimental nuclear power plant. President Eisenhower made him a vice-admiral.

You never heard of Muni Weisenfreund? Not surprising. His parents owned a little theater at Twelfth and Waller, just off Maxwell, and from the silent flickerings on the screen he learned to act. You know him from old movies on TV as Paul Muni, who starred in *The Good Earth, Louis Pasteur, The Last Angry Man*; if you're old enough and lucky, you saw him on Broadway in *Inherit the Wind*.

Al Capone's business manager, Jake "Greasy Thumb" Guzik, from just northwest of Maxwell Street, was prosperous enough to be convicted of evading $800,000 in income taxes. Small potatoes for a man the government said earned $970,302 in one year. Bootlegger, panderer, and inventor of the "Crime Syndicate," it was widely said. He claimed, "I never carried a gun in my life." But he knew how to keep the boss's books very well. And a Treasury Department official asserted that Guzik might have had as much as $150 million stashed away, back in the days when a million was worth several hundred thousand. His brother Harry owned brothels and unintentionally, said his friends and enemies, was instrumental in passage of the Mann Act.

William S. Paley, chairman of the Board of CBS, was the son of Samuel Paley who wrapped cigars in a storefront factory on Maxwell Street and eventually had 50 workers under him. His brand was La Palina. Bill made use of his father's money and business instincts and attended the Wharton School of Finance. On the side, he was admired as a great ladies' man. He became president of CBS before he was 27.

John L. "Jack" Keeshin owned a horse and wagon, used for deliveries in the Maxwell Street area. Then another horse and wagon, a truck, more trucks. Later, *Fortune* magazine said, "Besides muscle and guts he has brains and persistence and ambition and prodigious energy. [That could be a theme song for Maxwell Street.] For these reasons he also has money, and he flaunts the title of Keeshin Transcontinental Freight Lines."

Barney Ross started out as Barnet David Rasofsky. Not a good name for a boxer. After boyhood fights in the streets, he used to be beaten by his father with a cat-o'-nine-tails. Al Capone told him, "You couldn't be a hood if you wanted to." So Barney continued fighting and went on to championships in three weight classes.

Jackie Fields, born Jacob Finkelstein on Maxwell Street, was a pretty good boxer, too. Undisputed welterweight champion. So was Maxwell Street's King Levinsky—pretty good. But he made the mistake of living at the time when Joe Louis was the undefeated heavyweight. Joe, from Detroit, knocked out the Chicagoan. But he was knocking everybody out.

Benny Goodman's father was a Maxwell Street tailor. In a synagogue Benny and two of his brothers were lent musical instruments and given lessons, and a little later they played in a band at Hull House. At age 29 he played his clarinet in Carnegie Hall in its first-ever swing-jazz concert; among his orchestra members were Gene Krupa, Lionel Hampton, Harry James, and Count Basie.

Barney Balaban started by buying a nickelodeon (a tiny theater) for $750, raised by scraping together all the money his family and friends had. He went on to be co-owner of the huge Balaban and Katz theater chain, and president of Paramount Pictures. His father had run a small grocery-delicatessen close to Maxwell Street, and the big family had lived in four rooms behind it.

U.S.A.F. Major Sidney Barnett was the first American to bomb Berlin in World War II. He said about his boyhood on Maxwell Street, "I learned [to fight] the American way. Hit 'em first, knock 'em down, and make 'em know who's boss."

Born on Sangamon Street, just off Maxwell, Meyer Levin would become the author of *The Old Bunch*, a novel about Chicago's West Side. Better known: his dramatization of *The Diary of Anne Frank* and his psychological book called *Compulsion* that was made into a hit Broadway play.

Natal name: Jacob Rubinstein. Birthplace: Fourteenth and Newberry, just south of Maxwell Street. Better known as Jack Ruby. You would never have heard the name if he hadn't killed Lee Harvey Oswald, the assassin of John F. Kennedy. At age 11 he had been referred to the Chicago Institute for Juvenile Research because of "truancy and incorrigibility at home."

Joseph Weil, in the archives of crime, is better known as Yellow Kid Weil, who learned on Maxwell Street how to be a confidence man, separating fools and sometimes wise men from their money. His total take has been estimated as eight to ten million dollars. He died, a pauper, at age 100.

Arthur Goldberg was born in the 1300 block of Washburne, about a block from Maxwell. "He recalls," Ira Berkow tells us, "the continuous street fights between Jews and the neighboring Irish. 'I used to fetch bricks for my brothers to throw.' " He graduated high in his class at Northwestern Law School. At age 54 he was named by President Kennedy to the United States Supreme Court. Three years later he became U.S. Ambassador to the United Nations. Not surprising, considering all the things that can happen to a bright boy from Maxwell Street.

From Skunk's Misery Onward and Upward

Scranton, PA, has worked its way up. It started out as Skunk's Misery (perhaps the most unappealing name ever coined). That was followed by an unimaginative Harrison, a lazy-sounding Slocum Hollow, and a patriotic Unionville. Then to honor a prominent local family, it became Scrantonia and finally Scranton. Eventually one of the eponymous Scrantons (William) became governor of the state and a candidate for the United States presidency.

What Do You Call Somebody Who Lives in Moscow?

That depends. Residents of the Russian Moscow (which they call Moskva) are Muscovites. But people in Moscow, ID, aren't sure whether they are Moscovites, Moscovians, or Moscowites, with the majority apparently favoring the third choice.

There is disagreement about the most appropriate designation for many other Americans, too: Floridan, Alabaman, Arizonan, Indianan, and Oklahoman; or Floridian, Alabamian, Arizonian, Indianian, and Oklahomian? The i seems preferred in the first three, but not in the last two.

Is it Atlantan or Atlantian? The former, probably. Does one say, for New Orleans, an OrleANian or an OrLEENian? People who live in the Crescent City generally say the latter.

What does one call a person from Little Rock or Big Rock? Little Rocker and Big Rocker seem ambiguous. And are any names really suitable for residents of Elk River, Grand Junction, LaCrosse, Bumpus Mills? Most people from the hundreds of -villes want to avoid sounding like -*villains*. A person from Yellow Bluff, AL, might not like the designation Yellow Bluffer. The name Welcomer, for someone who lives in Welcome, LA, MD, MN, or NC, may appear too effusive to anyone who dislikes or distrusts strangers.

Years ago, in *American Speech*, George R. Stewart suggested these principles to designate residents:

1. For places ending in -*a*, add *n:* Oklahoman, Tacoman, Arkadelphian
2. For the ending -*on*, add *ian:* Washingtonian, Bostonian
3. For the ending -*i*, -*o*, a pronounced -*e*, or -*ie*, or -*ee*, add *an:* Miamian, Chicagoan, Albuquerquean, Ploughkeepsian, Tuskegean
4. For the ending -*y*, change to *i* and add *an:* Sanduskian
5. For the ending -*olis*, change to *olitan:* Minneapolitan
6. For a consonant ending or a silent -*e*, add *ite* or *er*, whichever sounds better: New Yorker, Brooklynite, Detroiter, Harlemite, Orangeite

Stewart's principles, although widely followed, are not accepted everywhere. So we have, in violation of the principles, Akronites, San Franciscans and San Diegans and Sacramentans, Angelenos, Cantabrigians (from Cambridge, MA), and Trojans (from any of the Troys). In Taos, NM, linguistically meticulous men call themselves Taoseños, and the women are Taoseñas.

Sometimes, of course, nicknames are applied, whether affectionately or derisively: Hoosiers (from Indiana), Jayhawks (Kansas), Cornhuskers (Nebraska), Tarheels (North Carolina), Crackers (Georgia), and Blue Hen Chickens (Delaware), but heard less now than a century or so ago are intentionally insulting names such as Maniacs (Maine), Bugeaters (Missouri), Leatherheads (Pennsylvania), and Crawthumpers (Maryland).

Why Kansas City Isn't Called *Fonda*

If Abraham Fonda hadn't insisted that he was a gentleman, one of the nation's large cities might have been named for him.

In the frontier days of Missouri, a man was expected to be a "real man"—loud-swearing, hard-drinking, gun-toting, unafraid to soil his hands. But Abraham Fonda wore fancy clothes and soft leather gloves, preferred wine to whiskey, had a jeweled stickpin, and when he wrote a letter he signed it "Abraham Fonda, Gentleman." He was one of the few self-styled gentlemen in the young state in the late 1830s.

Fonda had some money, and he and ten or twelve others pooled their funds to buy a ferryboat landing and a couple of hundred acres on the banks of the Missouri River. It was not far from the mouth of the Kaw and also near a trading post for western overland expeditions, set up earlier by a French fur trader, François Chouteau. The buyers got together after their purchase to discuss the name of the settlement, then only a few log cabins. They intended to promote it as a river port and as a gateway to the West.

One of Fonda's few friends suggested Port Fonda, arguing that Fonda had put up a considerable share of the money. But another partner, Henry Jobe, wasn't having any of that. Inspired by the whiskey passed around, he ranted and swore and patted his gun to signify what might happen to anyone who supported the soft-spoken Fonda.

The partners turned to other possibilities, leaving Fonda looking uncomfortable but probably relieved. They discussed Kawsmouth because of the proximity of that stream, and one orated facetiously on the merits of Possum Trot. A few Kansas Indians still lived in the area and across the river, and Native American names were being selected here and there for other towns. "Why not call the place Kansas instead of the less pleasant-sounding Kawsmouth?" someone asked. (At the time there was not even a Kansas Territory, and the state by that name would not be admitted to the Union until 1861.) So the Town of Kansas was what the settlement became in 1838, the City of Kansas in 1853, and Kansas City in 1889.

By the way, Kansas and Kaw are alternative names for the Native American tribe, so if Kawsmouth had been selected, it might conceivably later have become Kansasmouth. Maybe the verdict of history was best.

Why *Tallahassee?*

The story of Florida's capital is unclear in some details, but goes something like this: The capital cities of Spanish Florida were Pensacola and St. Augustine, near opposite sides of the upper part of the peninsula. After Florida became a U.S. possession, it was agreed in 1824 that two horsemen should set out—one riding east, one west—from those two places and that the midpoint, where they supposedly would meet, would be designated as the capital of the Florida Territory.

It turned out that no white people and only a few Native Americans lived at or very near that spot.

George Walton, secretary of the young Territory, asked his daughter Octavia to pick out a name. She did some research and found that near the chosen site a Native American village named Tallahassa Talofa had been shown on a 1767 map. *Talla*, scholars say, meant 'old,' and each of the remaining parts meant 'town,' suggesting that a still earlier town had once stood there.

Octavia liked both the historical association and the musical quality, according to onomatists Bertha Bloodworth and Alton Morris. She dropped *Talofa* and slightly changed the ending of *Tallahassa*, perhaps because Native Americans still living in the area were usually called Tallahassee.

Nicknames of Places

Most places, especially if they have long names, are familiarly or facetiously called by shorter ones: Frisco for San Francisco; LA for Los Angeles; P-town for Provincetown, MA; Hamp for Northampton, MA; Burgy for places ending in *-burg* (especially Williamsburg, VA); Philly for Philadelphia; Indy for Indianapolis; the Hut for Terre Haute.

Sometimes publicists use nicknames longer than the name of the place itself. New York's relatively few years of using The Big Apple has reportedly brought in billions of tourist dollars. Less inspired and less profitable are The Windy City for Chicago, and The Hub City for Boston. (Reportedly so called because some of its leading residents once considered Boston the hub of the universe; perhaps a few still do, such as the wealthy dowager who refused to travel, saying, "Why should I? I'm already here.") Incidentally, there has been at least one other Hub City: Stoughton, WI, because wagons and hubs for wagon wheels were once made there; it was also called Wagon City, but perhaps both terms became less frequent when it switched to making auto bodies.

Two-word names such as Cedar Grove, Green Bay, Wichita Falls, Cedar Swamp, Great Neck, Grand Rapids, and Walnut Point are likely to be known in the surrounding area as "the Grove," "the Neck," etc.: "I'm going down to the Point tomorrow."

Nicknames that are critical or opprobrious are likely to be mainly local, too:

Lake Quana-polluted (Lake Quanapowitt, MA)
Louseville (Louisville)
Merrimuck (Merrimack River)
Northwest Distressway (Expressway)
Sandy Kitty (Kansas City)
Sin Valley (Sun Valley, CA, ID)
Slumberland (Cumberland, MD)
Taxachusetts (Massachusetts)

The bigoted apply nicknames to places largely inhabited by any ethnic group other than their own, although that practice appears to be diminishing as general educational levels rise. There may still be occasional local references, however, to Swedetown, Little Italy, Frenchman's Flats, Hunkytown, Niggertown, Greaser Gulch, the P.V. (Polish Village), Dago Creek, and others for almost any place where "they" live and "we" don't.

❦ 22
This Is a Lovely Little Town, Wasn't It?

French Lick: Larry Bird's Home Town

French Lick, IN. Pop. 2,265. It would be 2,266 if one Larry Bird hadn't emigrated a few years ago. He has been spending time in Boston and elsewhere, wearing short pants.

"They ain't never been no better ball player," says a French Lickian, reminding listeners that the young Bird led an otherwise average Indiana State team to within a game of a national championship. On the winning Michigan State team was another pretty fair player called "Magic" Johnson, who later put on his own short pants in Los Angeles.

Back to French Lick. Deer and other animals used to lick salt at a spring in the area. Frenchmen in the eighteenth century built a trading post nearby. So arose the name. Much later a chairman of the Democratic National Committee named Taggart put up a large and ornate hotel and established a health spa and convention center there.

An old steam engine chugs its way along a weedy track, and the two conductors—of the same vintage as the engine—point out the sights to tourists in the three-car train. "Watch on the right. There! See that *Bird* house?" He laughs prematurely. "That's a *Larry* Bird house—one of 'em!" A few minutes later: "There's a waterfall over there, only it's dried up now."

At a rest stop at the edge of Cuzco (pop. 40, "You'll find soda, junk food, and one rest room"), the engine puffs its black smoke and in a few minutes starts to push its cars back home. Near a house on the east edge of French Lick, a boy in Celtic green is shooting free throws.

In an ice-cream shop not far from Larry Bird Boulevard, two beautiful little white-haired women, sisters perhaps, fill cones, taking turns using one cone-shaped dipper. One asks us not to be impatient, for the other dipper is broken. A young woman customer asks, "Do you know Larry Bird?"

The white-haired woman not dipping says, "Ever'body knows Larry."

Some of the Best Postmarks

Best rhyme: Solo, MO
Most affirmative: Okay, OK
Best refrain for a song: Walla Walla, WA
Best exclamation: Mio, MI

Hoosier Legends about Town Names

When the history of a place is unknown or at least forgotten by most of the present residents, someone is likely to make up a story to account for it. Although sometimes the stories are possible, other origins are more probable.

For instance, Galveston, IN, was probably named for the place in Texas. But local legend has it that its founder looked out the window and saw "a gal with a vest on" and that she inspired the name. (Sexist males loafing on Galveston's busiest corner used to make ribald remarks about Galvestoff.)

A similar story is told about Roann, IN. A father saw his daughter in a boat in a dangerous current and kept shouting at her, "Row, Ann! Row, Ann."

Slightly more amusing is the story of an earlier name of Lorane, another Indiana village. First called Steam Corners for the steam-operated sawmills there, it was later named Buzzards Glory. The local legend says that a traveler crossed a little stream late one day, saw some beautiful scenery, and was then invited to spend the night with a family named Lord. "The next morning," the legend continues, "he said he crossed the river Jordan, went through Glory, and stayed all night with the Lord, and from that time on the little place was called Glory. Someone added the name Buzzard. Why, no one knows." Maybe the stranger's name was Buzzard.

No legend about the name Lorane, though. It appears to be only a simplified spelling of Lorraine, a French province.

The Name Is Now *Correct*

When a post office was to be established in a village a few miles south of Versailles, IN, in the nineteenth century, Versailles postmaster William Will (so the story goes) was asked to suggest a name, a not-uncommon practice in those days. Because of a current and rather widespread interest in comets, Will recommended Comet. His handwriting was not clear, however, so the U.S. Post Office Department sent him a card with "Comet" on it and asked him to verify it. He wrote "Correct" on the card, and today's state maps still show Correct as the village name.

The name of another Indiana village, Siberia, is the result of another Post Office Department error—also based on good intentions. Father Isidore Hobi had named it Sabaria for the place where Saint Martin of Tours was born. A Post Office Department employee assumed that the priest could not spell well, and designated the place as Siberia.

Clerical errors by other folks resulted in the names of Perkinsville and Taswell, two other Indiana villages. The original intention had been to name them for early settlers William Parkins and James Laswell.

However, Scircleville, another Hoosier village, is not erroneous. It was named for George Scircle. (The first two syllables of the village name are pronounced like *circle*.)

Uprisings

Several U.S. places are Rising. Montana's Rising Wolf Mountain is named not for a lupine revolution but for a Blackfoot Indian chief. California's Rising River makes a sudden appearance from a large spring.

A few miles from Champaign, IL, is a sign that says Rising Road. Actually the road lies perfectly still. Its name is that of an early settler.

Indiana and Maryland each have a Rising Sun, and Ohio has a Risingsun, all so named because of a clear view to the east. For the Indiana town, which is a county seat overlooking the Ohio River, the formal explanation is this: "The name was suggested by the grandeur of the sunrise over the Kentucky hills above the town of Rabbit Hash, across the river."

A Texas community wanted to be a Rising Sun also, but for some reason the request was denied, so the residents now live in Rising Star.

College-Conscious Railroad Builders

In proportion to population, Idaho has more towns with college names than any other state. One reason is that builders of early railroads decided to apply such names to a number of stations. Some of the names have disappeared from the Idaho map, and most of the surviving villages still have no more than a hundred or a few hundred inhabitants.

College names that remain include Albion, Bennington, Cambridge, Fenn, Franklin, Georgetown, Harvard, Hope, Iona, and Princeton, as well as others such as Dayton that were probably named for persons or for places not known primarily for colleges.

Harvard and Princeton, incidentally, are in the same county. Yale is in Illinois, Iowa, Michigan, Oklahoma, South Dakota, and Virginia, but not in Idaho. Columbia, Brown, and other Ivy League institutions also don't rate there.

They're Going to Build the Depot Right Here

In the latter half of the 1800s, when railroads were built through many thinly populated parts of the Midwest, South, and West (built with speed barely imaginable in an age hampered by labor-saving machinery, computers, too little unoccupied land, and hungry lawyers), railroad officials chose the names of hundreds of places where they decided to locate their stations, called depots by almost everyone. Tiny villages or even bare spots on the prairie suddenly became minor shipping centers, their names actually appearing on maps, to the amazement of the residents.

Some village names were retained, others changed. As a rule, only the Post Office Department could veto the railroaders' choices, and it seldom did so.

The Illinois Central sponsored a contest for naming a place not far from Chicago. The winner was Floss-Moor, which soon lost its hyphen and the second capital. (The POD doesn't like hyphens, apostrophes, any other punctuation, or unneeded capital letters in names.) Residents weren't sure of the meaning, but some thought it might mean either 'gently rolling countryside' or 'dew on the flowers.'

Railroad surveyors in Indiana so much enjoyed boarding with the family of Bernardt Kouts (Kautz in Germany) that they named the place Kouts Station, later reduced to Kouts. In Kansas two villages, Greenfield and Canola, shared a depot and became Grenola; also in Kansas the *Colo*rado and *Wich*ita Railroad honored itself with a place called Colwich. When Kansas passengers wanted a ticket to Morrow, the agent might say, "All right. Come back tomorrow." So Morrow became Morrowville. Loogootee, IN, sounds like a Native American name, but actually results from combining the names of Thomas Gootee, who laid out the town plan, and a man named Lowe, the engineer of the first train to go through. (Of course, *everybody* was at the depot, cheering him and the train that symbolized the ending of near isolation for countless places like that of Mr. Lowe and Mr. Gootee.)

Two South Dakota spots competed for a railroad station. The winner selected as its name—Winner.

Farther west, in Utah, a helping locomotive was needed to pull heavy freight trains up a long, steep grade, so railroaders called the place Helper. In Texas a misreading of Primm and Plum, villages a few miles apart, caused a bad train wreck, so Primm's name was quickly changed to Kirtley, for its postmaster. In California, railroaders thought Dutch Corners too long; the name became Ducor. The Southern Pacific took over the name of a nearby village, Tres Pinos 'three pines,' for the terminal on its proposed Pacheco Pass route. Instances like these abound.

One conscientious railroad official, George Stewart reported in *Names on the Land,* developed a set of requirements for any name selected by the Milwaukee Road. Every name, he ruled, should be reasonably short, easy to spell, clear in Morse code, different in appearance and sound from names of all nearby places, satisfactory to the POD, and pleasant in sound. (Not bad criteria for almost any place name.)

There's No Business Like Our Business

"The business of America is business," Calvin Coolidge said. Hundreds of town names reflect agreement with that statement. Unfortunately, most of those names are unlikely to win any accolades for esthetic appeal. Consider these unbeautiful examples of post office names:

Bauxite, AR	Leadville, CO
Boron, CA	Limekiln, PA
Calcium, NY	Micaville, NC
Cement, OK	Nitro, WV
Cement City, MI	Oil City, LA, PA
Chloride, AZ	Oil Trough, AR
Concrete, WA	Oilville, VA
Creamery, PA	Ore City, TX
Crucible, PA	Petroleum, IN, WV
Dolomite, AL	Quarryville, PA
Firebrick, KY	Quartzite, AZ
Gas, KS	Radium, KS
Grindstone, PA	Radium Spring, NM
Gypsum, CO, KS, OH	Sulphur, IN, KY, LA, OK (and 7
Hematite, MO	combinations)
Lead Hill, AR	Taconite, MN

Versions of company names or their products often indicate a community's major business or industry, for example:

Alcoa, TN (Aluminum Company of America)
Atco, NJ (Atlantic Transport Co.)
Charmco, WV (Charleston Milling Co.)
El Segundo, CA (for a company's second refinery)
Excello, OH (Excello Paper Co.)
Guardian, WV (Guardian Coal and Oil Co.)
Hatboro, PA (home of an eighteenth-century hatter)
Katy, TX (Missouri, Kansas, and Texas Railroad—"Katy")

Latexo, TX (Louisiana-Texas Orchards)
Lobeco, SC (Long, Bellamy and Co.)
Millers Tavern, VA
Paramount, CA (movie studios)
Tolu, KY (local whiskey-based tonic)

Uncounted scores of town names are those of local business people. A smaller number, such as the following, merely pay homage to the idea of business:

Commerce, GA, OK, TX; Commerce City, CO; Commercial Point, OH
Enterprise (six states); New Enterprise, PA
Industrial, WV; Industry, IL, NY, PA, TX (may simply mean
    'industriousness')
Intercourse, PA (once a synonym for 'interchange, commerce')
Prosperity, PA, SC (originally Frog Level), WV
Success, AR, MO
Tariff, WV; Tariffville, CT (both in gratitude for protectionist tariff
    laws)

How High Is *High*?

High Point, NC, is by no means the highest point in the state. Mount Mitchell, almost a hundred miles farther east, would tower above it.

Highland City, FL, is in relatively flat central Florida, near Lakeland. The highest land in the state is about 250 miles northwest in the Florida Panhandle.

Low Moor, IA, is rather well named, but Lowgap, NC, Lowland, NC and TN, and Lowmoor, VA, are low-lying only in relation to their mountainous neighbors.

How Central Is *Center*?

Post office towns named Center are in Colorado, Kentucky, Missouri, Nebraska, North Dakota, and Texas. Center is also the first word in 45 combinations, and there are several Centrals and a few Centres and Centrevilles.

But don't make the mistake of thinking that Center and its variants are likely to refer to a central location in a state.

Centrahoma suggests central Oklahoma, but the village is actually near the southeastern corner.

Central City is close to Denver (fairly far east), and Center is in the southern third of the state. Center, Kentucky, is in the Bowling Green (southern) area, and considerably farther north are Centertown and Central City, both much closer to Indiana than to central Kentucky.

Centertown, MO, *is* close to the state's midpoint, but Center is in the northeast corner; Centerview can almost view the western border, and Centerville is down in the southeast, not far from Arkansas. Nebraska's Center is in the northeast quarter, Central City in the eastern third. Center, ND, is twice as close to the western edge as to the eastern.

Non-Texans may be confused to find Center Point not far from San Antonio, and Centerville hundreds of miles northeast, near Dallas. If people in Center, TX, stand on tall stepladders, they may look east across a big lake and see Louisiana, but they certainly can't see mid-Texas, several hundred miles west.

Why these oddities? Most of the names refer to county centers, business centers, or the like—not to state centers.

How Do You Spell *Lakes?*

A Swiss town with a name meaning 'between the lakes' is Interlaken, and that is the spelling used by its New York namesake. But Florida prefers Interlachen (German *lach* means 'pool, puddle, stagnant waters'). The famous Michigan music camp is at Interlochen—maybe influenced by Scottish *loch* as in Loch Lomond.

A Misnamed Minnesota Town

The town of Mountain Lake, in southwest Minnesota, has neither a mountain nor a lake.

Why Not *Snowbird?*

In Alaska, people tell how a place named Quail got its name. The settlers liked very much a local bird called a ptarmigan, a partridge-like grouse that thrives in cold areas. So they decided to name the place Ptarmigan.

"How do you spell it?" someone asked. Nobody knew. So they settled on Quail, which several of them could spell.

Okay, Nokay

There are villages called Okay in Arizona and Oklahoma, the latter having been named for the OK Truck Company.

There's a Nokay Lake in Minnesota, from the name of a chief of the Ojibway tribe.

Windy Weather

Gentle or strong winds move almost constantly across all parts of the globe, but few American town names reflect that omnipresence.

Breeze could often be used as a commendatory term, but Breezewood, PA, is the only post office town to take notice. Zephyr Cove, NV, and Zephyrhills, FL, perhaps profit from pleasant associations. Zephyr, TX, is an example of understatement: it was named following a bad storm called a "norther."

Tornadoes are often called cyclones or hurricanes, and all three words are used, though sparingly, as town names, usually to commemorate a destructive tornado. West Virginia has all three: Tornado, Cyclone, and Hurricane, the third of which was named for Hurricane Creek, on whose banks many great trees were blown down in 1774. The creek flows into the Kanawha River, whose Native American-based name may mean 'tornado' or 'hurricane.' There are also a Cyclone, PA, Hurricane, UT, and Hurricane Mills, TN.

Storm appears only in Stormville, NY, and Storm Lake, IA, for a lake whose stormy waters once threatened the life of a trapper.

Wind appears in Windgap and Wind Ridge, PA, and Windyville, MO. Wind Cave, KY, has a cave with an entrance about 50 feet high through which an outward-moving cool breeze provides natural air conditioning on a hot day. Windy, KY, is in a rather windy location and once was called Windy City (but the Post Office Department dropped *City*, perhaps fearing confusion with Chicago). Onomatist Robert Rennick says that another explanation of Windy is that "some local fellows called 'the Windy Bunch' . . . would gather at the store to swap tales."

Some Guys Named *Joe*

In Yuma County, CO, three men called Joe constituted a high percentage of the total population, so the villagers called the place Three Joes. Today the post office is simply Joes, CO 80822. How many Joes are there today is uncertain, but the population of all of Yuma County is less than ten thousand.

The names of two other Joes adorn Jo Jo Creek and Jo Jo Mountain in Wyoming, and Vermont has Joes Brook and Joes Pond.

Jolo, WV, however, doesn't fit in. It is named for a resident, John Lowe.

The Most Hospitable Town

The only post office towns in the United States with names starting with X are Xenia, OH and IL, although a postal substation in Cincinnati is named Xavier. Xenia, OH, is called that because of a suggestion made in 1803 by an educated preacher. He said that he thought the people in the community were unusually hospitable, and he told them that *xenia* is the classical Greek word for 'hospitality.'

Yes, My Darling Daughters

Hundreds of small towns got their names from those of early leading citizens, who perhaps otherwise would now be known only from their tombstones, if at all. Usually the *surnames* of men and the *given* names of women were chosen for towns.

The Minerva in New York honors the goddess of wisdom, but that in Kentucky stands for the first white woman settler. Emmalena, KY, honors both Emma Thurman, wife of a one-time teacher, and Orlena Morgan, a storekeeper and postmaster. Lynwood, CA, recalls both the first and maiden names of Lynn Wood Sessions, a dairy owner's wife. Jesse Veiley platted a town in Indiana and named it New Elizabeth for his wife, but the Post Office Department shortened and deformalized it to the present Lizton.

Daughters even more than wives were likely to be the honorees. Examples include Francesville, IN; Mayetta, KS (for Mary Henrietta Lunger); and Helechawa, KY. That last name was coined by a railroad president from the first letters of a daughter's three names: *Helen Chase Walbridge*. For another of his daughters, the railroad station name Adele had to suffice.

In Kentucky also, Robert Harrison donated the land for a town site, and the residents responded by calling the place Cynthiana for his daughters Cynthia and Anna. Indiana borrowed the name, and there's another Cynthiana in Ohio. Both the Mary Alice Coal Company and Mary Alice, KY, were named for Mary and Alice, daughters of the mine owner.

Idaho has a Juliaetta, for Julia and Etta, daughters of the first postmaster. Mineola, TX, got its name from the town mayor's daughter Ola and her friend Minnie, but Minneola, KS, is for two local women, Minnie Davis and Ola Watson. A Minnesota Minneola, however, doesn't refer to women at all. Its first two syllables are the Sioux word for 'water,' which appears also in *Minnetonka* and in *Minnesota* itself. (See also p. 198.)

The first postmaster in Bimble, KY, may have preferred animals to people. Local tradition says that *Bimble* combines the names of his prized oxen, Bim and Bill.

Peaceful Names

Maybe someday a sociologist will study the relationships, if any, between people's behavior and the names of the towns where they grew up or now live. For instance, are there temperamental differences between people who live in Savage (MD, MN, MS, MT) and those who live in Loveville (MD) or Amigo (WV)?

To help that sociologist, here's the start of a "peaceable," "friendly," and "loving" list. Perhaps you can think of additional names that belong:

Peace Dale, RI; Peace Valley, MO; Serena, IL; Dove Creek, CO; Accord, NY; Comfort, NC, TX, WV; Concord, AR, CA, GA, IL, KY, MA, MI, NE, NH, NC, PA, TX, VT, VA; Lake Placid, FL, NY; Idyllwild, CA; Harmony, CA, IN, ME, MN, NC, PA, RI, WV; New Harmony, IN, UT

Friendly, NC, WV; Friendship, AR, IN, ME, MD, NY, TN, WI; Friendsville, MO, PA, TN; Amity, MO, OR, PA; Amite, LA; Amityville, NY

Loveland, CO, OH, OK; Loving, NM, TX; Amo, IN; Amoret, MO; Amorita, OK

Maybe Tranquility, NJ, and Tranquillity, CA, should be on the list, too, but that's dubious. Those two places can't even agree about the spelling of the name.

The 24 Noisiest Towns in the United States

Bangor, CA, ME, MI, PA, WI	Guntown, MS
Bangs, TX	Hammer, SD
Bigbee, AL	Roaring Branch, PA
Big Falls, MN	Roaring Gap, NC
Bighorn, MT	Roaring River, NC
Boomer, NC, WV	Roaring Spring, PA
Cannon Falls, MN	Roaring Springs, TX
Drum, KY	Rumbley, MD
Drums, PA	Storm Lake, IA
Falling Rock, WV	Stormville, NY
Falling Waters, WV	Thunderbolt, GA
Good Thunder, MN	Yellville, AL

The Modest Ones

The town names given here suggest—rightly or not—that the inhabitants are or were modest, even self-deprecating. Although the modesty may sometimes have been genuine, often any unfavorable implication may have been unintentional.

Dinkey Creek, CA, for instance, does not belittle either the town or its creek: it memorializes a dog named Dinkey that unwisely tangled with a grizzly bear. And Ordinary, VA, isn't said to be an ordinary town. An old word for *tavern* or *inn* was *ordinary*, and near one such ordinary the town grew up. (In the same state there is also a Smoky Ordinary.)

The naming of Mousie, KY, is delightful. Postmaster Clay Martin, at the turn of this century, had two daughters, Kitty and Mousie. When he was asked to suggest a name for the post office (and thereby the village), he flipped a coin to see which of his daughters should be honored. The younger daughter won.

Here are some other apparently modest or even self-accusing town names:

Acorn, KY, VA
Bland, MO
Blanks, LA
Boca Raton, FL ('mouse mouth')
Boring, MD, OR, and Boreing, KY
Burden, KS
Cheapside, TX
Cloudy, OK
Crum, WV, and Crummies, KY
Dink, WV
Dowdy, AR
Drifting, PA
Dwarf, KY
Lower Peach Tree, AL
Lowpoint, IL
Little, KY (and about 60 more
   with Little as part of the name,
such as Littleton [7 states] or
   Little Silver, NJ)
Maybe, MI
Micro, NC
Muddie, IL
Novice, TX
Nuttsville, VA
Odd, WV
Oldenburg, IN
Peculiar, MO
Plain, WI; Plain City, OH;
   Plainfield (12 states); Plainview
   (6 states); Plainville (6 states)
Rowdy, KY
Shadow, VA
Weed, CA, NM, and Weedville,
   PA

Towns That Brag about Themselves

The namers of some towns (if the names are taken at face value) appear to have been boastful, and sometimes they were. Often, however, the names are deceiving. Ace, TX, for example, which seems to refer to itself as the highest-ranking card in the deck, was actually named for its first postmaster, Ace Emmanuel.

The following names are among those that seem to boast about the characteristics of the land or the scenery:

Broadlands, IA
Buena Vista (10 states)
Fairview (13 states)
Frostproof, FL (but oranges have
   frozen there)
Goodland (6 states)
Good Water, AL
Grand Island (3 states)
Grand Meadow, MN
Grandview (8 states, plus 2 Grand
   View)
Levelland, TX
Lovely, KY
Majestic, KY
Marvel, AL, CO
Nice, CA
Paradise (8 states)
Plentywood, MT
Pretty Prairie, KS
Richfield (14 states)
Scenic, SD
Waterproof, IA (but it was muddy
   when we were there)

Here are some that superficially, at least, appear to commend the early inhabitants or their life style:

Algood, TN; Allgood, AL
Brave, PA
Carefree, AZ
Champion (3 states)
Cornucopia, WI
Fairplay or Fair Play (5 states)
Goodwine, IL
Hardy (5 states)
Jolly, TX
Leader, MN
Lively, VA
Loyal, OK, WI

Niceville, FL
Noble (5 states)
Pleasant Unity, PA
Plush, OR
Rich, KS
Rising Star, TX
Smartt, TN
Smartville, CA
Star (4 states)
Superior (7 states)
Swift, MN
Valiant, OK

This last group includes some of the names that seem to praise miscellaneous virtues:

Aroma Park, IL
Balm, FL
Belle (40, usually with another word)
Blessing, TX
Bliss, ID
Bold Spring, TN
Bonnie, IL
Cool, CA
Darling, MS, PA
Diamond (4 states)
Dunmor, KY; Dunmore, WV
Faith, NC
Felicity, OH
Fine, NY

Gem (3 states)
Liberty Center (3 states, plus 3 Liberty and 24 others with Liberty as part)
Mammoth (4 states)
Marvel, OH, CO
Metropolis, IL
Miracle, KY
New Freedom, PA
New Haven (11 states)
New Hope (4 states)
Optima, OK
Premium, KY
Radiant, VA
Tiptop, VA

The Most Militant Names

Bellicose Park, AK
Cannon, KY (also Cannon Beach, OR; Cannon Falls, MN; Cannonsburg, MI)
Guntown, MS

Powderhorn, CO
Rifle, CO
Salvo, NC
War, WV

Names of Advice, Entreaty, or Command

Commenting on Do Stop, KY, George R. Stewart called it "one of the few hortatory advertising names to have received recognition on an official map."

Many other names, however, appear to give advice, to entreat, or to command. Actually, the appearance is usually false, for the names are often derived from personal names. For example, Dare, Virginia, which seems to be exhorting Virginia to be bold, was really named in memory of Virginia Dare, the first child born of English parents in North America.

But let's forget factuality for a few moments and have a little fun. Read this first group with a pause at the comma, so that you seem to be advising the people of the state—maybe on the Fourth of July or other patriotic occasion.

Advance, Indiana!
Duck, West Virginia!
Fly, Ohio!
Hustle, Virginia!
Huzzah, Missouri!
Muse, Oklahoma! (Pennsylvania!)
Ponder, Texas!
Reform, Alabama! (Mississippi!)
Rule, Arkansas! (Texas!)
Rush, Colorado! (Kentucky! New York!)
Smile, Kentucky!
Stay, Kentucky!
Switchback, West Virginia!
Wade, Mississippi! (North Carolina! Oklahoma!)
Zigzag, Oregon!

We'll read the names in this group without commas. In Bluff Utah, for instance, we are advising someone to make Utah think we have a royal flush.

Admire Kansas
Chase Alabama (Kansas, Louisiana, Maryland, Michigan)
Cook Minnesota (Nebraska, Washington)
Crown Kentucky (Pennsylvania, West Virginia)
Cut Off Louisiana
Dent Minnesota
Divide Colorado
Dodge Nebraska (North Dakota, Texas, Wisconsin)
Honor Michigan
Hurt Virginia
Mix Louisiana
Peel Arkansas
Purchase New York
Revere Minnesota (Missouri, Pennsylvania, West Virginia)
Shock West Virginia
Slaughter Louisiana
Surprise Nebraska (New York)
Tell Texas

Dying to Have a Place Named for You?

The Board on Geographic Names, which was created by federal law as an interdepartmental agency, decides which names are approved for federal use. You can't name a new village, for instance—not if you want to get mail delivery—unless the name has Board approval.

If the name you recommend is that of a person, the person must be dead. So you can't flatter your father-in-law, reingratiate yourself with your husband or wife, or immortalize your bright-eyed child by assigning that person's name to your village.

Goodnight, Roseann. Goodbye, Golden Pond

Every year, as population in some places dwindles and as the U.S. Postal Service tries to cut costs, post offices are closed. Most often the terminated offices are branches and substations, but sometimes post offices classified as Independent or Community are affected.

A single Post Office Directory of the 1980s reported that in the preceding two-year period a total of 234 "postal units" were closed.

So goodnight, Roseann, VA—love letters to Roseann have to be addressed to Grundy.

Goodbye, Golden Pond, KY. Cadiz is where the old folks now buy their stamps.

Goodbye, Valle Crucis, NC. The Postal Service says you belong to Boone.

The Apple Ridge, MI, and the Powderly, AL, substations are closed, and so are those called Echo Park, CA, Cherrelyn, CO, Pinehurst, TX, and about 20 in Puerto Rico with musical Spanish names such as Altamesa, Plaza Cortada, Villa Prades, Tiendas Deco, and branches called Las Flores and Barrio Cantito.

Send your mail not to the CPO (Community Post Office) in Saint Bernard, AL, but to Cullman, not to Jacob Lake, AZ, but to Fredonia (and don't forget that your zip code is changed to 86022). Farewell to once-ambitious Hope Valley, CA, and to Colorado Sierra, CO, although perhaps Golden is no less attractive. Goodbye to Round Oak, GA, and to Twin Lakes and Stonewall. Naf, ID, is so tiny it lost out to Malta, which itself is printed in the smallest road map type.

Chester, MN, succumbed to big brother Rochester, and Clearwater, MO, folks now get their mail from the little office in Sainte Genevieve, and so do those in Lake Forest. Do you feel abandoned—lost in nowhere—when you no longer have a post office?

Goodbye, six branch post offices in New Jersey. Bosque Farms, NM, lost 26 points from its zip code by shifting to Peralta. High Rock, NC, seemed to lose altitude by its change to Denton. People addressing mail to Geneva on the Lake, OH, saved time by sending it to Geneva, unadorned. Ormsby, PA, mail—was it blown away in Cyclone? Snowflakes are somewhat uncommon in southern Virginia; perhaps that's why the Snowflake CPO no longer exists.

And what should we make of this? The downtown station in Helena, MT, was eliminated and its mail had to be delivered to Last Chance.

❦ 23
Changing Times, Changing Names

Canada Desanctifies a Saint

M. and Mme. Belanger moved into a small settlement in northern Ontario in 1882. M. Belanger was employed by the brand-new Canadian Pacific Railway. Mme. Belanger's given name was Azilda. She was friendly, liked to nurse the sick, and was often helpful in other ways. She quickly became one of the best-liked people in the area. (Nick and Helma Mika, in *Places in Ontario*, have told about her, Andre LaPierre says.)

In 1890 a request for a post office for the nameless settlement was approved, and the Canadian government allowed local people—most of whom were Roman Catholics—to name it. On January 6, 1891, it opened under the name St. Azilda—of course for Mme. Belanger.

But a few years later, someone—no longer identifiable—looked into the register of saints and discovered that no St. Azilda was listed. And, of course, Mme. Belanger had not met the formal, rather rigorous qualifications for sanctification. So, on January 6, 1900, the post office was renamed Rayside Station. That's not the end of the story, and no one has recorded for posterity the details of what happened next. No doubt there were pro- and anti-St. Azilda advocates. On January 9, 1901, the post office again became St. Azilda.

Another change came just three days later. A compromise was reached, possibly to avert violence. On January 12, the post office—and the village—became Azilda.

Urpaign? Ono! Minnehaha? Wynot!

People in Lebanon County, PA, and Shasta County, CA, like to tell strangers how the town called Ono in each of those places got its name. Years ago when the village was to be incorporated, there was much discussion in village meetings about what the name should be. Whenever a new suggestion was made, someone would say "Oh, no!" At last someone said, "All right, let's give you what you want. We'll call it Ono." And so they did.

In all probability the story isn't true. The good settlers in each place knew their Bible, and some of them wanted a biblical name but not a frequently used one such as Goshen or Hebron. In one of the begat chapters of I Chronicles (8:12), there is a passing reference to a place called Ono, which is not mentioned again. It is almost certainly the source of the name that graces the two little towns as well as a few other, even smaller ones.

There is apparently some truth in a story told about Wynot, NE, and Whynot, MS and NC. This time, when in a name discussion someone said, "I don't like that name," someone else asked, "Why not?" And eventually those three places settled on Wynot and Whynot.

No place in the Bible has those names.

Other squabbles over place names, it is said locally, prevented the merging of Champaign and Urbana, IL, separated by only a street, and Minneapolis and St. Paul, MN, also right next to each other.

The Illinois merger talks aroused much interest, and general principles seemed reachable concerning the combination of governments, fire and police departments, tax assessments, and so on. But Elm Street in Champaign runs north and south, and in Urbana east and west, and the two don't come close to meeting. The avenue named Florida in Urbana becomes Kirby in Champaign, and residents on neither side of the dividing line wanted to change addresses. Even if those problems and other similar ones were soluble, what should the merged city be called? Chambana seemed a good choice, but residents of Urbana urged that because their city was older, it should come first; they didn't want to be the tail of an onomastic dog. And Urpaign didn't arouse anyone's enthusiasm, particularly after a professor discoursed learnedly on the sad fate of an ancient city named Ur.

The proposed merger of Minneapolis and St. Paul also ran afoul of the naming problem, a favorite local story says. A proponent of the plan suggested Minnehaha—the name of an attractive waterfall, creek, and park. A St. Paulite who opposed the merger saw his chance.

"Fine!" he said, "That's exactly what I thought someone would propose. It's *Minne* for Minneapolis and *haha* for St. Paul!"

What the English Did to the French Language

In parts of North America, especially in what is now called the Midwest, French explorers and sometimes settlers preceded the English. Since the best-educated of the English usually knew some French, many French names remained intact. We find, for instance in Wisconsin or Minnesota, places named Eau Claire 'clear water', Fond du Lac 'foot of the lake', and Lac Qui Parle 'the lake that talks' (one of the loveliest of place names). That last name, however, has deteriorated in pronunciation to something like "lackeyparl."

Larger changes occurred in other French names—sometimes enough to hide the original. Here are some examples:

Bob Ruly, MI: *Bois brûle* 'burned wood' was what the French called a place where there had been a forest fire. To the English, that sounded like a man's name.

Dishmaugh: a well-traveled Native American trail led to this lake in Indiana, which the French called *lac du chemin* 'lake at the road.' The English converted *du chemin* to Dishmaugh.

Glazypeau: a creek and a small mountain in Arkansas. *Glaise* was the French word for a salt lick, a deposit where animals could lick the salt they craved. One such lick was *glaise à Paul* 'Paul's lick.' The name went through various stages (Glazypool, Glazypole, Glazier Pole, Glacierpeau) and finally settled into Glazypeau.

Gnaw Bone: a village and a short creek in Indiana. Although local legends attribute the name to a person or persons who because of deep snow or other reasons were reduced to gnawing bones, the probable explanation is that early French settlers had called the place Narbonne, after a French town.

Lemon Fair: a Vermont river. Said to be an anglicization of *les monts verts* 'the green mountains.'

Loose: a Missouri creek. Possibly from *l'ours* 'the bear.' The same explanation has been offered for Louse Creek in Oregon, but George R. Stewart says that an early camp there was badly infested by lice.

Low Freight: an Arkansas creek. Originally, *l'eau froide* 'the cold water.' Understood by later English settlers as "low freight." Now it is officially L'Eau Fraise 'fresh water,' although *frais,* Stewart points out, should be *fraiche.*

Meredosia, IL: A *marais* was 'a pool or spring,' and *marais d'osier* was a pool near willows. Perhaps influenced by Greek names such as Theodosia, English speakers reworked the French. In other places, *marais* has taken other forms, as in Marie Saline Landing in Arkansas, from *marais saline* 'salty pool,' or in Mary Delarme Creek in Indiana, corrupted from *marais de l'orme* 'elm spring.'

Ozark Mountains in Missouri and adjoining states: the French referred to *Aux Arks* 'at the Arks,' from the Arkansa Indian tribe. Ozark is basically a respelling of the earlier name.

Picketwire, a Colorado creek: officially *Purgatoire,* but Picketwire is much easier for English-trained tongues. Originally a Spanish name, *El Rio de las Animas Perdidas en Purgatorio* 'the river of lost souls in Purgatory,' in memory of some Spaniards who were killed by Native Americans before they could receive absolution, it was for obvious reasons shortened to *Purgatorio* and then translated by Frenchmen into *Purgatoire.*

Skilligallee, MI: from *Ile aux Galets* 'pebble island.'

Smackover, AR: the French called it *Chemin Couvert* 'covered road,' perhaps because of overhanging tree branches. Try saying *shuh-MAA cuh-VAIR* a few times rapidly, and you too may come out with Smackover.

Swashing, a creek in Missouri: the French named it for Joachim, perhaps Saint Joachim. By folk etymology the pronunciation changed to Swashing.

Tar Blue is only one of a number of names in which French *terre* 'earth' was changed to *tar; blue* is obviously from French *bleue.* Stewart has also mentioned Pumly Tar from *Pomme de Terre* 'earth apple, potato'; Movestar from *Mauvaise Terre* 'bad earth'; and Turnwall, an Arkansas Creek, from *Terre Noire* 'black earth.'

Zumbro, a stream in Minnesota: In small streams, French voyageurs frequently encountered tangled tree trunks, tree limbs, and other barriers to easy passage. They called these *les embarras* 'obstructions.' Embarrass, MN, and the nearby Embarrass River, as well as the Embarras River in Illinois are named for them and called *EM-brah* or *EM-braw* by the knowledgeable, *em-BARE-us* by strangers. In southern Minnesota *les embarras* or *aux embarras* became Zumbro. A town on its banks is Zumbrota, which combines the revised French with a Siouan ending -*ta* 'on, at.'

Many French names were merely replaced by other names that the English preferred. Lac Saint Sacrement, for instance, became Lake George; Fort Carillon, Fort Ticonderoga; and Au Sable, Sandy Creek. La Rivière de la Famine was translated to Famine River.

How the Europeans Changed Native American Names

Novelist Thomas Wolfe wrote in *Of Time and the River:*

Where can you match the mighty music of their names?—The Monongahela, the Colorado, the Rio Grande, the Columbia, the Tennessee, the Hudson (Sweet Thames!); the Kennebec, the Rappahannock, the Delaware, the Penobscot, the Wabash, the Chesapeake, the Swannanoa, the Indian River, the Niagara (Sweet Afton!); the Saint Lawrence, the Susquehanna, the Tombigbee, the Nantahala, the French Broad, the Chattahoochee, the Arizona, and the Potomac (Father Tiber!)—these are a few of their princely names, these are a few of their great, proud, glittering names, fit for the immense and lonely land that they inhabit.

We tried to imitate the sounds the Native Americans made when they talked of rivers, lakes, and mountains, and we used imitations of what we heard to name hundreds of our towns, a score of our large cities, and about half of our states.

The Native Americans could not write the names, and white people's ears were sometimes faulty, their vocal organs untutored in forming the gutturals and other strange (to them) sounds that natives had learned to form with ease.

When we say that a place has a Native American name, all we can mean is that a modern word represents what white people once thought the natives were saying. Often, assuredly, today's name would be incomprehensible to a native of two hundred or so years ago if he or she could now be brought back to life.

Consider some of the Native American names that Wolfe included in his rhapsodic list.

French voyageurs encountered a rather small river that the natives seemed to call Ouaboukigon, which may or may not mean 'shining white.' The Native American name seemed ungainly, and the French shortened and altered it to Oubache. To the English that sounded like Wabash, and so it appears on modern maps. In the old books of favorite songs, the Hoosier brother of novelist Theodore Dreiser, who called himself Paul Dresser, has written sentimentally of "the banks of the Wabash." Could he have written—would he have written—"On the Banks of the Ouaboukigon"?

Kennebec 'long reach' was recorded in 1609 as Kinebeki. Apparently Penobscot 'sloping-arch-at' was originally just one small stretch of the stream above Bangor, ME, but the name was extended by whites to the whole river. The same seems true of Monongahela 'high-banks-falling-down,' a word of which Walt Whitman said, "It rolls with venison freshness on the palate." The name of North Carolina's Nantahala seems to mean 'noonday sun,' so called because in some places, although not along the whole river, the cliffs are so steep and high that sunlight reaches the water only at midday.

The Spanish wrote a Cherokee name as Tanasqui more than four centuries ago, and the English 150 years later thought it was Tinnase. For years it was the Cherokee River, but some secession-minded western North Carolinians in the late eighteenth century chose to call their new state, and the river, Tennessee.

In 1585 Chesapeake was first written by the English as Chesepiooc, which may have meant 'big-river-at' (*che* definitely meant 'big' in Algonquian). Susquehanna hasn't changed much from Sasquehanough, as John Smith wrote it as early as 1608, although the deleted final letters in effect deleted "men" from the meaning 'Sasque-tribe-stream-men' (*hanna* was 'stream' to the Algonquians).

Alabama's Tombigbee River of course has nothing to do with large makers of honey. The Choctaw was earlier written as *itombiikbi*, then respelled to appear more English and more pronounceable. It means 'coffin makers,' after a tribe who scraped the bones of their dead and made boxes to keep them in.

Virginia's Rappahannock 'back-and-forth-stream' was called that because it rises and lowers with the tides; Rapidan, a tributary, is a shortened form.

John Smith and other early settlers recorded Potomac as Patawomeck or Potowanmeac, which shortcutting English quickly reduced to Potomack and then dropped the k. Among the earliest written versions of Niagara were Unéaukara and Ongniaahra, short-ened by the French to Ongiara and then to the present form.

What happened to the Native American names of the rivers that Wolfe wrote so lovingly is similar to what has happened to countless other names borrowed from the earlier inhabitants. Here are early spellings of a few other familiar places:

Illinois: Eriniouai, later Aliniouek, Iliniouek. The French provided the
    final *s* to make it look more French.
Arizona: Ali-shonak 'little spring' in Papago; then Arizonac. (A recent
    theory, though, says that Arizona is a Basque name, not Indian, and
    that it comes from the Basque *aritz* 'oak,' which appears in a number
    of western place names.)
Milwaukee: Milo-aki
Wisconsin: Mescousing or Mesconsing, French Ouisconsing
Kansas: the name of the tribe was written as Escansaque by the
    Spanish.
Manhattan: Manna-hatta, possibly the same as a name by which
    Mohicans were sometimes called, Manhecan or Manahegan.
Schenectady: written Scheaenhechstede by the Dutch
Hoboken: Hopoakan-hacking
Roanoke: Rarenawok
Missouri: Ouemessourit
Michigan: Machihiganing

Eventually an anglicized version of a Native American name may be still further shortened. Thus, the Swatara, a creek with its name based on an Iroquoian word, is informally called the Swatty in southeastern Pennsylvania.

Walt Whitman, who loved most American names, and in par-ticular names of Native American ancestry, said, "What is the fit-ness—What the strange charm of aboriginal names?—They all fit. Mississippi!—the word winds with chutes—it rolls a stream three thousand miles long."

Maybe so. But American settlers were seldom content with a name that seemed three thousand miles long. They modified the long names, the hard-to-pronounce names, cutting a corner off here, a syllable there, often dispensing with endings or supplying endings that were more familiar. Inevitably in diminishing the original names they diminished the meanings, too—sometimes to no meaning.

But who is alive to know the difference?

The Power of Love in Gold Rush Country

In Amador County, CA, are places named Fiddletown, Kit Carson, Pioneer, River Pines, Sutter Creek, and Volcano.

But the most interesting onomastically is Ione—not because of what it is, but because of what it was. The place used to be called Bedbug. Women, however, could seldom be induced to marry men whose permanent address would be Bedbug, so the citizens got together and changed it to Ione—a woman's name said to mean 'violet.'

Such feminine influence or other forces of civilization resulted in other name changes in the gold-mining areas of California. Growlersburg, in El Dorado County, probably sounded too grumpy and so became Georgetown; Hangtown became Placerville; and Gouge Eye, in nearby Sutter County, is now the charming little town of Pleasant Grove.

Others of the once-flourishing gold towns have vanished or at least crumbled. Once there was Tin Cup, where miners boasted they could find that much gold daily. Whiskeytown is now a tiny village (some 50 places had Whiskey in their names). Stories are still told about other spots with such names as You Bet, Shirttail (a prospector carried his new-found gold in his shirttail), Tinkers Knob (teamster J. A. Tinker had a big nose), and Tinkers Defeat (which took place on a sharp curve), and Pinchemtight (where a pinch of gold was the price of a drink and a Swedish bartender, Big-Thumb Ole, was threatened when he didn't pinch his fingers tight enough—or so one version of the legend goes).

Bret Harte immortalized Poker Flat, but he didn't turn his genius loose on Cheese-Marie (perhaps from Jesus Maria), Hell Hollow, Murderers' Bar, Jackass Hill, Squaw Hollow, Sucker Flat, Humbug, and the Rattlesnake Bar and the Frogtown Bar. And Mark Twain reached California a little too late, although he did enlighten us about jumping frogs in Calaveras County, where Angel's Camp has been restored.

Should *Pikes Peak* Be *James's Peak?*

Who deserves the honor of having a mountain bear his or her name: its discoverer or the person who first climbs it?

In November 1806, Zebulon Pike, an army officer and explorer, led an exploring party to the southwest. West of what is now Colorado Springs, he found a previously unknown mountain over 14,000 feet high. He attempted to climb it, but cold weather and snow prevented him and his party from reaching the top. Nevertheless, his followers and then other people who went to the area began to call the mountain Pikes Peak.

Fourteen years later, in July 1820, an expedition led by Stephen Long was exploring the area. One mountain that he discovered he named for himself, Longs Peak. He sent a team to try to climb another, which was the peak that Zebulon Pike had been unable to master. The team members were Edwin James, J. Verplank, and Z. Wilson. After they successfully completed the ascent, Long said that the mountain should be named for James.

Since Long was an official of the U.S. Corps of Topographical Engineers, James's Peak would apparently be the accepted name. But to the people of the area it was Pikes Peak, and that's what they continued to call it, regardless of Topographical Engineers. Eventually officialdom gave in, and today Pikes Peak, although less tall than 30 other Colorado mountains, is probably the best known.

The Most-Used Street Name

In American towns and cities, the most-used street name is not Washington, Main, Elm, or First, as might be supposed. It's Second Street. Why? Because the street that would normally be First is often Main (which in England, by the way, is frequently High or "the High").

Street Names in Housing Developments

The term *housing development* has been defined as "a place where they cut down all the trees and then name the streets after them."

On the Street (Circle, Drive, Lane, Trail) Where You Live

Are there fashions in street names as in clothing and other things? John Algeo found that there are—at least in Athens, GA.

In 1859 about three quarters of the 46 street names in Athens were names of people prominent in the early days of the community or the university. The others were often directional: Oconee (for the river, which everyone would presumably know about), Factory (because there was a factory there), College, School, Rock Spring, Foundry, and so on.

But by 1978, although the early names for the most part still existed, the names of the rest of the 850-plus streets were generally "chosen for their pleasant associations and hence for their commercial value."

So modern Athens has street names such as Homestead Drive, Doe Run, Orchard Circle (no orchard there), Indian Lake Court (no lake), Deertree Drive (what's a deertree?), Woodstock Drive, Spruce Valley Road (no valley), Ravenwood Court, Arborview Drive (no arbors in sight), Mockingbird Circle, Horseshoe Circle (not shaped like either a horseshoe or a circle), Jockey Club Drive (no club, probably no jockeys).

As these names suggest, even the words *street* and *avenue* may now be superseded by other terms. In Athens, Algeo found 18 Drives, 10 Courts, 8 Circles, 3 Places, 2 Roads, 2 Runs, 1 Way, 1 Lane, and 1 Trail.

In other cities, many of the early names were those of national figures, other states, and trees. But their modern names resemble those that Algeo found in Athens, although sometimes they include more or less prominent, living, local people, not forgetting the developers and members of their families.

An example, from Gary Jenning's *Personalities of Language:* A street in Stamford, CT, was called Bubsey Lane, reportedly the nickname of a child of the tract developer. The residents petitioned to have the name changed to Club Circle.

❦ PART IV

Still More of These and a Few of Those

🍒 24
Still More of These

Early Automobiles

"Want a ride in my Seven Little Buffaloes?"

"I wouldn't ride in anything but a Geronimo!"

Those are two of the many makes of American automobiles—from decades before Japan ever built a car. Early in this century, there were more car makes than there are makes of computers today.

How about buying an Auto-Vehicle? or a Bi-Auto-Go, a Gearless, a Car-Nation?

Phillip R. Rutherford has made a hobby of collecting not cars but car names. He reported in Fred Tarpley's *Naughty Names* that he found 1,547 different ones, but he estimated that the total might reach 2,000. Most of the car makes and makers never became widely known; sometimes only a half-dozen or so of a brand were ever bolted and welded together.

In their search for immortality, car builders—over half of them—attached their own names to their creations. Surviving examples include Ford, Dodge, Chrysler, Chevrolet (who both designed and raced cars), and Oldsmobile (for R. E. Olds, who also tried to be remembered in a now almost-forgotten car called Reo).

, Eight U.S. Presidents' names are on the list: Washington, Monroe, Jackson, Lincoln (still being built), Johnson (Andrew), Grant, Roosevelt (Theodore), and Harding.

Many car builders liked to use boastful names: Marvel, Summit, Only (the Only car for you), Okay, Wonder, Superior, Success, Rex (Latin for 'king'), Paragon, Peerless, Ideal, Elite, Famous, Best, and Longest.

The towns or states where cars were built sometimes inspired the names. There was, of course, a Michigan, as well as a Detroit, a Jackson and a Jaxon, and a Flint. Kansas City, Birmingham, Los Angeles, Indianapolis, Tulsa, Rochester (which one?), Omaha, Akron, and Boston had cars named for them, as did smaller places such as Moline, Galesburg (the car was called Gale), Springfield (which one?), Amesbury, Auburn, Waco, Laconia, and Dubuque.

Obviously many other states competed with Michigan in car building. Auto-onomatist Rutherford found Texmobile, Texas, Alamobile, Lone Star, Ohio, Buckeye, Maryland, California, Illinois, Penn, Pennsy, and Bay Stater.

Among the few names from foreign place were Mecca, Alsace, Bethlehem, and Waterloo, although at least those last two may have referred to places in Pennsylvania and Iowa.

Some makers liked to brag about speed: Flyer, Dixie Flyer, Zip, Speedwell, Quick, Komet, and O-we-go, which probably should have been written with an exclamation mark.

Several early car names uncovered by Rutherford were based on mythology or ancient place names: Vulcan, Vestal, Olympia, Ajax, Centaur, Atlas, Roman, Phoenix, and Sparta.

A few were named for animals: Wolverine, Vixen, and Coyote; or for birds: Petrel, Black Crow, and Duck.

Some amusing and curious car names were Gadabout, Red Jacket, and Red Bug.

The name of a car made by the Knight Company suggests a pun: Silent Knight. (It didn't live up to its name.) A scarab is a kind of beetle, so the Stout Scarab sounds like a fat beetle, although it may have been made by a company or a man named Stout.

Fwick and Twombley sound like inefficient English butlers. Pungs-Finch could be a character in a P. G. Wodehouse story.

Perhaps Maytag could wash the owner's dishes or clothes as it drove along.

The Izzen is puzzling. Izzit or Izzent it? Peter Pan has a cheerful sound, as does Sprite Cycle-Car (maybe like an elf on a bicycle), but Norwalk Underslung suggests no nonsense.

Who would buy a car named Blood? or Hazard? or Savage? or even Klink, though that one belongs in a "funny" list.

Perhaps the most amusing name is the previously mentioned Seven Little Buffaloes. One can hear them under the hood, rushing their passengers across the trackless prairies.

On the Advantages of Learning Foreign Languages

A Chevrolet with the name Nova did not sell well to Hispanics. The reason: in Spanish, *no va* means 'it doesn't go.'

The Shortest Movie Title

It's hard to imagine a movie title much shorter than that of a picture directed by Fritz Lang in 1931: M.

A Record for Movie-Title Goofs?

How many errors can be made in a four-word movie title? Perhaps the record is held by a thriller called *Krakatowa, East of Java*, concerning the volcano that erupted disastrously in 1883. There are two errors. The conventional spelling of the volcano's name is Krakatoa, and it is west of Java, not east.

Why *Oscar*?

How did the Oscar, symbol of motion picture achievement, get its name? A frequent explanation is that in 1931, two years after the first were awarded, the librarian for the Academy of Motion Picture Arts and Sciences, Margaret Herrick, saw one of the statuettes and exclaimed, "It looks like my Uncle Oscar!" Ms. Herrick's uncle was Oscar Pierce, a wheat and fruit grower who lived in Texas, then later moved to California.

Behind the Silver Screen

Would you suppose that a common preposition could be a forbidden word in titles of movies? When the Hays Office in the early 1930s was busy inventing things that movie makers must not do or allow to be said, one of the words not permitted in movie titles was *behind*.

A New Spelling for X

Some newspapers or local mores or ordinances require that titles of certain X-rated movies (later NC-17) be modified in advertising. *Deep* or *Throat* may be acceptable, but *Deep Throat* may not. A gay film entitled *Stud Farm* was advertised as *Study Farm*. The theater probably lost money on that one.

How the 26 Major League Baseball Teams Got Their Names

1. Atlanta Braves The Braves inherited their name from Boston and Milwaukee. The Boston National League baseball team had been called, officially or unofficially, Red Caps, Beanies, Beaneaters, Doves, Rustlers, Pilgrims. Baseball club president Jim Gaffney, member of a political organization called Tammany, recommended Braves, honoring the Tammany "Wigwam." The name was accepted in 1912, and retained except for 1936 to 1941, when Bees was substituted. The name Braves followed the team to Milwaukee in 1953, and to Atlanta in 1966.

2. Baltimore Orioles The name was adopted in the 1890s. The oriole (formerly called the Baltimore oriole but now the Northern oriole) is Maryland's state bird. Nicknames: Birds, O's

3. Boston Red Sox Originally they were called Somersets (1901) for the owner, Charles W. Somers. Nicknames at the time included Speed Boys, Puritans, Plymouth Rocks. After the National League Braves, the other Boston team of the time, changed from red stockings to white, the American League team adopted red stockings and took the name Red Sox. Nicknames: Bosox, Sox

4. California Angels In 1961 they were the Los Angeles Angels, the name of the city's earlier Pacific Coast League club. On moving to Anaheim in 1965, they became the California Angels.

5. Chicago Cubs The team was originally called the White Stockings. From 1880 through 1886, the Chicago National League club won five pennants, but on the departure of their beloved manager, "Pop" or "Cap" (really Adrian) Anson, the team was called Orphans. Later, at a time when they had numerous rookies, they were nicknamed Babes, Colts, and Cubs. The last name stuck. Unofficially: Bruins.

6. Chicago White Sox In 1901, this team tried to take over the old name of the Cubs, which was White Stockings. On objections from the National League, they changed to White Sox. For short: Sox or Chisox.

7. Cincinnati Reds In 1866 they were Red Stockings, quickly shortened to Reds. In 1953, because of Joseph McCarthy's Communist-scare tactics, club officers changed to Redlegs, but fans thought the decision silly, so the team soon became Reds again.

8. Cleveland Indians The Cleveland team's pre-big-league name was Spiders because so many players were thin and gangling. When they entered the American League, they became the Blues or Bluebirds because of the color of their uniforms. In 1902 the players voted for Broncos, but fans liked Naps better, to honor their favorite player, second baseman Napoleon ("Nap") Lajoie. After he left to play for Philadelphia in 1914, the fans chose Indians.

9. Detroit Tigers The Detroit team was originally called Wolverines because Michigan is the Wolverine State, but their black and yellow stockings suggested the name Tigers. They were nicknamed Tygers during Ty Cobb's great career with them (1904-26). Nickname: Bengals.

10. Houston Astros In 1962 they were the Colt 45's or Colts, but the gun company objected, especially when they couldn't hit. In 1964 they became the Astronauts, which wouldn't fit headlines. Hence they are the Astros, who play in the Astrodome.

11. Kansas City Royals Vociferous protests and threatened legal action followed the 1968 move of the Kansas City A's to Oakland, but peace returned when baseball authorities permitted a new team to be formed two years later. The club asked for name suggestions and received over 17,000. The name should be "of significance to the area, and one that would be suitable for emblematic purposes, as well as appropriate in length for newspapers, radio and TV." The winner, a Kansan named Sanford Porte, referred to Kansas City's "nationally known American Royal parade and pageant" and added, "The team colors of royal blue and white would be in harmony with the State Bird, the Bluebird, the State Flag, the old Kansas City Blues baseball team, and our current hockey team."

12. Los Angeles Dodgers The name dates back to Brooklyn. Originally they were the Brooklyn Bridegrooms because that's what several of the first players were. New York Giants fans ridiculed them as "trolley dodgers" (a street kids' game of playing "chicken" with trolleys), and Dodgers stuck. Sportswriters also liked Robins (for a one-time manager), Kings, and Superbas, and fans lived and died with their beloved but often erratic Bums. The name Dodgers accompanied the team to the West Coast.

13. Milwaukee Brewers From 1878 to 1953 Milwaukee had Brewers alternately as a major and a minor league club, named for the city's most famous industry. In 1953 Milwaukee secured the Braves and kept that name. After the Braves moved to Atlanta, Milwaukee took over the Seattle Pilots and changed back to the name Brewers.

14. Minnesota Twins In 1960 a team secured from Washington, DC, was renamed the Twin City Twins, for Minneapolis and St. Paul. (In Washington the team had first been called the Statesmen, but was demoted to Senators. After that came the Nationals [the team from the capital city was supposedly the national team], the Nats, and then the Senators again.) The Twin City Twins' name was soon changed to Minnesota Twins to suggest that the team represented the whole state.

15. Montreal Expos In 1968, a year after the Montreal world's fair called Expo 67, the team was named Expos.

16. New York Mets The team is officially called the Metropolitans. In 1883 an American Association team had that name. The new version arrived in 1962, when New York had been without National League baseball for five years. Fans revived Metropolitans, which headline writers and conversationalists had to shorten.

17. New York Yankees The New York team was originally called the Highlanders or the Hilltoppers because of the highlands of the Hudson. New York sportswriters preferred the shorter Yankees. Nicknames include Yanks and, starting with the years of Ruth and Gehrig, Bronx Bombers. Once-numerous Yankee haters were known to call them Damyankees.

18. Oakland A's The Philadelphia Athletics, often called A's for short, have existed as amateurs or professionals since 1860. They were sometimes nicknamed the White Elephants, but not often while Cornelius McGillicuddy (better known as Connie Mack) was their manager (1901-1950). The name Athletics or A's followed the team to Kansas City, then to Oakland in 1968.

19. Philadelphia Phillies The name has been used most of the time since 1883, although Bob Carpenter, an owner from 1943 to 1950, unsuccessfully tried to foist the name Blue Jays on fans who preferred the short name of their favorite city. Nicknames: Phils, Quakers

20. Pittsburgh Pirates Originally they were the Alleghenies (for the river and the mountains), then Innocents (for unknown reasons). Since 1891 they have been the Pirates, so called because of their intensive efforts to lure star players from other clubs (now considered a legitimate part of the business).

21. St. Louis Cardinals The earliest St. Louis team was called the Browns, but the Browns of 1899 changed their colors to red, causing a female fan to refer to "that lovely shade of cardinal." So Cardinals they became, although another team in the American League took over the old name and existed (barely) as the St. Louis Browns into the 1940s, when they lost in their only World Series appearance—to the Cardinals. Nicknames: Redbirds, Cards

22. San Diego Padres An earlier Pacific Coast team had been the Padres, a popular name in an area with many priests and many speakers of Spanish, so the big-league team took it over during a time of expansion.

23. San Francisco Giants The team was originally the New York Giants, which had at first been called the Gothams. The name is sometimes attributed to President Benjamin Harrison, who thought the players looked like giants. It remained with the team when in 1958 it moved from the East to the West Coast.

24. Seattle Mariners They were preceded in Seattle by the Pilots, who moved to Milwaukee. In a contest open to fans,

Mariners was one of the names suggested and was chosen by the six owners. The older players are of course Ancient Mariners. Nickname: M's

25. Texas Rangers Formerly the Washington Senators of 1961 to 1971. They moved to Arlington, TX, (from Dallas) in 1972, and were named for the famous Texas lawmen.

26. Toronto Blue Jays In a contest to name the expansion team, 154 persons (out of 30,000) suggested Blue Jays, pointing out that Ontario has many of those birds and—this may have been decisive—that a beer called Blue was made by one of the owners, the LaBatt Breweries.

Mrs. Alice Jones,
Mrs. John Jones,
Ms. Alice Jones,
Alice Jones

Until about 1750 in the United States, *Mrs.* (Mistress) was used for both unmarried and married adult females, and *Miss* was for some time regarded as a possible slur on the woman's moral standards. So Alice Jones in that early period would not have been Miss Alice Jones or Mrs. John Jones. She could have been, however, Mrs. (Mistress) Alice Jones.

But late in the eighteenth century and early in the nineteenth, conditions changed and it became customary to write Mrs. John Jones, Mrs. Washington Post, and so on. If the husband had a high position, a wife might reflect his glory and enhance her own by being known as Mrs. General Jones, or Mrs. Judge Jones.

Not everyone was happy with this situation. French author George Sand and English author George Eliot, for example, took those pseudonyms as disguises of both their gender and their possession of one or more mates.

Lucy Stone, while organizing women's rights conventions in the United States, met and married Henry B. Blackwell in May 1855. For a year and two months, she was either Mrs. Henry B. Blackwell or Mrs. Lucy Stone Blackwell, but then, with Henry's enthusiastic support, she reverted to Lucy Stone. He abetted her, too, in her extended campaign for women's rights, helping her to found and edit several suffragist publications. Lucy's reversion to her maiden name caused her trouble with Massachusetts authorities, who allowed women to vote in local elections but were reluctant to let Lucy do so unless she used her "legal" name, Blackwell.

Stone and Blackwell established the American Woman Suffrage Association in 1869, started *Woman's Journal*, a suffrage weekly, and published numerous *Woman Suffrage Leaflets*, frequently considering the question of the "right" name for married women.

Long after they were dead, a Lucy Stone League was revitalized (in 1969), mainly because so many women objected to being called the equivalent of Mrs. John Jones or Mrs. Henry Blackwell.

A group with a still more specific function was founded in 1973, the Center for a Woman's Own Name. In 1974 it published a *Booklet for Women Who Wish to Determine Their Own Names after Marriage*, which covered not only the emotional issues but also legal questions and possible problems with the names of children.

Karla Taylor, writing for the *Indianapolis Star* in 1982, reported the comments of several women and men concerning their experiments with married names.

Donna Bays-Beinart: "Just because I got married, Donna Bays didn't stop existing."

Nancy Hartman Scott (who puts her maiden name at the end): "If I was Mrs. Worth Hartman, I'd be losing part of myself. . . . Sometimes people think he's my brother. And when people call me Mrs. Scott, I really feel like they're talking about my mother."

Worth Scott Hartman (who puts his wife's maiden name in the middle of his own): No other comment needed.

Teresa Adler-Phelps: "File it under Phelps, so Kevin and I can keep our records together."

Mary Beth Ramey, married to Rich Haily: "If we gave [our daughter] the name Ramey-Haily, God help her when she enters first grade and tries to learn to spell her name. And if it were Andrea Elizabeth Ramey-Haily and she married a Zabrowski—ugh!"

Genira Stephens-Hotopp: "What will they do if our son Brian Alexander Stephens-Hotopp grows up and marries, for instance, Katherine Anne Gallagher-Stewart? That will be up to them."

Bruce Stephens-Hotopp (who legally changed his name to include Genira's name and the hyphen): "For most men, the first reaction is 'Why in hell would you do a thing like that?' For me, it was based on an evaluation of who I feel like I am and my personal beliefs, which reflect that I enjoy my partner being equal with me."

Genira Stephens-Hotopp: "He's an exceptional human being."

The statutes of most states say in effect that a woman (or a man) may use any name she (or he) wishes, provided that the choice is not made with the intent of defrauding anyone. The Supreme Court of Alabama, a state that was one of the last holdouts, ruled in 1981 that even for drivers' licenses and voter registration, a married woman should no longer be required to use her husband's name. Lucy Stone finally triumphed.

Ms. has triumphed, too. In the 1950s a few people used it, mainly in corresponding with a woman whose marital status was unknown. Feminists in the 1970s urged its use as the counterpart of *Mr.*, but critics called it silly or unnecessary or said that it was no more than the Southern pronunciation of *Mrs.* Gradually, though, newspaper editors and more and more business letter writers found it a valuable addition to the language, and today it is used as a matter of course. (When a need exists, the language usually finds a way to meet it.)

The New York Times, the "newspaper of record," ran the following Editors' Note on June 20, 1986:

> Beginning today, The New York Times will use "Ms." as an honorific in its news and editorial columns.
>
> Until now, "Ms." had not been used because of the belief that it had not passed sufficiently into the language to be accepted as common usage. The Times now believes that "Ms." has become a part of the language and is changing its policy.
>
> The Times will continue to use "Miss" or "Mrs." when it knows the marital status of a woman in the news, unless she prefers "Ms."
>
> "Ms." will also be used when a woman's marital status is not known, or when a married woman wishes to use it with her prior name in professional or private life.

❦ 25
. . . and a Few of Those

Becoming Famous by Becoming Common

Sometimes the best way to become famous—maybe immortalized, in fact—is to have your name become a common noun, written without a capital letter. That, as is well-known, is what happened to the Fourth Earl of Sandwich (1718–92), who invented the sandwich so that he could eat without interrupting his gambling. And it's what happened to Governor Elbridge Gerry of Massachusetts who, to help his party in 1812, reshaped an election district that turned out to be salamander-shaped and gave rise to the noun (and verb) *gerrymander*.

Here are other examples, some of which may be a little less known.

Electrical terms
ampere (amp): André Marie Ampère (1775–1836), French mathematician and physicist, "father of electrodynamics"
joule: James P. Joule (1818–1889), British physicist
ohm: George Simon Ohm (1787–1854), German physicist
tesla: Nikola Tesla (1857–1943), Croatian-born American electrical engineer
volt: Count Alessandro Volta (1745–1827), Italian physicist
watt: James Watt (1736–1819), Scottish engineer and inventor

Flower names

begonia: Michel Bégon (1638–1710), governor of Santo Domingo
camellia: George Josef Kamel (1661–1706), Moravian Jesuit missionary
clivia: a Duchess of Northumberland, *nee* Clive
dahlia: Anders Dahl, eighteenth-century Swedish botanist
fittonia: Elizabeth and Sarah Mary Fitton, botanists
fuchsia: Leonhard Fuchs (1501–1566), German botanist
gentian: probably for Gentius, king of Illyria in second century B.C.
lobelia: Matthias de Lobel (1538–1616), Flemish botanist
magnolia: Pierre Magnol (1638–1715), French botanist
poinsettia: discovered by J. R. Poinsett (1799–1851), U.S. Minister to
   Mexico
wistaria or *wisteria:* Casper Wistar or Wister (1761–1818), American
   anatomist
zinnia: Johann Gottfried Zinn (1729–1759), German botanist

Miscellaneous

blanket: possibly for Thomas Blanket of England, said to have been the
   inventor in 1340; more likely, though, from French *blanc* 'white'
bobby: Sir Robert Peel (1788–1850), British prime minister who helped
   to establish London's police force
boycott: Charles C. Boycott (1832–1897), British land agent driven out
   by tenants when he refused to lower their rents
bowdlerization: Thomas Bowdler (1754–1825), English editor who
   expurgated Shakespeare
cardigan: Seventh Earl of Cardigan (1797–1868), British army officer
chauvinism: Nicholas Chauvin, nineteenth-century French soldier
   extraordinarily devoted to Napoleon
derrick: a hangman, Derick (c. 1600) at Tyburn, England; the gallows
   was named for him, then other suspension devices
diesel: Rudolf Diesel (1858–1913), German mechanical engineer
dunce: contemptuously used by opponents to ridicule followers of John
   Duns Scotus (1265?–1308), Scottish philosopher and theologian
fermium (a synthetic element): Enrico Fermi (1901–1959), Italian-born
   American physicist
guillotine: Joseph Guillotin (1738–1814), French doctor who
   recommended its use
guy: Guy Fawkes (1570–1606), British conspirator whose effigies are
   burned each Guy Fawkes Day (November 5)
hoodlum: of doubtful origin, but sometimes said to be based on
   Muldoon, a ruffian on San Francisco's once notorious Barbary Coast
jimmy: Jemmy or Jimmy, a conventional name for an assistant in the
   late Middle Ages; a jimmy, to pry things open, is a "thief's assistant"
kaiser, czar, tsar: Julius Caesar and other dictators who followed him
lynch: Charles Lynch (1736–1796), Virginia planter and justice of the
   peace
masochism: Leopold von Sacher-Masoch (1836–1895), Austrian novelist
   who described the abnormal condition

maudlin: old pronunciation of (Mary) Magdalene, a symbol of tearful repentance

mausoleum: Mausōlus (d. 353 B.C.), king of Caria, whose widow built an elaborate tomb for him

maverick: Samuel A. Maverick (1803–1870), unconventional Texas cattleman who did not brand his calves

nicotine: Jean Nicot, sixteenth-century French ambassador credited with introducing tobacco to France

pants, pantaloons: Pantaleone, fourth-century Venetian doctor who was made a saint; later became a stock figure in comedies, wearing a garment including tight-fitting breeches and stockings

pap smear, pap test (sometimes still capitalized): George Papanicolaou (1882–1962), American scientist of Greek descent

pasteurization: Louis Pasteur (1822–1895), French chemist who invented the process

pompadour: Marquise de Pompadour (1721–1764), mistress of French king Louis XV; she wore her hair brushed straight back

praline: invented by the cook of French Count du Plessis Praslin (1598–1675)

ritz (putting on the): César Ritz (1850–1918), Swiss hotelier

sadism: Comte Donatien de Sade (1740–1814), French novelist and libertine who praised sexual violence

saxophone: Adolphe Sax (1814–1894), German maker of musical instruments, who invented it in 1846

silhouette: Étienne de Silhouette (1709–1767), briefly a French controller-general, but no one is sure of what his association is with the word

sousaphone: in honor of John Philip Sousa (1854–1932), American bandmaster

spoonerism: William A. Spooner (1844–1930), English clergyman who frequently transposed sounds in his speaking, for example, "well-boiled icicle" for "well-oiled bicycle"

tawdry: Saint Audrey (died A.D. 679), queen of Northumberland, whose throat tumor was blamed on her liking for necklaces

teddy bear: Theodore Roosevelt (1858–1919), whom some people ridiculed because he once refused to shoot a bear cub

varnish: Berenice II (c. 269–221 B.C.), queen of Egypt. The Greek city of Berenike, in Libya, was named for her, and a smooth, glossy finish for wood was developed there. The name was changed to Latin *veronix*, Old French *vernis*, Middle English *varnisch*, our *varnish*.

In all, the English language has about six or seven hundred of such persons' names made common. They are sometimes called *eponyms*, although that word has other meanings also. In addition, many personal names have been made into adjectives—for example, *ritzy* and *sadistic*, from the same sources as *ritz* and *sadism*.

How do Authors Name Their Characters?

Margaret Mitchell's Scarlett O'Hara was originally going to be named Pansy, but an editor insisted on a change. Beyond little doubt, *Gone with the Wind* owed part of its financial success to the inspired names of Scarlett O'Hara, Rhett Butler, and the saccharine-sweet Melanie.

Literary onomastics (the study of characters' names) is a growing part of literary criticism, probably because most professional authors do choose names with care. As one example, Erwin C. Brody made an analysis of names used by Fyodor Dostoevski in *Crime and Punishment* and another novel.

Raskolnikov's name, according to Brody, means 'schismatic, dissident, heretic,' and as readers of the novel will recognize, those words are a pretty accurate character sketch. (The full name, incidentally, is the alliterative Rodion Romanovich Raskolnikov.) Marmeladov, a "tragicomical small government clerk," is based on *marmelad* 'a candied fruit jelly,' and, says Brody, shows the man's fundamental weakness. Raskolnikov's sober, thoughtful friend, Razumiklin, has a name derived from *razum* 'reason, intelligence.' And Amalia Ivanovna Lippewechsel, who is of German ancestry, is as her name suggests a "lip-changer," a gabble-mouth.

Twentieth-century authors may not use names quite so obviously to indicate character, preferring suggestiveness instead. A glamorous leading man is not likely to be named either Mark Brown or Aloysius Heffelfinger, but he may be called—well, how about Rhett Butler?

How Do You Name a Boat?

Paddling his kayak in waters off the east coast of Florida, John McNamara tallied and classified the names of one thousand yachts, cabin cruisers, charter-fishing boats, and sailing vessels, and whenever possible chatted with people aboard concerning the boats' names.

The favored types of names, with examples, were these:

1. Picturesque (144): Moonraker, Spindrift, Windchime
2. Sea-going (75): Sea Angler, Sea Scamp, Sea Witch

3. Children (67): Gekiven (*George, Kim, Steven*)
4. Geographical (67): Arkansas Traveller, Souix [*sic*] City Sue
5. Birds (63): Flamingo, Ibis, Pelican
6. Man and Wife (62): Dot-N-Mike, Jack-Lynn
7. Foreign (61): (Italian names defeated Spanish, 25 to 23)
8. Whimsical (50): Mi-Yot, Pade-IV, This-L-Du
9. Alcoholic (45): Rheingold Express, B & B
10. Fictitious (40): Davey Jones, Lorelei, Poseidon
11. Zoological (40:) Crashing Boar
12. Men (38): Sneaky Pete

Other categories were Ethnic (Italian Stallion), Fish, Initials, Ladies (Fast Lady, Shady Lady), Numbers (Three Pals), Reversals (Rolyat), Risqué (Muffdiver, Rut Cry), Surnames, Unexplained (Fat City).

Under the heading of Wrong Assumption, McNamara reported a Full House, which turned out to refer not to poker but to the seven children in the family.

One name, selected as Dullest, was Investment Broker.

The Bible That Ordered Adultery

Ever since printing was invented, printers have occasionally made mistakes and proofreaders have sometimes failed to notice them. Not even the Bible has escaped error-free.

Generally the errors are inconsequential. For instance, the first printing of the Authorized Bible, in Ruth 3:15, referring to Ruth's departure from Boaz, says "... and he went into the city." As a result that printing was nicknamed the He Bible. The next printing, called the She Bible, got it right: "... and she went into the city."

Another printing, in 1717, had *vinegar* instead of *vineyard*, and so was named the Vinegar Bible.

British Tories had a little fun when one edition appeared in which Matthew 5:9 said "Blessed are the *placemakers*" instead of *peacemakers*. Because the Whig leaders of the time were often accused of creating "places" 'easy jobs, sinecures'" for their party hacks, the Tories promptly nicknamed the version the Whig Bible.

One of the Ten Commandments, as several people know, says, "Thou shalt not commit adultery." But in one version, called the Wicked Bible, Exodus 20:14 not only condones adultery but requires it: "Thou shalt commit adultery."

Other Bibles have been nicknamed not for printers' errors but for eccentric translations. For instance, the Breeches Bible (which officially is the Geneva Bible) says in Genesis 3:7 that Adam and Eve "made themselves breeches." The conventional translation is "made themselves aprons." Perhaps to the conservative British Puritans who were responsible for that translation, breeches seemed more decent, less revealing apparel than aprons for our ancestors to wear.

Another translator, whatever his reason, altered "strong drink shall be bitter to them that drink it" to "beer shall be bitter to them that drink it." His version was named the Beer Bible.

How Did She Call Her Husband?

A woman named her dog Dammit. Sometimes her penetrating voice could be heard throughout the neighborhood as she called, "Dammit! Come here, Dammit!"

Palindromes

Ava is a palindrome—it's the same whether you read it backward or forward. Others include Anna, Hannah, and—a rare masculine example—Otto.

If a surname can be successfully inverted to suggest a given name (not many can), a two-word palindrome results. A professor of classics at the University of Illinois in Urbana-Champaign was named Revilo Oliver.

If his middle name had been Otto, his name would have been a three-word palindrome: Revilo Otto Oliver.

When most surnames are spelled backward, the result either is unpronounceable or sounds like a character in science fiction: Senoj, Strebor, Sirrom, Nameloc, Zepol, Nadroj, Nodrog, or Rednaxela. (Try your own name. Is it as good as Kooh?)

Real or Fictional?

Does each of these names represent a real or a fictional person?

Johnny Appleseed	John Henry
King Arthur	Sherlock Holmes
Billy the Kid	Robin Hood
Daniel Boone	Jack the Ripper
John Brown	Jesse James
Buffalo Bill	Casey Jones
Paul Bunyan	Captain Kidd
Crazy Horse	Jean Lafitte
Davy Crockett	Pecos Bill
Robinson Crusoe	Peter Pan
Febold Feboldson	Pocahontas
Frankenstein	Long John Silver
Lemuel Gulliver	Sitting Bull
	Rip Van Winkle

Johnny Appleseed Real. Actual name John Chapman (1774–1845). He
did not scatter apple seeds randomly, but did plant apple orchards
from the Alleghenies westward.

King Arthur Uncertain, although there may have been a Welsh Arthur
who won important battles from the Saxons. Most of the Round
Table stories, however, were made up centuries later.

Billy the Kid Real. Actual name William H. Bonney (1859–1881). A
bandit in the Southwest.

Daniel Boone Real (1734–1820). American explorer and pioneer.

John Brown Real (1800–1859). American abolitionist leader who was
executed.

Buffalo Bill Real. Actual name William Frederick Cody (1846–1917).
Frontiersman and showman.

Paul Bunyan Basically fictional, although there appears to have been a
French Canadian named Bon Jean whose exploits were greatly
exaggerated in the tales.

Crazy Horse Real. Actual name Tashunca-Uitco (c. 1849–1877). Sioux
leader who participated in the Battle of Little Big Horn.

Davy Crockett Real (1786–1836). Frontiersman, congressman. Killed at
the Alamo.

Robinson Crusoe Fictional, although author Daniel Defoe got his idea
and some of his facts from the story of the marooned Alexander
Selkirk.

Febold Feboldson A fictional Paul Bunyan-like "Big Swede" of Nebraska,
developed by Don Holmes and Wayne T. Carroll.

Frankenstein Fictional. A mad scientist created by Mary Wollstonecraft
Shelley (wife of the poet Percy Bysshe Shelley). Trivia question:
What was Frankenstein's first name? (Victor)

Lemuel Gulliver Fictional. The leading character in Jonathan Swift's
satire *Gulliver's Travels*.

John Henry Uncertain. The exploits of the powerful black railroad
worker, "a steel-drivin' man," have been celebrated in countless
stories and songs, some of them possibly based on fact.

Sherlock Holmes Fictional, although author Sir Arthur Conan Doyle
fashioned the character in part on Dr. Joseph Bell (1837–1911),
under whom Doyle had studied medicine.

Robin Hood Mainly fictional, although some scholars say that he
actually lived in the twelfth century, that his true name was Robert
Fitz-Ooth, and that he was reputed to be the Earl of Huntingdon.

Jack the Ripper Real, although the actual name of this vicious murderer
of London prostitutes (1888) is unknown.

Jesse James Real (1847–1882). American outlaw.

Casey Jones Probably real. A popular ballad was written about this self-
sacrificing railroad engineer, whose original name may have been
John Luther Jones. There had been, however, a somewhat similar
earlier ballad about a black fireman, Jimmie Jones.

Captain Kidd Real. Actual name William Kidd (1645?–1701). Scottish-
born pirate who was hanged.

Jean Lafitte Real (1780–1826). French pirate who was an American
hero in the War of 1812.

Pecos Bill Fictional Southwestern hero, credited among other things
with digging the Rio Grande.

Peter Pan The fictional boy who never grew up, created by Sir James
Barrie.

Pocahontas Real. Original name Matoaka (1595?–1617), later called
Lady Rebecca. In Captain John Smith's account (which some
historians say was romanticized), when Powhatan's men were "ready
with their clubs, to beate out his [Smith's] braines, Pocahontas, the
Kings dearest daughter . . . got his head in her armes, and laid her
owne upon his to save him from death."

Long John Silver The fictional one-legged pirate leader in Robert Louis
Stevenson's *Treasure Island*.

Sitting Bull Real. Native American name Tatanka Iyotake (1834–1890).
Dakota-Sioux chief who annihilated General George Custer's forces
in 1876.

Rip Van Winkle The fictional creation of Washington Irving, whose
story of the famous long sleep shows how many changes may occur
in 20 years.

We're Not Superstitious, But . . .

For many years large numbers of British sailors have cher-
ished the belief that Friday is an unlucky day, and as much as
possible they try to avoid any unusual or innovative activities on
that day.

Earlier in this century, British navy officials decided to disprove
the superstition by providing a dramatic example of its falsity. They
began building a ship on a Friday, never missed a Friday during its

construction, finished it on a Friday, named it Friday, officially christened it on a Friday, and started it on its shakedown cruise on a Friday.

The ship was never seen again.

Sometimes numbers substitute for names. Pampa, TX, numbers its police cars. Late in 1980, Car 13, in use only a few days, was in an accident. A little later, another; then another; five accidents in all, some of them serious enough to keep Car 13 off the street for weeks.

In April 1982, Police Chief J. J. Ryzman finally decided to take action. He changed 13 to 25.

In September he told United Press International, "We've got some superstitious people here. We haven't had an accident since."

Skiing Down the Spiral Stairs

Some of the America's ski slopes seem especially well named. *Outside* magazine, identifying the twelve most difficult ski runs in America, included these four:

Elevator Shaft (Aspen, CO)
Gunbarrel (Heavenly Valley, CA)
Spiral Stairs (Telluride, CO)
Exterminator (Crystal Mountain, WA)

Who Is Waltzin' Matilda?

Wrong question. The Matilda of Australia's enduringly most popular song is not a *who* but a *what*.

The composer of the song was Andrew Barton (Banjo) Paterson (1864–1941), an Australian lawyer and poet. Lawyer Paterson might long since have been forgotten, but the poet—or at least one of his products—lives on and on. As early as 1900, a British *Literary Yearbook* said of him, "No living English or American poet can boast so wide a public, always excepting Mr. Rudyard Kipling."

The Anzacs marched to World War I singing "Waltzin' Matilda," and their sons sang it in World War II. The British named a kind of tank "Matilda," while their little children at home were learning to sing the song in their nurseries.

Paterson, riding with a friend into Winton, Queensland, had heard the expression "Waltzin' Matilda" and learned that it refers to a pack or "tucker bag" such as a peddler, wandering worker, or tramp (a "swagman") might carry. The term fascinated him, and he improvised verses as they rode along. That evening, in Winton, he composed music to fit, not knowing that he was writing what has been called Australia's unofficial national anthem.

So a waltzin' Matilda is a pack carried by a swagman. This swagman stops in the shade of a coolibah tree (a kind of evergreen) and starts a fire under his "billy" (a kettle or pail used for cooking). Along comes a "jimbuck" (a sheep) to drink at the "billabong" (a water hole).

The swagman grabs the jimbuck "with glee" and shoves it into his tucker bag, singing, "You'll come a-waltzin' Matilda with me." But the jimbuck's owner—presumably a rancher but called a "squatter"—rides up with three troopers to arrest the itinerant thief. He refuses to give up his freedom, however:

> Up jumped the swagman and dived into the billabong.
> "You'll never take me alive!" cried he,
> And his ghost may be heard as you pass by that billabong,
> Singing, "Who'll come a-waltzin' Matilda with me?"

The song owes its undying popularity in part to the rollicking tune, but perhaps more to the universal desire for freedom, for lack of regimentation, for independence of authority. Moralists rightly lament the swagman as a poor guide to conduct, but an Australian novelist, Kylie Tennant, declared, "There is no sweeter mutton than what has been stolen, killed, and hung in a fig tree overnight and cooked next morning."

Z for *Zany?*

Why a Z-shaped bridge? An unproved guess is that midwestern bridges which approximated that shape were built in honor of Ebenezer Zane, who was responsible for clearing Zane's Trace, an important road for Ohio and Kentucky pioneers. More likely the Z shape, really closer to S, was intended to reduce the force of the water. (Zanesville, OH, named for Ebenezer Zane, gained renown for having what may have been the only Y-shaped bridge in the country.)

Henry Clay, Punster

Statesman Henry Clay of Kentucky was in a stagecoach that upset close to Uniontown, PA. He was unhurt but got dirty. As he brushed off his clothes he said, "I'm mixing the Clay of Kentucky with the limestone of Pennsylvania."

Maybe He Had a Poetic License

"I'll Take You Home Again, Kathleen," generally supposed to be an Irish song, was actually written by a Virginian with the un-Irish name of Thomas Paine Westendorf.

His wife's name was Jennie.

Cutie-Pie Commercial Names

The Wearhouse (clothing store)
The Meating Place (butcher shop)
Den of Antiquity (antique shop)
Turtles Pantyhose—They Never Run
Wallpapers to Go
Merrys' Little Lambs (David and Mary Merry, sheep raisers)
Evil People Lounge (Fort Pierce, FL. It advertised "the finest in topless entertainment" but would admit no one wearing jeans and no males in collarless shirts.)
Squid Row (tavern in Seattle, WA)
Ash Kickers (chimney cleaners, Wichita Falls, TX)
Julius Scissor (hairdressing shop, Albuquerque, NM)
Lettuce Entertain You (restaurant chain based in Chicago)

Tall Corn

Places in Iowa we may have to patronize sometime:

Flatt Tire Service
Little Charm Motel

One John Isn't Enough

The most often misspelled and misspoken name of a university may be that of the Johns Hopkins University. The reason for the *s* in *Johns* is that a large part of the original endowment for the university and hospital came from a Baltimore banker named Johns Hopkins.

The most often incorrectly worded name of a university is probably that of Indiana University. That's the official name, *not* the University of Indiana.

The, by the way, is an official part of the names of several universities and colleges, for example, *the* Ohio State University.

Old Names for Our Months

The Anglo-Saxons, an agricultural people, used names for the months which were much more descriptive than our Latin-derived ones.

January, Wulf-mōnaþ 'wolf month,' when people had to be especially fearful that hungry wolves might invade their villages
February, Sprote-kalemōnaþ 'sprout cabbage month'
March, Hlyd-mōnaþ 'boisterous month,' because of the wind
April, Easter-mōnaþ
May, þrimilce-mōnaþ 'month of three milkings,' because grass was then so lush that cows could be milked three times a day
June, Sēre-mōnaþ 'dry month'
July, Māēd-mōnaþ 'meadow month,' when meadows were blooming
August, Wēod-mōnaþ 'weed month,' when weeds flourished
September, Hāērfest-mōnaþ 'harvest month'
October, Wīn-mōnaþ 'wine month'
November, Blōt-mōnaþ 'sacrifice month,' when a calf might be sacrificed; also Wind
December, Midwintra-mōnaþ; also called, by Christians after about A.D. 600, Hālig-mōnaþ 'holy month'

Native American Indians spoke many languages. The names given to their "moons" by two Midwest tribes were translated in these ways by English settlers:

January Valor; Spirit, Great Spirit
February Cats; Eagles
March Bad Eyes; Snow-Crust
April Game; Putting Away the Snowshoes, Maple Sugar Making
May Nests; Flowers
June Strawberries by both tribes
July Cherries; Raspberries
August Buffalo; Whortleberries

September Oats (wild rice); Wild Rice
October Second Moon of Oats; Falling Leaf
November Roebuck; Freezing
December Budding of the Roebuck's Horns; Little Spirit

Anybody for *USan*?

As is generally agreed, *American* is inappropriate as a designation of a resident of the United States. *United States*ian, though listed in dictionaries, has never caught on. (Perhaps USan, pronounced, *you-esś-an*, would be more manageable.)

All the Way to Zzzyrmidgeon

The current Manhattan White Pages telephone directory starts with 6½ pages of business names ranging from A (nothing more, just A) through AAAAAAAA, which is what the Transamerica Stretch Limousine Ltd calls itself. After that we find the first personal name, Aaarman.

At the far end of the fat book, we find these four personal names: Zyzykin, Zyzzmjac, Zzzyandottie (two of these), and Zzzyrmidgeon.

🍎 Bibliography

Adams, James N., *Illinois Place Names*. Springfield, IL: Ill. Hist. Soc., 1968.

Algeo, John, "Changing Fashions in Street Names." *Names*, March, 1978.

– – – "The Australianness of Australian Placenames." *Names*, Sept., Dec., 1988.

Alsberg, Henry G., ed. *The American Guide* [by the WPA Federal Writers' Project]. New York: Hastings House, 1949.

American Council of Learned Societies, *Surnames in the United States Census of 1790*. Baltimore: Genealogical Pub. Co., 1971.

Ashley, Leonard R. N., "Flicks, Flacks, and Flucks." *Names*, Dec., 1975.

———, Source of "Ask for Him by His Right Name." *Blackwood's Magazine*, 1842.

Baker, Ronald L., and Marvin Carmody, *Indiana Place Names*. Bloomington, IN: Indiana U. Press, 1975.

Bardsley, Charles W., *Curiosities of Puritan Nomenclature*. London, 1880.

Berkow, Ira. *Maxwell Street*. Garden City, NY: Doubleday and Co., 1977.

Bloodworth, Bertha, and Alton C. Morris, *Places in the Sun: The History and Romance of Florida Place-names*. Gainesville, FL: The U. Presses of Florida, 1978.

Boone, Lalia, P., *Idaho Place Names*. Moscow, ID: U. of Idaho Press, 1988.

Brody, Erwin C., "Naming and Symbolism in ... Dostoevsky." *Names*, June, 1979.

Browder, Sue, *The New Age Baby Name Book*. New York: Warner Books, 1974.

Carlson, Helen, *Nevada Place Names*. Reno, NV: U. of Nevada Press, 1974.

Carney, Joseph D., in *Oregon Health Trends*. April, 1987.

———, *A Century of Population Growth, 1790–1900*. Baltimore: Genealogical Pub. Co., 1970.

Cheney, Roberta, *Names on the Face of Montana*. Missoula, MT: U. of Montana, 1971.

Dickson, Paul, *Names*. New York: Delacorte Press, 1986.

———, *The Dictionary of Maine Place-Names*. Freeport, ME: Bond Wheelwright Co., 1970.

Dietrich, R. V., and L. T. Reynolds, "The Name Is *Not* the Thing." *Names*, Dec., 1973.

Dingman, Lester F., in *Naughty Names*, ed. by Fred Tarpley. Commerce, TX: Names Institute Press, 1975.

Duckert, Audrey, "Place Nicknames," *Names*, Sept., 1973.

Dunkling, Leslie, *First Names First*. Detroit: Gale Research Co., 1982. Selections from *First Names First* by Leslie Alan Dunkling. Copyright © 1977 by Leslie Dunkling. Reprinted by permission of Gale Research Inc.

Espenshade, Abraham M., *Pennsylvania Place Names*. State College, 1925.

Ewen, C. L'Estrange, *A History of Surnames of the British Isles*. Baltimore: Genealogical Pub. Co., 1968.

Felton, Gary S., "Addendum to 'The Name Is *Not* the Thing.'" *Names*, March, 1977.

Fitzpatrick, Lillian, *Nebraska Place Names*. Lincoln, NE: U. of Nebraska Press, 1960.

Foscue, Virginia D., *Place Names of Alabama*. Tuscaloosa, AL: U. of Alabama Press, 1989.

Gaffney, William G., "Tell Me Your Name." *Names*, March, 1971.

Gallagher, John S., and Alan H. Patera, *Wyoming Post Offices, 1850–1980*. Burtonsville, MD: The Depot, 1980.

Grossman, Ron, "Slicing Up a Tradition," *Chicago Tribune*, March 20, 1990.

Gudde, Erwin G., *California Place Names*. Berkeley, CA: U. of California Press, 1969.

————, *Halliwell's Filmgoer's Companion*, 7th ed. New York: Scribners, 1980.

Hanson, R. M., *Virginia Place Names*. Verona, VA: McClure Press, 1969.

Harder, Kelsie B., *Illustrated Dictionary of Place Names: United States and Canada*. New York: Facts on File, 1976.

Imboden, Stanley F., in *Valley Record* (Lebanon Valley College, PA), Summer-Fall, 1988.

————, *Information Please Almanac*. New York: Simon and Schuster, 1981. Boston: Houghton Mifflin, 1990.

Janssen, Quinith, and William Fernbach, *West Virginia Place Names*. Shepherdstown, WV: J and F Enterprises, 1984.

Jennings, Gary, *Personalities of Language*. New York: Atheneum, 1984.

Kaganoff, Benzion C., *A Dictionary of Jewish Surnames and Their History*. New York: Schocken Books, 1977.

Kenney, Hamill T., *The Origin and Meaning of the Indian Place Names of Maryland*. Baltimore: Waverly Press, 1961.

Kirkham, E. Kay, *A Genealogical and Historical Atlas of the United States of America*. Providence, UT: Everton Press, 1980.

Krakow, Kenneth, *Georgia Place Names*. Macon, GA: Winship Press, 1975.

Laird, Charlton, *Language in America*. New York: World Pub. Co., 1970.

Lambert, Eloise, and Mario Pei, *Our Names: Where They Came From and What They Mean*. New York: Lothrop, Lee & Shepard, 1960.

LaPierre, Andre, "Post Office Names in Ontario." *Names*, June, 1983.

Leighly, John, "Biblical Place-Names in the United States." *Names*, March, 1979.

Loughead, Flora H., *Dictionary of Given Names*. Glendale, CA: Arthur H. Clark Co., 1974.

McArthur, Lewis A., *Oregon Geographic Names*, 4th ed. Portland, OR: Oregon Hist. Soc., 1974.

McNamara, John, "Reflections on Nautical Onomastics." *Names*, March, 1979.

McWhiney, Grady and Forrest McDonald, "Celtic Names in the Antebellum South." *Names*, March, 1982.

Manguel, Alberto, and Giannini Guadalupi, *The Dictionary of Imaginary Places*. New York: Harcourt Brace Jovanovich, 1987.

Matthews, C. M., *How Surnames Began*. London: Lutterworth Press, 1967.

Mencken, H. L., *The American Language*. New York: Alfred A. Knopf, 1965.

– – – *Supplement One*, 1965.

– – – *Supplement Two*, 1962.

Names. (References to this journal are listed here under authors' names.)

――――. "News Affects Naming," *Harper's*, Jan., 1976. Copyright © 1975 by *Harper's Magazine*. All rights reserved. Used by special permission.

Odelain, O., and R. Seguineau, *Dictionary of Proper Names and Places in the Bible*. Garden City, NY: Doubleday and Co., 1981.

Pearce, Thomas M., *New Mexico Place Names*. Albuquerque, U. of New Mexico Press, 1965.

Perkey, Elton A., *Perkey's Nebraska Place Names*. Lincoln, NE: Nebraska State Hist. Soc., 1982.

Phillips, James W. *Washington State Place Names*. Seattle: U. of Washington Press, 1971.

– – – *Alaska-Yukon Place Names*. Seattle: U. of Washington Press, 1973.

Puckett, Newbell Niles, and Murray Heller, *Black Names in America*. Boston: G. K. Hall & Co., 1975.

Pukui, Mary K., and others, *Place Names of Hawaii*. Honolulu: U. of Hawaii Press, 1984.

Pyles, Thomas, "Bible Belt Onomastics." *Names*, June, 1959.

Ramsay, Robert L., *Our Storehouse of Missouri Place Names*. Columbia, MO: U. of Missouri Press, 1973.

Read, William A., *Louisiana Place Names of Indian Origin*. Baton Rouge, LA: The University, 1927.

Reaney, P. H., *The Origin of British Place Names*. London: Routledge and Kegan Paul, 1960.

Reed, A. W., *Place Names of Australia*. Sydney, Australia. A. H. and W. A. Reed, 1973.

Rennick, Robert M., *Kentucky Place Names*. Lexington, KY: U. Press of Kentucky, 1984.

– – – "Hitlers and Others . . . ," *Names*, Sept., 1969.

– – – "The Alleged 'Hogg' Sisters . . . ," *Names*, Sept., 1980.

Rode, Zvonko, "The Origin of Jewish Family Names." *Names*, Sept., 1976.

Romig, Walter, *Michigan Place Names*. Grosse Pointe, MI: 1986.

Rosenkrantz, Linda, and Paula R. Satran, *Beyond Jennifer and Jason*. New York: St. Martin's Press, 1988.

Rydjord, John, *Indian Place Names* (of Kansas). Norman, OK: U. of Oklahoma Press, 1968.

--- *Kansas Place Names*. Norman, OK: U. of Oklahoma Press, 1972.

Scherr, Arthur, "Change-of-Name Patterns of the New York Courts." *Names*, Sept., 1986.

Schorr, Alan E., *Alaska Place Names*. Juneau, AK: The Denali Press, 1987.

Schuessler, Raymond, "Oops! All-time Great Bloopers." *Modern Maturity*, April–May, 1982.

Shirk, George H., *Oklahoma Place Names*. Norman, OK: U. of Oklahoma Press, 1974.

———, *The Scottish Tartans* (William Semple, ill.) Edinburgh, Scotland: Johnston and Bacon, 1945.

Sims, Clifford S., *Scottish Surnames*. Baltimore: Genealogical Pub. Co., 1968 (reprint of 1862 ed.).

Smith, Elsdon C., *American Surnames*. Philadelphia: Chilton, 1969.

--- *New Dictionary of American Family Names*. New York: Harper & Row, 1973.

Smith, H. Allen, *People Named Smith*. Garden City, NY: Doubleday, 1950.

Sneve, Virginia, *Dakota Heritage: . . . Indian Place Names in South Dakota*. Sioux Falls, SD: Brevet Press, 1973.

Stewart, George R., *American Place-Names*. New York: Oxford U. Press, 1978.

--- *Names on the Land*. Boston: Houghton Mifflin, 1945, 1967.

Swift, Esther M., *Vermont Place Names*. Brattleboro, VT: Greene Press, 1977.

Tarpley, Fred, *Naughty Names*. Commerce, TX: Names Institute Press, 1975.

Taylor, Karen, (Material for "Mrs. Alice Jones . . .,") *Indianapolis Star*, 1982.

Thomson, Christine, *Boy or Girl? Names for Every Child*. New York: Gramercy Pub. Co., 1974.

Trogdon, William (William Least Heat Moon), Excerpts from *Blue Highways. Atlantic*, Sept., 1982.

Trumbull, James H., *Indian Names of Places in Connecticut*. Hamden, CT: Archon Books, 1974.

Tuchman, Barbara, (material for "Name Trouble for Historians") *Atlantic*, Dec., 1975.

Upham, Warren, *Minnesota Geographic Names* (reprint ed.). St. Paul: Minnesota Hist. Soc., 1969.

U.S. Immigration and Naturalization Service, *Foreign Versions, Variations, and Diminutives of English Names*. Washington, DC: U.S. Gov't. Printing Office, 1973.

U.S. Postal Service, *National Post Office Directory*. Washington, DC: U.S. Gov't. Printing Office, 1986.

U.S. Social Service Administration, *Distribution of Surnames in the Social Security Number File*. Washington, DC: Office of Program Operations, 1974.

Vogel, Virgil J., *Indian Place Names in Illinois*. Springfield, IL: Ill. Hist. Soc., 1963.

– – – *Iowa Place Names of Indian Origin*. Iowa City, IA: U. of Iowa Press, 1983.

————, *Who's Who*, London: A. & C. Black, 1989.

————, *Who's Who in America*, Wilmette, IL: Marquis Who's Who, a Macmillan, Inc., Co., 1989.

————, *Who's Who in Canada*. Toronto, Ont.: International Press, Ltd., 1989.

Williams, Lena, "Ambition and Pride in Names of the 80's." *New York Times*, Jan. 10, 1990.

Williams, Mary Ann, *Origins of North Dakota Place Names*. Washburn, ND: Bismarck Tribune, 1966.

————*World Almanac and Book of Facts*. New York: Pharos Books, 1988.

Writer's Program (WPA), *The Origin of Massachusetts Place Names*. New York: Harian Publications, 1941.

❦ Index

To avoid making the book tail-heavy with a tremendous index, only about 2,700 of its approximately 7,500 names are indexed. Common variants are omitted; so, for example, the entry 'Ann, etc.' covers such variants as Anna, Anne, and Annette. Names of many small cities and towns have not been indexed, but can be found by glancing through the entries for their states. General topics, such as ACTORS AND ACTRESSES, ORIGINAL NAMES, are set in capital letters.